W9-DCW-619

"Clean, clear, and unpretentious . . . as sharp, stark, and powerful as the best b&w photographs of the time."

—*Kirkus Reviews*

THE FIRST OF THE FIRST . . .

SERGEANT "CAUTIOUS" CRAWFORD: As forward observer for the murderous "Four Deuce" mortars, he learned that living through direct enemy fire is always as tough as the first time . . .

THE FUNNY GUNNY: If God wanted the men of the Four Deuces to be outstanding Marines, he would have made them short, fat, and disheveled —and named them all Funny Gunny . . .

"Told with convincing authenticity . . . *THE FOUR DEUCES* is poignant and irreverent, solemn and funny, all the while describing in . . . vivid detail what it's like to fight and die in the service of your country in a war no one really understands."

—*Wichita Falls Times Record News*

"Very personal, frequently profane, sometimes humorous, more often shocking—and extremely well-written throughout. Recommended."

—ALA *Booklist*

RED: The 81mm forward observer and World War II veteran played the blues, carried all his possessions attached to strings, and taught young Crawford the first rule of war: Keep moving!

THE CANDY BAR KIDD: On rifle ranges around the world he proved the best shot. Now, in a state worse than death where no rifle could help him, he put his buddies to the ultimate test of heroism . . .

"Crawford is a marvelous teller of tales."
— *Rochester Post-Bulletin*

"A prized contribution to Korean War narratives."
— *The Midwest Review of Books*

"(A) collection of wartime anecdotes and tall tales. . . . Marines of all ages will enjoy Crawford's yarns."
— *Publishers Weekly*

CORPORAL ALBERT TRUELOVE: He called himself the Armenian Jew, though he was neither Armenian nor Jew. The men of the 1st came to miss his cooking and the highly unconventional ways he looked out for them . . .

FIRST LIEUTENANT LESTER ABLE: After their first firefights, most young grunts stopped thinking of war as an adventure. The confident, hymn-humming officer never did—which made him an exceptional soldier in the eyes of his men . . .

"A war story as only war stories can be, filled with character and the special friendships men form with each other. . . . A remarkably vivid performance."

—*The Book Reader*

"Crawford's book is a winner!"

—*Leatherneck*

THE FOUR DEUCES

A KOREAN WAR STORY

C.S. CRAWFORD

POCKET BOOKS

New York   London   Toronto   Sydney   Tokyo   Singapore

For my wife, Joann

POCKET BOOKS, a division of Simon & Schuster Inc.
1230 Avenue of the Americas, New York, NY 10020

Copyright © 1989 by C. S. Crawford

ISBN: 0-671-70562-8

First Pocket Books printing December 1990

10 9 8 7 6 5 4 3 2 1

POCKET and colophon are registered trademarks of
Simon & Schuster Inc.

Printed in the U.S.A.

"My old man was in World War Two," said Pike. "His stories are just the same old bullshit."

"Maybe you ought to listen to them," I said. "Maybe he's still got something on his mind."

JACK FULLER
from his novel
Fragments

War stories aren't really anything more than stories about people anyway.

MICHAEL HERR
from his novel
Dispatches

PROLOGUE

The Korean War began late in June 1950 and for the first fifteen months raged fiercely up and down and across the peninsula of that country. Both North Korea and South Korea were devastated. After the war machines of the United Nations command, of the Chinese communist forces, of both North Korea and South Korea had chewed up the country, spitting out only waste, much had been lost and very little had been gained by either side. The fight to gain land—for one side or the other—ended almost exactly where it began along the 38th Parallel.

Although great masses of land were taken and lost again by both sides during the first fifteen months of the Korean War, the beginning of peace talks saw the war stagnate following a last major engagement in 1951, an action called the Punchbowl. The war stagnated with combatants on both sides living in trenches. War was a matter of reconnaissance and combat patrols, a matter of fierce firefights with small arms, a matter of howitzers and mortars fired discriminately and indiscriminately.

Many books detail the history of early Korean battles, of engagements both large and small, of men and machines of war, of the way and manner and fighting abilities of all concerned with the war, especially during the first fifteen months of the Korean War. Justifiably so; this was fierce warfare and needed to be recorded.

Very few books have been written of the months that followed, from October 1951 until the end in July 1953. In those twenty-one months, many men died in the trench warfare that existed—warfare likened to that of World War I, but which was fought in a more modern manner. Although still a shooting war, a dying war, the Korean War came virtually to a standstill, degenerating in 1951 into dreary and seemingly endless battles for the same hills. Although the war came somewhat to a halt, the men fighting it did not.

War is often quite unconventional, and fighting in a trench warfare situation is often bizarre. One of the last recorded instances of an engagement in the Korean War is perhaps the oddest of all. Some forty minutes before 2200 on July 27, 1953—the hour the shooting stopped—marines on a hill near Panmunjon saw Chinese digging in a trench less than a hundred yards away. They asked if they should shoot and were ordered not to. Lieutenant Colonel Joseph Hill, their battalion commander, summed up the entire war when he allegedly said: "Don't start anything you can't stop." The marines did not shoot; instead they spent the last few minutes of the Korean War throwing rocks at the Chinese.

The Korean War cost the United States 142,091 casualties—33,629 men were dead; 103,284 were wounded; and 5,178 were captured or missing. This book is about some of the grunts who died or were wounded from September 1951 through September 1952.

These memoirs are not an attempt to answer, solve, or resolve the problems arising from or about the three-year-long Korean War or the much longer stalemate that followed that war. This story was written to let you know how one very young, very scared marine saw his very first war and how he reacted to the killing and the mayhem of it. The stories are my view of that war, a war gone to ground in the trench lines. Dig into the stories and you may find some-

2

thing you were not expecting. I am well aware that my view of the Korean War has no historical importance. Still, it is my view, and I want to share it with you. I do not have a cause to plead or an ax to grind, and that alone ought to count for something. My memoirs are selective and most certainly tainted with time. My recollections are a lot like boot mines, and ought to be approached with caution. I was a grunt, a Four Deuce forward observer, assigned to duty with a marine infantry company every time the 1st Marine Regiment went back up on line. During the time I was in Korea, my boondockers were firmly planted in trench-line mud. When I came home in September 1952, I was proud that I had helped in the attempt to stop communism in Korea. I was proud of all the men I served, and served with, and I was a little bit proud of myself, too. I was very young and naive back then; I believe we all were very young and naive.

C. S. Crawford
Burlington, North Carolina

BOOK I

*From Line
to Line*

CHAPTER
1

I was one of the relatively few men to be promoted to private first class right out of boot camp. I must have shown the Parris Island drill instructors something, maybe perseverance, maybe stubbornness.

I first joined the marines in November 1948. After a lifetime of waiting to be old enough to join, I was permitted to join for just one year. I had to enlist in the USMC-V program. There was a reason for such short-term enlistments.

Recent history had shown that the United States was always caught short without a proper reserve unit of trained men to call upon in the event of war. Prior to World War I the marines had less than 10,000 officers and enlisted men, and after the war was finished, peacetime attrition saw the ranks fall back to 16,000 enlisted men in 1920. When the Japanese struck Pearl Harbor in December 1941, there were just slightly more than 4,000 officers and just a bit more than 66,000 enlisted men; four years later there were more than a half-million men in the marines with a wartime strength of 37,664 officers and 485,113 enlisted. Peacetime cutbacks saw the marines reduced to just 7,254 officers and 67,025 enlisted men, the on-board strength as of June 30, 1950, when the Korean War began.

Having studied the problems inherent in bringing reduced strengths to peak effective strengths in a short time period, the Marine Corps developed its own plans to have an effective combat force. A select cadre of combat-experienced officers and enlisted men, the Old Salts, would be retained on active duty. New blood in the form of enlistees would be permitted to join for just one year, and would then stay for eight years in the Marine Corps Reserve, a force trained in marine ways and readily available to be drawn upon. That's the position I was in during June 1950.

I wanted to reenlist at the end of my first year. Hell! Why not? I liked being a marine. Besides, times were tough on the outside. Men were having trouble finding a job and then keeping it. Nobody in the Democratic White House was admitting it, but everyone thought we were heading into another depression.

Anyway, a major shook my hand, made a big production out of handing me a lapel button called a "ruptured duck," and handed me a set of honorable discharge papers saying I was a World War II veteran entitled to wear the National Defense Service Ribbon. I didn't understand any of it, but I didn't question it either. Young Pfc's, men "prayin' for corporal," hardly ever question majors. All I knew was that during the past year I had fought mosquitoes and ticks and chiggers in the swampy parts of Camp Lejeune. I had distinguished myself learning basic skills in how to identify and avoid copperhead snakes, water moccasins, and NCOs looking for people to put on shit details.

One day I was a marine and the next I was a civilian looking for work. I went home to an economy that was depressing. During the next eight months I worked as a carpenter and yard boy at four lumber companies and saw three of them fold due to bankruptcy. The fourth company, the one where I was then employed, was on very shaky legs.

That's when the North Koreans came barreling and shooting over the 38th Parallel early in the morning of June

25, 1950. I first heard about it over the radio and then read about it in the newspapers. I headed straight to the marine recruiting station in Wilkes-Barre, Pennsylvania. I wanted to see family friend Marine M. Sgt. Walter Fletchko, the man who had filled out my first set of enlistment papers.

If there was going to be a war—and from what radio broadcasters were saying it seemed that feisty President Harry Truman wasn't going to stand for any shit from communist North Korea—then I wanted to be in on it. I had no idea where Korea was located, and I couldn't have cared less. I only knew that I still remembered my General Orders for a marine sentry on guard duty, remembered most of the lessons I had learned in basic infantry training, and was well aware of the fact that I was tired of working for peanuts in civilian outfits fast going broke. This was my chance to live a life of adventure, the hell-bent-for-leather life I had watched Wallace Beery play in the movies. This was my chance to join the marines for longer than just one year. Hopefully, this would be my chance to earn some NCO stripes.

While I was filled with the high ideals of youth, realistically I must admit that my convictions at that time were perhaps just as shallow as those of the next man. I was an idealist. I felt that a foreign war—especially this war against communism—might require sacrifices because it was for a just cause. Later, when I took the time to examine more closely my Don Quixote ideals, I figured out that it just might be me ending up on the sacrificial block; it just might be me inside the windmill that was being tilted.

However, in the first moments of my militaristic enthusiasm, I eagerly accepted the four-year enlistment contract that Sergeant Fletchko offered me.

During the next thirteen months I volunteered each and every month to go to Korea. I'd get myself into the first sergeant's office; sidle up to the company clerk; ask for, receive, and fill out completely all the necessary paperwork seeking transfer to a combat assignment; and then hand everything over to the first sergeant.

"What the fuck are you doing here in my office again,

9

Crawford?" the first sergeant would snarl at me, his mild-mannered way of welcoming me and my transfer request into his small office area.

"Sir!" I would belt out as loud as he had in his greeting, getting my voice down as low as I could, manlike, letting him hear the timbre of my vocalization. "I joined the marines because I was told the marines were the finest fighting outfit in the world. There's a fight going on over in Korea. Marines are fighting in it. I want to fight in it, too. I want a transfer to Korea, sir!" I felt like hot stuff.

"Now you cut out this bullshit, Crawford. I'm on to you. What are you tryin' to get out of?" the first sergeant would thunder back at me, exasperatedly, his barbed words bursting my balloon.

"Nothing, sir! Just volunteerin', sir!"

"You goddamn snuffies are all alike! Did you know that? Here we've got a goddamn war going on over there in Korea, and we need every man we can get over there. And here you are peckering up my office, filling out blank forms, screwing up my day.

"You and the rest of your punk buddies ought to start acting like marines instead of filling out these goddamn transfer papers, trying your level best to get out of doing your duty." He tried to shoo me away, waving his hands at me.

"You just go on and leave those papers there on my desk. Then you get your ass out of my office, you hear me?" The first sergeant was a reasonable, understanding career man filled with suspicion about everything a younger enlisted man did.

I never got my transfer as long as I volunteered for it. After thirteen months of this kind of treatment, I was definitely at the low point of my less-than-illustrious marine corps career.

It was small stuff that kept screwing me up. I could not understand the reasoning behind some of the nitpicky stuff that my officers and staff NCOs set such store by—things like keeping my bunk made up so tight with the dark olive green marine blanket stretched across it to such a degree that when a coin, say a quarter, was dropped on it, why that quarter would bounce up into the air; or maybe it was for not having the proper spit shine on my shoes for an inspection.

Actually, it was the spit-shined-shoe-routine that turned me off on everything the officers and NCOs set such store by. To compensate for my lack of effort in preparing my shoes for inspection, I would, while standing in ranks, rub the toe of first one shoe and then the other on the calf area of the opposite rear trouser leg. This would get me a sort of shit-brindle-brown kind of a shine on my shoes. What it really accomplished, however, was to smear whatever polish I had on the shoes to the back area of my trouser legs. I'd get chewed out in every inspection for smudged shoes and dirty trousers. With every ass-chewing inspection my promotion potential would further diminish.

But it was getting my hair cut to the acceptable Quantico marine style that really held up my promotion to corporal. Before each and every inspection, officers and NCOs alike would seek me out and tell me specifically to get a white-side-walled haircut.

A white-side-walled haircut is self-describing. The barber would run his clippers up the side of your head, removing everything but skin. Then the barber would take all but about a quarter inch of hair off the top, tapering it down to nothing in the back.

Only I wasn't having anything to do with a haircut like that. Okay, I'll be honest; I was vain, very vain about my hair. My hair was very curly, growing in tight ringlets. Those ringlets fitted my head like a tightly woven skullcap. In my imagination I figured it gave me an aristocratic kind of look.

I'd pay my two bits and get my inspection haircut every week. But as far as my officers and NCOs were concerned, I wasn't getting my twenty-five cents' worth of hair removed. When the barber asked me how I wanted my hair cut, I would point to the pictures posted on the barbershop wall and insist on getting my hair cut regulation style and not another snip more.

I would have just enough hair removed from the top and sides of my head to justify myself at inspections. Can't you just picture my platoon lined up for inspection, and everyone has a white-side-walled haircut but me? I'd stand out like a sore thumb.

Naturally when the inspecting officers hurried down to where I was standing rigidly at attention in ranks, they wanted to find fault with me. I made it easy for them. All they had to do was look down and there would be my smudgy shoes. Those officers could gig me on my shoes and my trousers but not on my haircut. Marine regulations permitted me to have hair two inches long, neatly tapered on the sides.

The day after the North Korean invasion, President Truman said, in so many words, that he wasn't going to tolerate that kind of crap. He called for intervention on the part of the United States and other United Nations countries. Truman, at first and for about a week, called his intervention a police action. Later, better informed and knowing that his army troops were getting the shit kicked out of them, he called the situation what it really was; he called it war.

I volunteered to go to Korea because that was where the action was located. It followed that where the action was located, there also would be promotion opportunities. I figured there would be mighty few parade-ground type of inspections in an area where men were fighting, shooting, and dying. I also figured I could fight and shoot as well as the next man; I made no plans for dying.

To be completely honest, however, another reason why I kept asking for a transfer was actually because of the type of duty I was doing at Quantico. I was a telephone switchboard operator on the main telephone exchange at the Quantico Marine Corps Base.

Damn! Can't you just picture my position in life? Here's a war going on with marines involved in it doing all kinds of things, winning all kinds of medals and honors. And you put in your telephone call to Quantico and you get me on the line as your telephone operator. At that time just about every telephone exchange in the world had female telephone operators.

Imagine how I felt when people asked me what I did in the Marine Corps.

12

"Why, uh, I'm in the Communications Platoon at 'G' Barracks" is the way I would respond, sort of nonchalantly, hoping that no other questions would follow. But, no, questions always followed.

"What do you do there?"

"Well, uh, actually I'm a wireman. My occupational specialty number is 2511. That stands for basic marine corps wireman. You know, like a telephoneman."

"Oh, my, isn't that interesting. Then you climb telephone poles and that type of thing, don't you?"

"Well, uh, no, not exactly. My job is more technical than that. But I use those telephone lines in my work, though," I would admit, hoping the questioning would stop.

"Oh! How exciting! And just how do you use the telephone lines?"

"I USE THEM BECAUSE I AM A GODDAMNED TELEPHONE OPERATOR!" I would snarl back. "I sit at a goddamned switchboard with my little telephone headset on, just like the girls in the big cities do, and I answer the goddamned incoming telephone calls!"

Generally my yelling out loud and my cursing and the look of hate I gave to my questioner would cut off any further chitchat. The first time it happened at home, I hated to answer my mother's questions like that, but it always cut me to the quick to have to admit that I answered telephone calls at Quantico when marines in Korea were having all the fun.

Actually, other than to have other marines poke fun at you, you know, the raised eyebrows and the la-di-da smirks, I had to admit that duty as a male telephone operator at Quantico was really pretty good duty after all. It sure had a lot of advantages and benefits. Good liberty hours in nearby Washington, D.C., were greatly enhanced by the contacts made with real telephone operators who worked for Ma Bell, young and sometimes not-so-young females who all had those soft, dulcet-sounding, sexy voices.

Females worked the switchboards in telephone exchanges in the big and little cities throughout the United States. There had to be thousands of those females. And when you had thousands and thousands of women working night

13

shifts, chances were very, very good that you would get connected with a couple of them who were hot to trot. Those females liked the idea of placing a telephone call to Quantico and getting a marine on the other end who was always guaran-goddamned-teed to be eager and ready for sex, any kind of kinky sex with a female telephone operator.

Each of us marines working the switchboard at Quantico had a little black book. We filled the pages in our little black books with the names and addresses of female telephone operators who indicated they would like to see us if we ever got around to their neighborhood. When we went out on liberty to see one of those female telephone operators, we hoped, we eagerly anticipated that we would get connected in all the right places. Still, whenever I had to own up to the type of work I was doing while other marines were fighting in Korea, well, I always felt a little bit limp wristed.

So it was really the combination of a lot of different factors that prompted me to volunteer month after month for combat duty in Korea. It was also the combination of a lot of other factors that prompted my officers and NCOs to turn down anything I requested. I guess none of them figured they owed me anything.

Every month for thirteen months, I had been asking for a transfer to Korea—to the Land of the Morning Calm where ever since I had reenlisted there were no calm mornings—when I just thought, well, fuck it. All I was doing was pissing off the first sergeant and aggravating the company commander because they had to turn down my requests. I couldn't understand why, if I was such a pain in the ass to them, they just didn't get rid of me by transferring me.

I had done some figuring. I figured the war in Korea had gone through three phases so far.

Phase one was that the strong southern drive of the North Koreans had been checked by both the United States and United Nations troops. The drive was further checked by the brilliant landing of marines on September 15, 1950, at Inchon, on the west coast of Korea and just below the 38th Parallel. An extremely successful and winning drive north started with this landing. By October 20 the North Korean capital city of Pyongyang was taken by UN forces. Exactly

14

one month later, on November 20, soldiers of the U.S. Army 7th Division reached the Manchurian border. General Douglas MacArthur—who operated so brilliantly in the Pacific during World War II—told the American public that their soldiers would be home for Christmas. But that wasn't the way things worked out.

Phase two of the Korean War started with the November 26, 1950, counterattack by 200,000 Chinese communist "volunteers" who crossed the Yalu River from Manchuria and forced the evacuation of 105,000 United Nations troops and some 91,000 Korean civilians at Hungnam on about Christmas Day. The Chinese viciously pushed down and across the 38th Parallel, driving nearly seventy miles south into South Korea. When Marine Col. Lewis B. "Chesty" Puller—then commanding a regiment of marines, a man who won all the combat medals his nation could award a fighting man, all except the Congressional Medal of Honor —was told that he was surrounded by Chinese, he is alleged to have said, "Good! Now my men can shoot in any direction and hit the fuckers!"

Some journalists, many of them writers who never left their safe stateside desks, callously called the pullback to Hungnam a retreat. Other journalists, some who walked the frigid roadway from the frozen Chosin Reservoir to the sea, wrote warm words with frozen fingers using the military term "retrograde movement" to describe the pullback, calling it an attack in a different direction. No matter what name was applied, the soldiers and marines who fought the Chinese in ice-coated gorges and on ridges in freezing North Korea knew it to be a killing war. For the marines, the rearward march to the sea—from November 28 through the night of December 11–12—was a fifteen-day lifetime cut short for far too many. The marines faced eight Chinese divisions commanded by veteran communist Gen. Sung Shi-lun; his mission was to destroy the marine division. Fierce hand-to-hand combat raged endlessly day after day, marines crouching low in hastily scooped-out fighting holes and numbed nightly as massive artillery duels heated up the dark. General Sung Shi-lun failed in his task; the marines reached Hungnam bloody but intact. True to their word, they brought out their honored dead, their terribly wounded, and their battered equipment. Later, on Christmas Eve, the last of the ships involved in the seaborne evacuation cleared Hungnam, headed for southern safety.

The following spring, a strong United Nations force would again push the Chinese and North Koreans backward, back across the 38th Parallel. The really big action would take place in the Punchbowl, in the craggy mountains of eastern Korea. The Punchbowl fight would signal the halt to an offensive that had been carried out by some 600,000 Chinese soldiers and ended in combat action that raged day and night during the final eight days of April 1951.

Phase three of the Korean War actually started about mid-April 1951—on April 11 to be exact—the day when President Harry Truman "fired" General MacArthur from his command of the war. With new commanders in the war operating under orders direct from President Truman, with the cessation of the Punchbowl operation, negotiations for a truce in Korea began in earnest on July 10, 1951.

It was that same day, after reading about the truce talks in the base newspaper, that I told the company clerk that no, I did not want to put in for a transfer to Korea.

"How come, Crawford? You'll be breakin' up a long string of turndowns," the company clerk smirked.

"How come? I'll tell you how come! You've been readin' the newspapers, the same as me. You've been lookin' at the pictures in the newspapers. You must've seen all those clean-faced soldiers being inspected by those bandbox generals.

"Shitfire, man! There ain't gonna be much of a war goin' on over there anymore. All those people are gonna do from now on is stand inspection.

"They're gonna be livin' in the field, and they're gonna hafta shave in cold water outta their helmets, and some asshole first sergeant or company clerk is gonna be on their asses about makin' them get white-side-walled haircuts, and maybe makin' them spit shine their goddamned combat boots and all, and I'm tellin' you true, I got a bellyful of all that stuff right here at Quantico, where at least I got clean sheets on my bunk and weekend passes to go out and screw around with telephone operators!"

I really had examined closely recent photos and pictures coming out of Korea. At earlier times in the past year the photos played it big, showing battle-weary men with drawn faces and weary-looking, sort of spooky eyes, the men dirty with wisps of beards and mustaches, each man with a thousand-yard stare and untidy hair that grew heavy into ragged sideburns.

Well, now all you saw was those happy, smiling faces of barracks soldiers with clean uniforms and their bright looks, and every one with a short haircut.

So when the peace talks started, I stopped asking for a transfer to Korea. It was my failure to ask for a transfer that was one of the reasons why the front office later transferred me. Where once the officers and NCOs in my company had thwarted all my efforts for a transfer, now they plotted to get me on a draft quota. There was no way to prove it, but I just knew that, collectively, my officers and NCOs had agreed to give me everything I particularly did not want. I had the feeling that my officers and NCOs had all agreed that on the occasion of my next fuck-up, that would be the occasion for giving me the mean green wienie. It almost happened that way.

It was the middle of the week, a Wednesday. It was 2000 (8:00 P.M.) and I was working the midwatch at the main telephone exchange. The day was June 11, 1951, and I was working on my thirteenth month of reenlistment. The watch I would be standing would stretch to 0800 (8:00 A.M.)—twelve hours of ho-hums, of head-nodding and neck-snapping, of my chin bouncing off my chest, of eyes burning, stomach churning sour, and my mental faculties at zilch.

Militarily speaking, every message of importance had already been sent and answers received; everything of importance had already been discussed by late Monday or early Tuesday and was being acted upon. Anything that would need to be further discussed would wait until late Thursday as it worked its way through to all day Friday. This was how the Marine Corps worked.

17

Wednesday afternoons had the colorful term "rope yarn Sunday" attached to them. An earlier seagoing phrase, the term meant time off, so that web and rope gear of the fleet could be cleaned, mended, and repaired. Wednesday afternoons were a time for general relaxation for the troops, especially seagoing marines, who faced rigorous routines throughout the remainder of the week.

Because Wednesdays were notoriously slow, I came to work prepared. I carried a couple of steak sandwiches bummed from a mess cook on the promise of the name and address and phone number of the next hot-to-trot female telephone operator. I also brought a couple of bars of candy, some books and magazines, and a small metal coffee percolator as well as the grounds to brew in it.

"Who's got the backboard watch?" I asked of the man I was relieving on the switchboard.

"Technical Sergeant Eoff," said the man being relieved of duty who was already halfway out the door.

A quick look at the log informed me that only three long-distance telephone calls had come in during the past three hours. I noted that Sergeant Eoff had marked down his home telephone number; he was the first man contacted if something went wrong with the switchboard. He lived at an off-base housing location in the nearby town of Triangle. His telephone line was on an emergency circuitry and did not go through the switchboard I would be operating. It was guaranteed safe even in wartime situations. I thought all of that preparedness was a bit much, but, what the hell, I wasn't paying for it.

Sergeant Eoff was constantly on call. That was the reason for him having the special telephone line. He was a big, grim Swede.

The constantly snapping noises, sounds, and movements of the automated telephone switching system located in an adjoining but separate soundproof room was the kingdom of Technical Sergeant Eoff.

Most technical sergeants were called "Gunny," a term that was a holdover from an earlier time when there was such a rank in the marines. Scuttlebutt had it that Headquarters, Marine Corps was thinking about reinstating that

18

rank. I hoped they would. It had class. It sounded tough. Gunnery sergeant! Damn, when you got to saying it and thinking about it, that rank had a better ring to it than the term "Top" or even "first sergeant."

I was dreaming again.

"The first thing I gotta do is get promoted to corporal. And then to buck sergeant, and then to staff sergeant, and then right on up to Jesus Christ and God before I get to be a gunny sergeant," I muttered to the switchboard.

I busied myself by making things comfortable. I filled my small eight-cup percolator with water and then put the coffee grounds on top. I plugged the percolator into a nearby wall socket, and then I set it down right on top of the flat work area of the adjacent telephone switchboard which was connected internally with the switchboard I would be using.

While the percolator sputtered, I read the admonishing sign posted on the wall above the dual switchboards:

NO LIQUIDS WILL BE CONSUMED
BY TELEPHONE OPERATORS
SEATED AT THESE CONSOLES!

The sign, in big black block letters penned in India ink by the wire chief, was a PYA sign, a protect-your-ass sign. Marine NCOs had a fetish about PYAs. They were posted conspicuously around every working area at Quantico.

If something went wrong, and something always did go wrong, the senior NCO present would point to his PYA sign as if to say, "I told you not to do it!" I always thought the signs were of dubious value, the specialty of men who had been promoted beyond their level of competency.

I was fascinated by the workings of the automated switching system. Whenever I saw Gunny Eoff making repairs or replacing worn-out parts, I'd ask him if I could help, if only by fetching and carrying his tools. I was awed by the erratic clicking and snapping sounds, the rapid movement of all the switches.

Alone now in the switchboard area, my coffee perking frantically, I found out the true meaning of the statement that time sure passes fast when you're having fun. No telephone calls came into the switchboard during the first two hours of my watch. I heard the muted sound of taps being played down at the main area in front of the MP barracks; it was a beautiful, haunting sound telling the base to go to sleep. Because of the small size of its main encampment, Quantico was one of the few bases where you could actually hear taps played at night.

I had already finished reading one of the paperbacks and had eaten one of my steak sandwiches, and now, as I tried to pour another cup of coffee, I found nothing but dregs in the bottom of the pot.

I ducked out of the switchboard room with the coffeepot in my hand and headed to a nearby toilet facility with a sink to refill the percolator. I took my time and even tapped my kidneys while I was there; a man can only drink so much coffee without seeking relief.

It's going to be a long night, I thought as I returned to the switchboard room. I busied myself putting a few spoonfuls of coffee right on top of the wet grounds of the first pot and then plugged the electrical cord into the wall socket. I didn't notice that the electrical cord had become wrapped around one of the wheeled legs of the office chair I was sitting on.

I didn't realize it but my transfer to Korea was coming up.

I sat back and started to read another book. Fifteen minutes later the fresh smell of newly perked coffee filled the switchboard room. I looked about for my cup. It was at the far end of the dual switchboard. With a push against heels that were firmly planted on the deck, I shoved, propelling the chair I was sitting on by its wheels toward the coffee cup. The movement tightened the electrical cord, pulling the eight-cup percolator sideways and spilling freshly brewed coffee and wet grounds across the circuitry of one switchboard, which shorted out both of the interconnected switchboards with a quick blue flash.

Zzzzzzzzzt! went the quick blue flash.

"Sheeeeiiittt!" I yelled.

Right away I was in a world of shit, and didn't I know it.

In less than five minutes I had all the external mess cleaned up. I cleaned the floor below the switchboards of dripping coffee and coffee grounds. A few drops of coffee seeped out from beneath the switchboard.

Hoping, and I already knew I would be hoping in vain, I threw the switch on the switchboard to the on position. Nothing. The switchboard lights did not light up. I really had not expected them to.

I removed the dozen or more setscrews that held the heavy plastic switchboard faceplate in position. In the cavity below, dark brown and rich-smelling coffee and coffee grounds puddled around tangled masses of multicolored wires. I definitely had shorted out the switchboard.

I knew this mess was a job beyond my cleaning capabilities.

Half an hour later, Gunny Eoff was looking down into the mess I had created. Rich coffee odors wafted upward. Eoff touched a finger to the puddle of coffee in the middle of the whole mess and tentatively raised the finger to his lips.

"The coffee's not bad, Crawford. But you picked a hell of a place to brew it," Eoff said.

I had anticipated a royal ass-chewing. I had not expected humor.

Continuing in his mild manner, Eoff said, "Now what I'm gonna do is show you how those different-colored wires interconnect between the telephone central and this switchboard. Between the two of us, we're going to have to dry every one of those wires and then check to see if they've been burned out." He was acting like he was holding school.

The job of wiping all the wires, of replacing one or two that had been burned with an arc of electricity, took nearly seven hours. Working with Eoff, being informed by him, shown by him, and helping him with the job gave me a taste of what it was like to be a telephone technician.

Eoff and I even brewed another pot of coffee or so to see us through that long night. This time the coffee was made in the approved area of the switchboard room.

Finally, with the last of the wires wiped, with the last bit of coffee grounds vacuumed up by way of a small hand-held unit, with the last of the many tiny screws tightened again, Eoff plugged the switchboard back into the wall circuitry.

21

The whole unit lit up like a Christmas tree.

Quickly I plugged into each jack, disconnecting the circuit when I received no answer to my "Quantico operator" query. I hesitated and then placed a call to the telephone centers in Richmond and Washington, checking to see just how many telephone calls had been made to my inoperative switchboard throughout the night.

"Nope, no calls from here. Is that you, Crawford? When you coming up this way again, sugar? Show you a good time, honey."

I couldn't believe it. No calls had been made through either switchboard. Chances are if a telephone call had not been routed through these two boards, then the probability was great that no telephone calls had been made at all to my switchboard.

I was home free.

Well, almost home free.

I saw Gunny Eoff making an entry in his switchboard logbook.

He looked at me with tired eyes.

"You know I've got to make a report of this, don't you?"

"Yessir, Gunny. I know."

"Okay. Just so you know. Nothing personal in it."

"It's okay, Gunny. You've been great. I got no complaints against you. I'm just sorry I caused you to stay up all night working on that switchboard."

"No big thing. It's my job. I like doing my job."

He looked up from his writing and gave me a big Swedish kind of a grin.

"You can bet your ass, though, that something like this could really fuck up any kind of promotion possibilities you might have had going for you, right?"

I chuckled a little bit, nervously.

"Right, Gunny. But I'll tell you straight. I never figured I had many promotion possibilities going for me here in this command."

We both sipped coffee, giving that statement the time it needed to be thought over.

"Somehow, Crawford, I get the feeling that you're blaming somebody else beside yourself for your not getting promoted to corporal. It's easy enough to shift blame. But it's kind of hard to accept responsibility for your actions, after you've gotten used to shifting blame."

"I do my job, Gunny," I said, trying hard to convince myself that I really did do my job.

"I don't know about that, the way you've been fuckin' up lately, pissing off the company commander every time we got an inspection and you not being marine enough to even get a white-side-walled haircut and all. That's part of your job. You just haven't been cuttin' the mustard. You do a good job workin'; nobody's going to find fault with you there. It's just that you only put yourself out about halfway on military decorum, and that don't hack it at all. And, personally speaking, I didn't figure you had too much of a chance on making corporal on the next promotion cycle, which, by the way, is coming up real soon. There's just too many Pfc's out there hustlin', keepin' themselves squared away."

Eoff paused to sip his coffee. That was the single-most longest spell of words he ever said to me since I had known him. Not talking now, he was evidently waiting for me to respond.

But I didn't have anything to say. I realized right at that tiring moment at the end of a long, frustrating night that I had not been giving my best to the Marine Corps, that I had been bucking the system, trying to make the system do things my way. Fat chance I had of succeeding. I realized then that you can't fight city hall.

"I'll tell you what," Eoff said. "You keep yourself squared away most of the time what with your uniform usually clean and neatly pressed, except maybe for those stupid shoe-polish stains on the back of your trouser legs. The only thing that really gives the company commander an itch where he can't scratch it is the way you carry on about haircuts, you not gettin' white-side-walls for inspections and all, making him look bad to the people who mark his fitness reports.

"When that kind of an act pisses off the company commander, he gets a case of the ass and takes it out on the first sergeant. And we both know the marine corps law of gravity is that shit rolls downhill. When the first sergeant

23

catches hell, you can bet all the money you have that the company NCOs will catch hell. And we in turn hand out our own brand of crap to all of you peons. Let me clue you in on something: Good NCOs don't like to see their men getting shit on because of the really stupid actions of any one man."

Eoff made sense. I was dog-tired, but his words got through to me. I sort of nodded my head in agreement. I did not say anything. I really had not taken the time to see my actions through the eyes of the person who was in charge of my life. Tired as I was, I now realized that stupidity can really blind a guy. Before, all I could see was that I wanted things to go my way, and by being bullheaded about it, I forced the issues. I was being an independent. I really was not part of the marine corps team. How did I ever get to thinking I could do it my way?

Eoff was speaking, breaking into my thoughts. "You did a good job, helping to clean up the mess you made earlier. And you seemed interested in what you were doing; you asked questions and all about everything. That counts a lot—somebody being interested in their work. And we did get a long-overdue job of preventive maintenance done on the switchboard. It's a job I've been meaning to do but just hadn't taken the time to get around to doing it."

He looked at me slyly over his coffee cup.

"You ain't plannin' to make coffee over here again, are you?"

I was suddenly so tired I just mumbled out a reply.

"No, sir, Gunny. Not for quite a while. I might be hardheaded, but I learn my lessons well."

"That's good. Now let me ask you, have you ever thought about becoming a telephone central repairman? The military occupational specialty number is 2516. You'd be doing the type of work we just did on the switchboard, plus working in the telephone central. I could put you in an on-the-job training cycle right here. That way you wouldn't have to go away to a school for an MOS change."

"I never thought about it before, Gunny. All I really wanted to do these past couple of months was to pull a hitch in Korea and maybe pick up my corporal's stripes there. I keep on askin' for a transfer and the main office keeps turnin' me down. And now the war's almost over, what with the truce talks and all."

Eoff shook his head. He looked out the window at the dawn's early light coming up, filling the sky overhead.

"Get your head out of your ass, Crawford. That war in Korea will be going on for quite a while. And let me tell you something else: The old man here is not the kind of a commander who transfers out his fuck-ups; he deals with his own problems.

"A couple things, now. Maybe I can help you, if you want to help yourself, and maybe I can help myself as well. First things first: Right after you're relieved here, without any questions or back talk, I want you to get your ass down to the barbershop and I want you to get a boot-camp, no-fucking-around-about-it white-side-walled haircut, and I want it real short on top, do you understand me?"

I was surprised at the way this conversation was going. I didn't exactly answer Eoff, but I sort of raised my left eyebrow in a way that meant I'd like to hear more before committing myself to something as rash as getting a white-side-walled haircut.

"I'll be going in to see the company commander just as soon as he comes aboard. I'll tell him what happened here. And I'll ask him to assign you to me as a retrainee for the 2516 MOS."

I was definitely surprised at the way this conversation was going. For the past couple of hours I had feared the coming of dawn. I had been thinking about how much brig time I would get for fucking up the switchboard. Now here was the repair chief talking about getting me a military occupational specialty (MOS) change so I could work for him.

I do not know what Eoff told the commanding officer and the first sergeant. All I know is that when I returned to the barracks from the barbershop with my real short haircut, I was told to report to the communications officer's office, immediately. I was given a retraining assignment. I was told to report to Technical Sergeant Eoff the following morning.

I worked for Eoff for exactly two weeks.

And then I was told to pack my seabags. My orders to Korea had come in. I was to be in Camp Pendleton in ten days' time for intensive training as an infantryman. I was part of the 13th Draft going to Korea.

I shook hands with Eoff. I stammered out that I was grateful to him. Then I headed to the company office to pick up my transfer orders.

The desk of the company commander was clear of everything except my set of orders at one corner and a single sheet of white paper that had a large black marine corps emblem embossed on it. The heavy bond paper was a promotion warrant.

The company commander handed me my transfer orders without a word. Then he made a motion with his hand toward the promotion warrant.

"Do you know what that is?"

"No, sir," I said, in all of my innocence.

"I wouldn't doubt that, seeing as how it's been a long time since you've been near one. It's a promotion warrant, Private Crawford. It's a promotion warrant to the rank of corporal. And it has your name on it. Do you think you rate being promoted to the rank of corporal?"

"Oh, yes sir. Indeed I do, sir," I mawked out.

The company commander picked up a clean, unsharpened pencil from his desk drawer. With the eraser end he pushed the warrant across his shiny desktop to me.

"I'm not so sure you do rate it, Crawford."

He was looking me right in the eye when he said that.

"But a man I respect thinks you rate it. Technical Sergeant Eoff recommended that you be promoted."

I looked down at the promotion warrant. Shit! It was dated two weeks earlier than the present date. I looked at the commanding officer.

"I don't promote fuck-ups or hard-asses, Corporal Crawford. And I don't transfer shit out of my command to commanders in a combat zone. I live with what the Marine Corps gives me. And I will tell you, Corporal, you have been a pain in the ass to me for a long, long time."

Suddenly a light went on in my mind. Now I knew why I had been turned down on my transfer requests over the past thirteen months. Good commanding officers, guided by the best judgments their first sergeants can make to them, do not transfer out their fuck-ups; they deal with them; they square them away, somehow.

"But over the past two weeks I've been getting good reports about you," my commanding officer said. "It seems that someone, somewhere along the line, finally got through to you about a lot of things, but especially about haircut regulations, which, as you well know, are my pet peeve."

The commanding officer took a big breath and held it, and so did I hold mine.

"Okay, enough said. Since you look like a marine, and since you've been working like a marine, then maybe you just might make a good marine NCO.

"One final word before you leave. I was the man who trained Technical Sergeant Eoff in his skills as a backroom man. I got my opportunity to work back there for exactly the same reason Eoff got his chance, and for the same reason you got your chance.

"Go ahead. Pick up that promotion warrant, Corporal. There are no coffee stains on it." And then, for the first time, he smiled at me.

I went home on a brief leave. Two weeks later at Camp Pendleton in training with the 13th Draft, the hair around my ears was just as long as it always had been. I had found out that NCOs had certain little perks and privileges.

The men of the 13th Draft put in a lot of hours in combat training of all types. Our standard uniform of the day was utilities, field pack, helmet, and rifle. No one looked under the steel edge of my helmet to check whether or not I had long hair.

CHAPTER
2

At home on a ten-day leave, I contacted a high school buddy, Sgt. Tom Posty. He had also been assigned to the 13th Replacement Draft. Our transfer orders indicated we were both to be trained as infantrymen at Camp Pendleton, California, and then be sent by ship to Korea. Posty and I pooled our travel pay and bought an old car, a 1936 Dodge, for a hundred bucks even. We changed the oil and the spark plugs, put some Marvel Mystery Oil in the crankcase, hung a "California or Bust" sign on the back, and headed west.

I admit I felt a little bit guilty as Posty and I drove out of town trailing a great cloud of exhaust smoke behind us. We both waved good-bye to my wife, Joann. Joann was hampered a bit in her enthusiasm to wave good-bye to us; she was holding our crying year-old son, Michael, in her arms and she too was crying. I was torn between desires as I went off to war. Sure, I loved my wife and, sure, I wanted to be with her and our son. But I was a young marine eager to know the world; I wanted horizons farther away than the next town, the next state. I was quite willing to trade time at home with my family for the opportunity to go to a far and distant land to fight a war. I viewed war as an exciting adventure. The thought never occurred to me that I might get killed. I had too much to live for; I was young and I was filled with the optimism of youth.

Joann and I had met each other at her June 1948 high school graduation dance. She was quite thin but had a nice shape. I knew right away she was the girl for me. We danced together that first night and then dated, almost continually, from that time on. We were married less than a year later, soon after I finished my one-year hitch in the marines.

I might have had esprit de corps on my mind the first time I joined the marines, but the second time around I looked for security for my family in exchange for my four-year enlistment.

For a guaranteed monthly paycheck all I had to do was put my body and soul in hock. I think Joann realized more than I that that was just what I was doing, putting my body and soul in hock, as Posty and I headed for California.

The drive west was long and monotonous. Posty and I devised a hundred different games to play to occupy our time on the road. One of those games was to use the odometer of the car in guessing how far away a viewed object was from our present position.

I discovered I had an unusual ability; I knew almost instantaneously the distances involved. I was seldom ever wrong, even when the distances involved guessing at points just barely visible through the car windshield. I was guessing —more accurately put, I was stating exactly—the distance that needed to be traveled. I was right on the money, time after time. I would find out soon enough just how I could put this ability to work for me.

Word had been passed during advanced infantry training at Camp Pendleton that peace might come to the Far East before the 13th Draft got into the war. That was the way newsmen were referring to Korea, calling it the "Far East," picking up on the phrase, I guess, because it had a smoother, more sophisticated sound.

I wasn't one for reading newspapers or magazines on a daily basis. I depended instead on getting my news from scuttlebutt, the unverified word passed along by other marines or, maybe, through listening to local radio stations. By mid-June the word that was passed was that Eighth Army doggies were really kicking the shit out of the Red Chinese Army. No one in the marine training camps had a high opinion of the army, so I just figured if the army could kick the shit out of the Far Eastern armies, then maybe the war was really running out of steam.

Someone had tacked a magazine photo on the company bulletin board about the middle of June. The caption and story line below the picture almost made a believer out of me about the war winding down. The words jumped right off the page, saying the Eighth Army was literally slaughtering the Red Chinese Army. Tens of thousands, the caption read, had been either killed or taken prisoner since April 22, right after the communists had launched their spring offensive. The photo showed two long, ragged lines of Orientals following one after the other, a line on each side of a winding roadway in Korea with only an occasional GI— and most of them not carrying a rifle or anything—telling them where to go.

I carefully examined the photo. The POWs were all of a kind, a ragged, emaciated-looking bunch in sacklike cotton tunics and baggy trousers. Each of them, except maybe those with head-wound bandages, was wearing a nondescript cloth hat, its rumpled visor pointing at an off angle. Many had arm and leg wounds wrapped with dirty gray bandages. The Chinese were slogging along a dirt roadway, churning footing below into mud with their all-of-a-same-size rubber sneakers. I examined the faces of my enemy in that photo. There was no conquering look to them. They all had dejection, despair, and defeat mirrored in their eyes. Some of their faces, of the wounded ones anyway, showed signs of great pain. All their faces had a hungry look. The caption said they had not eaten in a couple of days. The caption said the recent Eighth Army offensive had pushed the Chinese back to positions north of the 38th Parallel. The caption spoke confidently about how, this time, the army had "broken the Chinaman's back."

About the third week in June, my company had just come

in from a grueling twenty-mile Saturday morning training hike up and over those goddamned Camp Pendleton mountains out at Tent Camp Two, carrying field marching packs on our weary backs. All of us were sweaty and tired and pissed off because the conditioning hike was one missed earlier that had to be made up. We griped it was a hell of a way to start a liberty weekend. None of us needed any bad news when a local radio station gave us the bad news anyway.

Even though Russia disclaimed any part in the Korean War, the country's United Nations delegate, Yakov Malik, had just made a proposal calling for an armistice in Korea. Malik recommended that the opposing generals "arrange a cease-fire in the field." Malik said, in part, "the Soviet peoples believe that discussion should be started between the belligerents for a cease-fire and an armistice."

"I'll be damned," I said, angrily parroting other marines when I heard the news. My earlier fears of not getting into a shooting war were rapidly returning.

"I'll be damned," said Army General Van Fleet, probably more in amazement than anything else, when he was apprised of Malik's statement, his hopes quickening for stopping the war before more men were killed. Fearing a trick, he ordered the Eighth Army to continue patrolling. By dusk Sunday, talk of the armistice was put on a back burner as soldiers shakily returned from reconnaissance patrols, which had snaked along the fringe of the Chinese lines. Wide-eyed—as only the sound of bullets zinging close by can turn a man wide-eyed—the patrols reported that the Chinese Reds were still shooting.

A day later Peking Radio broadcasted word from Kim Il Sung, the North Korean premier, and Peng Teh-huai, the Chinese Army commander, saying they agreed to meet with United Nations representatives on the 38th Parallel near Kaesong. According to the radio broadcast, the communists were ready to talk about "a cessation of military action and the establishment of peace."

From his Tokyo headquarters, Gen. Matt Ridgway, USA, commanding general and army administrator in Japan, selected Vice Adm. Charles Turner Joy to be his chief UN truce negotiator. Joy would be aided by Adm. Arleigh Burke and Maj. Gen. Laurence Craigie, USA.

The communists would be represented by North Korean General Nam Il and Chinese General Tung Hua.

The truce talks were scheduled to begin July 10. Word was passed to the United Nations troops to hold in place, to patrol in order to be knowledgeable, to fight back but not to antagonize. No one in Korea wanted to chase away those white doves.

The patterns of war in early July were small-scale skirmishes, punctuated occasionally by violent flurries when larger units met in bloody clashes.

Monsoon winds from the ocean brought heavy rains, the rains turned the parched land into a morass of mud, and soldiers on both sides were the worse for the weather. The rain restricted flying. The planes that got into the air found reconnaissance negligible due to poor visibility.

The restricted combat situations did not hamper the Chinese or North Korean forces in any way. By August 6, four weeks after the peace proposal, aerial and ground reconnaissance located fresh Chinese troops entrenched at west coast positions. These troops had recently arrived on line in the form of two new Red armies and numbered an estimated 150,000 men. On the east coast a new North Korean army, estimated as being twice as powerful as the one that had attacked in June 1950, was in position and ready for a new offensive. Reconnaissance provided the frightening news that a lot of Russian T-34 tanks had been sighted rolling south. Additionally, quite a few heavy artillery units had been moved to frontline positions.

My enthusiasm for war waned slightly when I figured the odds; during August, the 12th Replacement Draft of about 950 marines was prepared to ship out to Korea, and my draft, the 13th, composed of about the same number of marines, was scheduled to leave during mid-September. Simple arithmetic led me to believe we were facing odds of about seventy-five to one. All through training I had been taught that one marine was worth any ten of the best troops the communists had to offer. Still, I figured I better train a lot harder than I had been doing.

During late August, with the peace talks sputtering, with the communists putting up one stumbling block after another, with Matt Ridgway getting angrier and angrier at the situation, the watchful soldiers of both armies on rain-fogged peaks or in muddy valleys fitfully prodded and jabbed at each other. The prodding and jabbing and sparring was firm but not forceful. Whatever limited offensive action occurred was carried out under heavy artillery fire. United Nations forces belted out brisk punches and assaulted communist positions in the monsoon rain–soaked mountains north of the Hwachon Reservoir and in the area east of the Iron Triangle.

Three days before the 13th Draft boarded ship, more enemy strength information was received. The communist armies were said to have 500 or more tanks in position, more tanks now than they had when they started the war. More than a thousand planes were spotted on fields and could be launched to strike targets anywhere in South Korea. Ample artillery units and supplies had been noted, their locations and coordinates marked on UN artillery maps. On the eastern front, where my draft was headed, four new North Korean divisions had been verified as being in position behind the front lines. This new strength report was figured in and the results were astronomical; altogether the communist forces on line amounted to about forty divisions fully refitted and resupplied; another thirty divisions were in reserve.

Korean peace prospects dwindled as the peace talks stalled. Daily newspapers said the U.S. military dead in Korea was rapidly reaching a figure close to 14,000 men. There was no doubt the war was continuing as bloody as ever. Because of the renewed fighting in the Punchbowl area, coupled with an alarming increase in casualties, an urgent need existed for the 13th Draft to get to Korea to supplement losses in marine units.

I had just one major grievance. My birthday was less than two weeks away. I would soon be twenty-one years old.

When ships or planes cross the international date line, those aboard them must change the date of their calendars to correspond with the area into which they are moving. Troop ships headed west to Korea advance the date by one full day.

So when the USS *Marine Lynx* passed the international date line at about 2358 on September 23, it automatically became 2358 on September 24. And since it was past taps, with everybody in their bunks except the fire watch, well, shit, by the time reveille sounded I had already missed my twenty-first birthday, all two minutes of it. I felt cheated somehow.

Earlier, the urgency to get to Korea diminished somewhat when, a few days out at sea, the ship developed engine trouble. Don't ask me any technical questions about it because I don't have any answers. All I know is that thick, black, oily smoke billowed sluggishly out of her stacks and we were barely making enough headway for it not to settle down upon us. Finally, thirteen days after leaving the States, we limped, trailing smoke behind us, into Kobe, Japan.

There on the docks were some five hundred soldiers lined up with their individual weapons, transport packs, and seabags. They were waiting to come aboard. We were informed through a ship's broadcast that the soldiers were to be billeted topside and forward on the USS *Marine Lynx*.

Following right on the heels of that announcement we were told bitter news: Because of the delay in crossing, there was no time for liberty; we were scheduled to back out of port within five hours' time.

My first look at Japan was from the rail of the docked transport. I had no idea what I thought I would see, but it was entirely different from what I had anticipated. I think I was expecting, well, something out of the *Mikado*.

There were some majestic light blue mountains in the background, their peaks white with snow. Nearby, in the foreground, were flimsy-looking shanties perched on top of firm-looking docks. Some Chinese junk type of boats flitted like dragonflies all around our ship.

Everybody lined the rails and got a real charge out of some Japanese women—called josans—who were on the

34

docks. Dressed in colorful kimonos, each carried a beautifully painted but flimsy-looking umbrella. The josans were calling out and waving good-bye to the soldiers as they went up the gangplank.

You would think with that many soldiers aboard—and they were really cramped up on deck—there might be some trouble between them and the marines. I'll tell you right now there wasn't so much as an argument, much less a fight. I guess it is okay for soldiers and marines to act like assholes when there is little prospect of a real fight around, but with Korea just a day away everything was quiet.

The anchors came up and we maneuvered away from the dock, raising black smoke high overhead. Really huffing now, the ship headed southwest, hooked a right turn up to the Strait of Korea, and headed into Pusan, where the soldiers off-loaded some twenty-four hours after they had boarded ship. We lined the rails and wished them luck.

The USS *Marine Lynx* was really hurting as she hit the high seas, heading up to the Sea of Japan and then northwest into the area of the east coast of Korea near the 38th Parallel. We continued to leave a long black track of greasy, heavy smoke behind us. I was glad when it got dark. I was also very glad that we had established air supremacy over the skies and that North Korea did not have any more Yak airplanes. We would have been a sitting duck instead of a lame one.

At around 0300 on September 28, reveille went for all hands. Buck sergeants roamed the sleeping quarters bellowing: "Let go of your cocks and grab your socks! Reveille! Reveille!"

Chow bumps sounded out and we snaked our way through corridors to the mess hall. We had a great feed—the best since we had boarded ship. Steak, eggs, french-fried potatoes, hot home-baked bread with a good yeasty smell and taste, plenty of butter, and hot coffee, although a lot of us were calling it "java" because, I think, it sounded tougher that way, at least to our ears. Eating was done as it always is done on troopships—standing up at narrow metal tables.

Quickly, then, everyone again hustled below decks to pack seabags a final time, to prepare field transport packs and then shoulder them, and to check and double-check everything one more time.

There was a valid need to be certain that we carried the required items in our packs. In any military operation, supplying the fighting man with what he needs is possibly the most crucial and critical problem facing a commander. Initially, any time a marine unit changed positions or assumed a new position, the individual grunt carried everything he needed to that position on his back.

Now that the United States had been at war in Korea for more than a year, it was already a known fact that we had set up what was considered to be the longest supply line in the history of warfare. And while we all joked about the supply system, every mile of it and every pound of equipment in it had the most serious meaning.

Most of us grunt marines had already learned the seriousness of hauling around only the most necessary of weight on our backs as we humped up and down the hills at Camp Pendleton, and sometimes even the essential items weighed too much.

What it all boiled down to was this: Whatever we were going to use—for the next twenty-four hours or longer—whatever we were going to eat, or wear, or sleep in or under, or shoot with, whatever we were going to change into if what we were wearing got soaked, anything and everything we would need or possibly have a use for, well, that's what we packed into our field transport pack. We packed everything in our haversack and our knapsack, and then we wrapped it all around with a blanket roll, we put belt suspender straps on it, and then we hooked it onto our back and tried to walk with it.

The scabbard for the bayonet could be hooked on the top left side of the haversack. A lot of marines spent days and days sharpening their bayonets to a razor sharp keenness on both sides. We had been told: "The most important member of the modern amphibious assault team is the individual marine. It is the individual marine, with his rifle and bayonet, who closes with the enemy and destroys him." Damn!

36

We had been taught that skill and confidence in the ability to use the bayonet gave the marine the spirit to make a bayonet assault. Hot damn!

Our instructor had said: "The rifle and bayonet, in your hands, can become a deadly combination of spear, sword, club, and shield. At night this combination weapon can kill silently and with surprise. In hand-to-hand fighting when the rifle cannot be reloaded and the use of grenades would be impractical, the bayonet is the decisive weapon." So it was small wonder we spent so much time devoted to sharpening our bayonets.

Our entrenching tool was hooked in its cover at the top of the haversack and strapped down by its handle on the knapsack. This small shovel with its collapsible blade, almost overlooked in the scheme of things, was perhaps the one item most constantly used in Korea, both as a tool and as a weapon. As a weapon it far overshadowed the bayonet.

A man usually needed help in getting the field transport pack on his back. It was cumbersome, bulky, and awkward to carry, and the straps that permitted it to ride high on a man's back desperately tried to cut off blood circulation to hands and fingers, seeing as how the straps came over each shoulder and went immediately to the rear again after passing under the armpits.

Heavy? You bet your ass it was heavy. But there was still more to carry. Each of us had a cartridge belt with its ten pouches filled with ammunition clips. We carried two canteens for water, a small first-aid packet, and either a compass or wire cutters attached to the cartridge belt. Squad leaders and NCOs armed with the .45-caliber automatic pistol still had to hook a holster on their belt.

Add the weight of a steel helmet, put a rifle or a Browning automatic rifle (BAR)—they were heavy but everyone wanted one—at sling arms on a marine, and he knew right away what heavy was all about. The whole kit and caboodle weighed about eighty pounds.

Clumsy is only a word. It is the word that best describes how a marine feels when, after he has harnessed himself into his field transport pack, he must still strap himself into a

Mae West, the light, sky blue, kapok-filled navy life jacket. The standard life jacket for debarking troops at that time had a half-moon, contoured and tapered pillowlike affair that fit behind a man's head and that, by connecting strong cloth, attached itself to two fat sausagelike tubes that extended down both sides in the front. Everything was all tied together with blue cotton stringlike ties affixed in front.

Scuttlebutt at breakfast said we were going to make an amphibious landing above the 38th Parallel. Everyone had been issued a full ration of ammunition. We were to put ten clips in our cartridge belt, and load a clip into our rifles and then lock our weapons in the safety position.

If you think that locking and loading our rifles in the small metal living compartment way below decks in a ship that was being rocked from side to side by ground swells wasn't a bit hairy, well, I've got news for you.

Live ammunition! Oh, mother, I've come home to die!

Suddenly, to the sound of a shrill boatswain's pipe screaming, demanding notice, to the sound of an off-key marine bugler blatting out the call for attention, someone spoke loudly, excitedly, into the ship's intercommunication system and set everything in motion: "Attention, all hands! Attention, all hands! Now away the special sea and anchor detail. Away the special sea and anchor detail. Coxswains, man your boats! Coxswains, man your boats! Marines, report to your debarkation station! Marines, report to your debarkation station!"

The rat race began with those words and like rats leaving a sinking ship we scurried up the narrow ladderways. We had to quickly climb up three, sometimes four decks on those narrow, cleated metal ladderways that were very slippery even when dry, going up, up, up toward topsides.

On reaching the sweet salt smell of sea air, feeling the soft breeze dry our sweaty faces, we began to mill around like pregnant hippos trying to find our debarkation station. It all seemed different, somehow, from the practice run. It was about as fucked up as a Chinese fire drill on New Year's Eve in Times Square.

Damn! We were informed someone took the wrong turn on the ladder coming topside. Our debarkation station was on the other side of the ship and forward. The acrid taste in my mouth was nothing but the bitterness of frustration.

Officers loudly called out debarkation station numbers. Staff NCOs hustled about, harassing the troops. Navy enlisted on upper decks laughed and pointed out marine fuck-ups. The PA system blatted and whistled.

Move to the rail. Lift a leg, robotlike, and throw it over the rail. Follow it through with the rest of your body. Hold on tight to the rough, inch-thick hemp rope of the debarkation net. Steady in position until your group of five marines are all on the net and lined abreast of each other. Down! Go down one shaky step at a time. Just like marching! Your left leg, and then your right leg. Another group of five marines is forming above you on the net. And another group of five is waiting, and another is waiting, and another is waiting.

At one time there were as many as eight groups of marines in rows of five men each, forty men in all, inching their way down just one of the debarkation nets on rope steps supported by rope risers. There were eight debarkation nets being used on each side of the ship. If things went right—and marine officers and staff NCOs make things go right—some 632 men would move down the debarkation nets and into the peter boats at the same time.

I was bobbing in and out on the ropes and I had a death grip on the vertical strands, the saving factor. I trusted my feet to find a rope step below, but I couldn't look down. I could only look forward at the scabrous gray paint of the ship's hull as it closed to my face and then receded, closed and receded, moving in and out without rhyme or reason. We were all on the same rope step, yet we bobbed back and forth indiscriminately.

We had it drilled into us time and time again: "If someone above you falls, grip tightly to the vertical rope and cradle that person in your arms until help can get to you." Just who is shitting who? I could barely hold onto the ropes myself, barely bring up courage enough to do the clutch-tight dance on the rope moving one step down, slowly. If someone fell down on me I swear I would have bitten him on the ass and would keep on biting until he got off on his own.

It was over. After a last yawing, swelling, rising, and

falling step, I was off the rope ladder and on the deck of a bouncing, jouncing peter boat. I was too scared on the debarkation net to consider my gobbled-down breakfast; now I headed to the side of the peter boat where other men were heaving their cookies.

Fighting a war had to be a whole lot easier than getting to it.

CHAPTER
3

I purposefully did not make a movement forward, to the rear, or sideways. All my movements were involuntary during the lurching, bucking-up-and-down roller coaster ride as we headed toward the beach in uneasy waters made all the more choppy by erratic forward maneuverings. I found myself in a sort of at ease posture, with my knees bent slightly forward, the better to accept the vicious thrashings of the constantly yawing boat.

I was more or less in the center of the peter boat and just a bit forward, at that point where the deck begins to slope slightly upward. I was well away from the gunwales of the boat, its gray-painted sides, with no chance at all to better my stability by extending an arm and bracing a hand against a side. My mind focused inward; I mentally attempted to push my toes down through the half-inch leather soles of my boondockers to gain purchase, a tight grip, by clamping them forcefully to the slick, wet corrugated metal deck of the peter boat.

Consciously, I was very much aware that I was holding my body rigidly upright. I tried to keep myself in a steady position, my feet widespread, by bracing my legs rigidly in place. For the most part I was able to do so, excepting only an occasional quick-step lurch caused by particularly vicious sea movement, by waves smashing alongside.

I permitted myself to sway in an almost circular pattern, from front to side to rear to side and then back to the front again, monotonously, in harmony with all the other wretched bodies packed tightly. We hypnotically swayed, with our feet anchored tightly while our rigidly upright bodies all slowly moved in unison to the creaking of the boat, to the small, secret sounds of leather rubbing and canvas chafing, to the sound of heavily starched utility uniforms whispering softly, coming in contact with those of other marines in the boat.

For there was contact, physical, crowded-together contact that results from bodies packed closely against other ill-at-ease bodies, with life jackets and packs rubbing. I was ashamed when I realized that the contact seemed sensual, and that I was semihard.

My shame was short-lived. It was replaced by a throat-clamped-shut seasick sensation that I felt throughout my sweat-soaked, tired, miserable body, which ached in so very many known and hidden places.

I could feel the quickening movement of the rushing water below the peter boat through the thick soles of my heavy, rugged, ankle-high boondockers as we made our run to the beach. I listened to the ocean talk to me through the cleated steel deck. Without rhyme or reason I mumbled the words of the sea, mouthing the words softly, sensuously, in proper cadence: "BOON-dockin' MUTHA-fuckah! BOON-dockin' MUTHA-fuckah!"

I was aware again of the sensuality of the moment, of the soft rising and falling of the deck, a sensation that had a sick manliness to it, and I was again aware of my half erection. I snickered to myself and wondered if this was why they call these crafts "peter boats."

The day seemed hazy blue. The sun was up and hot, trying to burn away the gray between the peter boat and the beach. I was aware of the sick-sweet sweat odor of perspiring bodies with fear in them of things unknown and still to come, of the nauseating salt taste of the ocean, and of the rushing waves as they punished the sides of the boat and then splashed high overhead in small showers, with each shower accompanied by a rainbow. I made a wish and I kept it to myself; I knew that wishes would not come true if they were shared with others.

I had a mind flash: What was the last thing I heard over the ship's PA system?

"You marines will be the first draft contingent to Korea to make an amphibious landing from the sea above the Thirty-eighth Parallel," the bodiless voice of the PA had intoned while I concentrated on not falling from the debarkation net. "Meet your enemy on his home ground and defeat him. Good luck, marines! May the luck of this vessel go with you!"

I brought the words to the surface of my mind, realization finally setting in. Shitfire, man, all along I had been told that heavy fighting was going on just above the 38th Parallel.

I felt all over biting-tingling with parts of my body asleep and parts just awakening. I was suddenly aware of the fact that I was no longer seasick. I was uneasy, sure, but not sick.

I was in the first wave scheduled to hit the beach. The boat team commander was a buck sergeant. I did not know him. He was in the rear, near the coxswain. He was bellowing out orders. He seemed to be enjoying himself.

All of us in the landing party were soaked with the heavy splashes of cold seawater coming in over the side. Our lips were cracked and our throats were parched with the constant swallowing, retching, and gagging. None of us grinned or even thought it was funny when someone guffawed, "If it tastes hairy, you better swallow it, 'cuz it's probably your asshole."

Just then the buck sergeant bellowed out: "Okay, you fuckers! Lock and load your weapons! Don't waste your ammo! Don't shoot unless you have a target."

"Oh, shit!" I said aloud, all uneasiness departing from me at the sound of the sergeant's voice. I was trying to force another clip of eight rounds into my already-loaded rifle.

43

When I hauled back on the operating rod handle to open the chamber, the clip that I had loaded earlier ejected out and in doing so knocked the fresh clip of ammunition I held in my hand to the bouncing deck.

About a dozen more marines who had also loaded their weapons earlier shouted out "Oh, shit!" along with me. Clips of ammunition clattered to the steel deck.

One rifle discharged straight up into the air with a hellacious roar.

"Oh, shit!" said a sailor. He was hanging on tightly to the side of the peter boat as he inched his way forward along the foot-wide outer shelf. His job was to kick down on the chain and sprocket that lowered the ramp at the front of the peter boat.

"When that ramp goes down," yelled the buck sergeant, "I want to see nothin' but assholes and heels headin' into that beach! You people be sure to jump off the sides of the ramp. That ramp might surge forward and break your legs if you don't.

"And point those goddamn rifles forward at all times! Don't shoot unless you have a gook target!"

I was now up in the front facing the ramp. I don't know how I got this far forward. I just was there. I saw and heard the sailor kicking and cursing at the sprocket that had locked itself in place. And then the ramp was down, aimed at the beach.

I was floundering in water higher than my knees. I was floundering and lurching in the frothy surf like some kind of sick whale coming ashore to beach itself.

"Oh, mother! I hope I can come home to die!" I cried out, loudly.

Marine corps training is second to none; it is the best in the world. All marines learn to do things by the book, and they learn to keep on doing those things, the same way every time, until they arrive at the point where they just naturally respond to a situation, doing the right thing at the right time. My infantry training came into play as I slammed down on my gut as I had been taught to do after I had trudged the mandatory ten steps forward. My next movement was to roll either left or right in order to disrupt the enemy's aim. I tried to roll to my right as I had been taught and I could not roll to my right. I tried to roll to my left and could not roll to my left. Why the hell couldn't I roll?

Damn! That fucking life jacket! I still had on that soggy, soaked, ten-thousand-pound life jacket. I had never trained in one and I had forgotten the last-minute shipboard instructions to remove it at the water's edge. I was bobbling around on top of it, my feet, legs, hands, and arms all off the ground. I was scrabbling around on top of those two sausage-shaped pods like some kind of wounded walrus.

I bobbled backward, forcing my knees to make contact with the sand. I propped my elbows in close, forming a tripod, pulled the rifle butt plate to where the hollow of my shoulder should have been, and snugged the stock close against my cheek. I quickly lined up the front and rear sights of my rifle.

I was looking at the soles of two pairs of worn boondockers. I raised my sights a hair upward and looked at two of the scroungiest marines I had ever seen. They both were wearing what was termed a Fu Manchu mustache, and both had wispy chin hair barely noticeable because of the grit and grime on their faces.

Both men wore soft covers on their heads, the bills folded back like you would a baseball cap. Their herringbone twill dungaree uniforms were torn and ratty looking and were extremely filthy with what looked like oil stains.

I had never seen either of them before in my life, yet I immediately identified them. They were your average run-of-the-mill motor transport truck drivers. Those guys, even if they had access to soap and water, would shun washing as a vampire shuns clear, clean, crisp daylight.

Anyway, there I was eyeballing them, my sights lined up on them.

"I think that gung ho fucker is gonna shoot us, Willie," the man on the right said.

"Damned if I don't think he might, Joe," the man on the

left said. Smirking, he raised his hands high overhead and simpered, "Lawdy! Lawdy! I surrender! I surrender!"

"Shit!" I said, disgustedly.

"Shit!" sounded off that loudmouthed buck sergeant who had been my boat team leader. "They ain't nothin' worth shootin' here. They's just a bunch of asshole marines."

CHAPTER
4

Loudspeakers set up strategically inland above the high-water mark of the beach sputteringly informed us in a loud metallic voice that the 13th Replacement Draft had come ashore at a place called Sochiri, a small fishing village located about seven miles below the front lines but still above the 38th Parallel. The metallic voice rattled on, saying the 13th Draft had come in as an amphibious landing force strictly for the experience. Marines on the draft had not been told the landing would be unopposed in order for it to be more realistic.

The grating voice on the loudspeaker continued. Who was to say when an experience such as this might not be beneficial? Almost one year earlier, on D day, September 15, 1950, the 1st Marine Division (less the 7th Marine Regiment, which was to be used for inland operations around Seoul) made up the bulk of troops that composed the landing force of the army's X Corps at Inchon, the South Korean port city.

That earlier amphibious landing had been a daring operation, brilliantly conceived and executed by Army Gen.

Douglas MacArthur, who overcame all military planning objections, and time-and-tide odds, in order to make it a success. Using marines because of their expertise in amphibious operations, MacArthur pulled elements of the 1st Marine Division out of Pusan; they half-circled war-torn Korea to the west and, after a difficult and hazardous landing by a small marine unit at Wolmido Island, completed the assigned mission in less than a half-hour's time. Courageous marine grunts of the 1st and 5th Marine Regiments climbed out of peter boats and then, using handmade wooden or metal ladders, scrambled up those ladders to capture Seoul, South Korea's capital city, after brisk and dangerous street fighting.

Simultaneously, marine elements had seized nearby Kimpo Airfield and began using runways there as a base of operations for the 1st Marine Air Wing. Continuous combat operations on land had been supported by Corsairs of Marine Fighter Squadrons 214 and 323, who alternately attacked, screened ground action with smoke, observed, and kept the skies free of enemy aircraft. Within a few short months, following a series of hard-fought land engagements, contested land areas were cleared of the enemy all the way up to the Yalu River and the nearby Manchurian border.

On the white sandy beach at Sochiri, armed with information explaining why the Marine Corps did things the hard way, as presented by the strident squawks of the loudspeaker, I stumbled up the beach, collecting a ton or more of sand on my soaking-wet utility trousers and boondockers. A hundred feet away and just over the berm, the metallic voice continued harshly, would be a road where a convoy of six-by-six trucks, the workhorse of the motor transport system, was located. I studiously ignored all the remarks coming out of those two scroungy-looking marine truck drivers and, walking away, left them and their derisive laughter far behind.

At the truck site there followed an incredible two hours of fuck-up after fuck-up as the men of the 13th Draft were sorted into four different units. Bullhorns competed with each other in blatting out countermanding instructions, moving sections and bodies of men in and around the trucks waiting there on the backroads of Korea. The calm of the morning was rent first with group muttering and then with an occasional, individually shouted curse.

It was the sound of dismemberment. The 13th Draft was being segmented. Friendships formed in training-cycle days were split up. The draft was being formed into four different units. Three of the units were destined either to be grunts—infantry replacements—to the 1st, 5th, and 7th Marine Regiments or to be cannon-cockers to the 11th Marine Regiment. I went to the 1st Marine Regiment.

Finally, after climbing aboard three different trucks and dismounting from two because of conflicting orders, the 1st Marine Regiment part of the incoming draft was off with a powerful roar of engines. Tandem fashion, they raced like a thundering herd of turtles up and down narrow and rutty Korean roads at speeds that often exceeded fifteen miles per hour. The truck I was on didn't miss a pothole in the road; it passed all those shocking, jarring sensations to the spines of those of us seated on the wood-slatted seats situated above shock absorbers that had long lost their ability to respond properly.

I remember little about that truck ride except that it was very uncomfortable. My sea-soaked utility trousers had not yet fully dried out. Damp, they chafed my crotch, legs, and feet. The sun overhead provided scant warmth, which was quickly blown away by an early winter breeze that swept the land. The four-hour drive was both tedious and tiring. Thoroughly uncomfortable, I grew indifferent to the passing scene, even to the Oriental-looking structures built of blue, green, yellow, and orange brick topped with curved red tiles, all perched precariously on steep hillsides. All seemed intact. There was very little evidence of war in the areas we passed. I feared again that I had arrived in Korea a day late and a dollar short. I knew my worst dreams would come true. I pictured myself as a clean-cut, shined and starched marine in the field, suffering barracks-type inspections.

The sun was low in the afternoon sky when the trucks growled into a bowl-shaped area located between craggy mountains. We had arrived at the headquarters of the 1st Marine Regiment. The truck stopped moving and, while waiting for orders to dismount, I stood up and stretched and then leaned over the cab of the truck to better my first real look at Korea.

The headquarters area was ringed farther out by stark, sharp mountains piled like slag heaps of coal refuse such as those in eastern Pennsylvania and West Virginia. The tops of those steep, mile-high mountains cut sharply into the soft underbelly of wispy clouds. The slopes were stacked irregularly one behind the other and seemed to go on into infinity. The mountains were beside, behind, and in front of each other, like marines packed in a peter boat, and seemed placed without thought or care, all jaggedly thrusting upward like devil dicks going after angels.

There were no green growing things on these mountains. On those closest to view I could see just occasional snapped-off trees spotted in and around large areas of blackened granitelike stone outcroppings. The only word to properly describe the area was desolate. Once I thought of the area as being desolate, other words came quickly to mind—dangerous, frightening, war-ravaged. Later, after I studied maps of the area as part of my duty, I would determine that the 1st Marine Regiment was located in a section of the Taebaek Range, one of the four main systems of mountains that covered Korea.

The Marine Corps had been assigned to fight a trench war in and around the Kumgang-san mountain area, a place referred to as the Diamond Mountain Range, along the eastern coastline and among great spikes of mountains surrounded by the many Buddhist monasteries built on the slopes. I had spotted the monasteries as we traveled inland to our present location.

The backbone of the Korean peninsula is the great mountain chain near the east coast. From this backbone the terrain descends gradually to the west into a piedmont plain. To the east the mountains drop abruptly to the Sea of Japan. Diamond Mountain was, perhaps, the most well-known of the mountains close to the east coast and not too far north of the 38th Parallel. The celebrated 12,000 peaks of the mountain area around Diamond Mountain form a cluster nearly fifty miles in circumference. Part of this cluster was known as the Punchbowl, the scene of some of the war's most vicious fighting. That fighting had just stopped; it had been a small war inside a larger one.

At the tag end of my first long, weary day in Korea, I ignored the beauty that was still in the deep canyons of the Diamond Mountain area, in the winding ravines, the oddly shaped rocks, and the crystal waterfalls. I was told that when the fighting for the area began in the spring of the year, the mountains had been covered with the fragile colors of wild azaleas, with delicate lilac blossoms, with great white flowers bursting forth amid the vividly green leaves of stately magnolia trees. Now it was the fall of the year; the foliage had turned the entire mountain into a blaze of color. Marines unwittingly helped nature by adding the quick blossoming of their white phosphorus shells, by sending out autumn colors in briefly erupting spouts of red and yellow and black as bursting high-explosive artillery shells impacted, by adding streaming red arcs of incendiary bullets connecting the hillsides one to the other.

The large shallow basin of land ringed by craggy mountains where we had stopped seemed peaceful at first, with wisps of smoke rising from small fires scattered about the area. Dispersed in an almost haphazard fashion, which I later learned was designed to add protection against incoming mortar and artillery rounds, were many one-story-high and very crudely but very substantially built wooden frame dwellings. These crude dwellings were covered with sheets of corrugated metal and then heaped high with sandbags. Scattered around and about these structures were canvas tents, both pyramidal and long squad tents. All had sandbags packed thickly to a height of about four feet. There were also a few self-contained metal structures, similar to those carried around on the truck beds of heavy transportation vehicles.

Around each of these buildings, tents, or shelters were strategically placed individual and crew-served foxholes. These fighting holes all had a parapet of sandbags and some were covered over first with heavy wood planking, then perhaps with corrugated metal, and finally with layer after layer of sandbags. Every one of these fighting holes had

51

some type of weapon sticking out of their firing ports—a rifle, perhaps a BAR, and occasionally the snout of either a light or a heavy machine gun.

Surprisingly, there was even an occasional Korean-built house made of wood and stone with a thickly woven rice straw–thatched roof. These houses inside the perimeter site were at first shunned like toadstools; they were often knocked down or demolished. Later, during the freezing-cold winter months, these dwellings came into high demand. The Korean homes were heated by flues located under the floor. Connected to the wood- or coal-burning kitchen stoves, the flues transferred warmth expeditiously and evenly to all the rooms of the house.

The sun was just barely hanging in the sky when the last of the convoy trucks drove into the headquarters area. The NCOs hustled from all over to meet the trucks, all of them bellowing out orders, calling out names, assigning marines to this or that place. It was almost like the Chinese gang bang we had suffered through down at the beach. Just when it seemed like it couldn't get worse, it didn't, and it all came together. I had to admit the rear-echelon headquarters NCOs had their shit together; they got the job done.

New replacement marines were hustled to fighting holes, mainly those on the inside perimeter of the camp. We settled down and NCOs came along and assigned us fields of fire, areas, usually to the front of the position, that a weapon or a group of weapons covers efficiently with fired rounds.

Dusk was rapidly coming on. We were given the password: "It can be any type of fruit that you can think of, and let's get it straight right now that I am personally going to kick the ass right off the silly shit who sounds out with 'pomegranate' or somethin' like that," said the huge staff sergeant instructing my group.

"We are done playin' games! People get shot with real bullets here if they fuck up! And don't you forget it!"

"Now it's gonna get colder'n a well-digger's ass in Alaska in a couple of hours. You people break out your blankets and ponchos and wrap up in them after you make a head call. I don't want nobody walkin' around when it gets dark here, tryin' to find a piss tube. Anyway, around midnight, it'll get cold enough to freeze your tally-whackers off," the staff sergeant said.

He waited until we had broken into our packs and gotten the gear we needed for the night watch.

"Now you people take turns sleeping. I want a fifty percent alert tonight. The gooks always try some shit when we get new people in, so be alert.

"And if any of you people breaks fire discipline, if any of you fires his weapon tonight, you better be prepared to show me a body when it gets to be morning, and if you can't do so, then I'm going to get very, very angry!" This staff sergeant had already impressed me with his huge gorillalike demeanor and manner. He looked mean enough to mean just what he said. I didn't know about anyone else, but I resolved that I wasn't going to be the first man to crank off a round, no matter what.

But I was wrong. Looks are sometimes deceiving. The staff sergeant might have looked as ugly and ornery as Hogan's goat, but he seemed genuinely interested in looking out for us. Throughout the early part of the evening, he went from fighting hole to fighting hole talking to us, calming us down. He checked our names off a roster that listed our name, rank, serial number, and military occupational specialty.

"Are you Corporal Charles S. Crawford, 1092787, MOS 2561?"

"You've got everything right except my MOS, sergeant. I'm a 2516, not a 2561. I'm a telephone central backroom repairman trainee."

He nodded his great gorilla head and made a notation on his paper with a huge hand that had black hair growing between the knuckles of his fingers.

"You got any idea what the hell a 2561 is?"

"Nope! Beats me, sergeant."

"Well, maybe it's a typographical error. From what it says here, you're gonna go up to the Four Deuces. You tell the company gunnery sergeant up there about this MOS fuck-up. It probably don't mean much, anyway."

53

"Okay, sure, I'll do that, sergeant. Now let me ask you something. What the hell is a Four Deuce?"

"Are you shittin' me? You mean you don't know?"

"I'm not shittin' you, I really don't know."

"Well, hell, Corporal. The Four Deuce is really the 4.2-inch chemical mortar. It's an army weapon that the marines have adapted to our specific use.

"A chemical mortar is designed for the purpose of projecting gases, smokes, and other chemicals. As a secondary mission, the Four Deuces use high-explosive shells in close support of the infantry. You know the marines. We'll tie a bayonet on it somewhere and use it as an offensive weapon.

"Seriously, though, the Four Deuce is probably the biggest and best goddamn mortar the marines ever had. Headquarters staff officers here call it 'the company commander's artillery.' You're going to a great outfit; a good skipper is up there, and a friend of mine is the company gunnery sergeant.

"But I'll tell you straight, I sure don't understand why they would want a telephone central backroom repairman trainee up there."

"Well, sergeant, I guess I'll find out tomorrow."

"Yep, corporal, I guess you will."

That first night in Korea stretched out to be about two months long, or at least it seemed that long to me and maybe to a whole lot of other replacements. I heard and interpreted every sound made in the black of night.

I heard gooks. There was no doubt about that in my mind. I knew there were gooks all around, crawling in, sneaking in, walking in, or whatever the hell gooks do when they come at you at night. I had my finger on the trigger of my M1 all night long. I wanted to fire at every clink and rattle I heard. I wanted to fire at everything the wind blew against and rattled against. Once, when a guy in a fighting hole a couple yards away let go with a great ripping fart—and there was absolutely no doubt about the fact that it was a great ripping fart—hell, I wanted to get a shot off at it, too.

I did not sleep at all that first night. There were three of us replacements in the fighting hole. We shivered the night away. I was sure glad to see the first gray light of day cutting around those sharp mountains.

With the dawn came Tom Fuhs. He came with a question, initially, and with answers later on.

"Which wunna you guys is Corporal Crawford?" It was cold enough for the words of the question to hang in midair, caught in the breath vapor of the extremely filthy marine who had voiced them, who had pushed them past about three weeks of whiskers on his face. The question was directed at a bunch of us new replacements. It was morning and although I had just spent my first sleepless night in Korea, I wasn't tired. I was too keyed up to be tired. But my eyelids were sticky with whatever it is that forms on them when I don't get a full night's sleep.

The dirty marine smiled, showing me a mouthful of teeth yellow with nicotine stain, mossy gray at the roots.

"I'm Fuhs. Pfc Tom Fuhs. I'm the regimental runner for the Four Deuces. You're goin' up to the Four Deuces with me," Fuhs said. "Where's your gear? I'll help you load it on the jeep. The Old Man said he's gonna be awfully happy havin' you join the outfit."

Fuhs gave me another one of his dirty, wolfish smiles. "And so will I be."

He grabbed my knapsack and haversack, the two pouchlike canvas bags that had made up the bulk of my field transport pack. I had used my poncho, my shelter half, and my blanket while I was on guard duty. I made a quick bundle of these items and, slinging my rifle over my shoulder by way of its leather strap, I followed Tom Fuhs to a mud-spattered jeep. I was glad enough to be following someone who seemed at least to know just what he was about, even if he was only a Pfc.

As we settled into the jeep, I asked him the same question I had earlier asked the regimental security sergeant: "What the hell is a Four Deuce?"

Tom Fuhs was already bouncing the jeep out the rutted dirt road heading away from the regimental area. He had been to see the personnel officer and arranged that I be picked up on the Four Deuce daily report sheet, so we did

55

not need to waste any time at all getting on the road. Fuhs had muttered something about crowded areas attracting incoming fire.

Now, responding to my question, Tom Fuhs said: "It's a mortar. A really big fuckin' mortar. It shoots a shell just a hair smaller than a 105-howitzer round. Only I think the Four Deuce shoots more accurately and a whole hell of a lot faster than a howitzer."

He negotiated a narrow part of the road carefully, letting a truck pass him coming into the area. "Anyway, our outfit provides both close and far high-angle support fire to the rifle companies up on the line. We usually dig the mortars in about a half mile behind the lines. Sometimes closer, depending on the situation." I liked the way Tom Fuhs had included me in by saying "our outfit." This was the kind of thing he automatically did.

He continued talking. "Usually the 81-millimeter mortars set in place between us and the lines. And right up there on line with the grunts are the 60-millimeter mortars, which ain't much bigger'n a popcorn fart. Even though we're positioned farther back than either of them, we can shoot out a whole helluva lot farther than them.

"But," Tom Fuhs said, "we can't get out as far as the artillery."

He turned his head slightly and nodded toward the rear. "Back there is where the 105-millimeter guns, the heavy 150-millimeter guns, and I guess the 8-inch self-propelled guns are located. Every gun has its own job."

Tom Fuhs drove in silence a minute or two. He looked at me and said, "Look, I'm just a driver, that's all. I'm not an expert on all this stuff. I'm just sort of telling you how the Four Deuces fits into everything, so don't go askin' a whole lot of technical questions or nothin' like that, because I don't know a whole lot more than what I just told you."

He was driving the jeep very carefully, looking at the road ahead and shifting his eyes from side to side.

"I know we can shoot high-explosive antipersonnel rounds—we call it HE—and those rounds explode into small chunks of shrapnel that'll kill you if you're standin' up within twenty-five yards of where they impact.

"And we shoot a lot of WP, that's white phosphorus, but we call it 'Willie Peter.' They're like smoke shells. You get a big thick white cloud when you shoot them.

"And we got a lot of other shells, some of them kind of technical, like flares, for when you need light at night, but I don't know too much about the rest of the stuff. Like I said, I'm just the company driver."

I thought about his answer as he navigated the jeep along some very rutty dirt tracks. Both driving and steering were becoming more and more difficult.

"What kind of telephone central switching equipment do you have in the Four Deuces?"

Tom Fuhs looked at me like I wasn't packing a full seabag. "Are you shittin' me? All we have in the company are EE-8 telephones and some sound-powered telephones we use between the gun pits. But only the EE-8s are hooked into the switchboard we have. You know, one of them small field switchboards, one of those BD-72s that can handle up to about a dozen telephone calls at one time."

He navigated a particularly bad stretch of road, carefully giving all his attention to driving. Then he said, "We've got radio equipment, some of the really heavy SCR-300s, that the radiomen assigned to FOs carry up on the hill. They're really heavy sons of bitches that don't work for shit most of the time, if you know what I mean. Batteries keep going bad in them."

I nodded my head like I knew what he was talking about, but I had absolutely no idea what an SCR-300 looked like, never mind how it worked.

"And we've got some of them PRC-10 radios." Tom Fuhs looked over at me and smiled, saying, "They call them 'Prick Tens.' They're pretty good over short distances. You can hold one in your hand or carry it over your shoulder by its strap. Again, the big problem with them is getting a good battery, or at least one that will last overnight."

Tom Fuhs drove in silence again for about a mile. Then he said, "And, of course, you know that we have the Haggler."

"Of course," I said. I had no idea what it was that he was talking about. I could identify with the EE-8 and the BD-72, but that was all. I had trained with them more than a year earlier in California when I was learning to be a wireman. Both pieces of equipment were powered by flashlight batteries. An instructor in wire school had said they were both antiquated but were tough as nails and would work under almost any circumstances. The telephone was tied into the switchboard by way of telephone wire W-110B, two separate metallic lines enclosed in a protective rubber and canvas covering.

"The telephone wires are cut or broken lots of times," Tom Fuhs said. "When that happens our wiremen get to go out and find the break in the line and splice it, restoring the line. To find the break they wrap their hands around the telephone line, which is usually just lying on the deck, and let it run between their fists. That's what they call 'hand-fucking' the line. It helps them spot where there's a break in the line or where it's been cut."

Tom Fuhs looked at me again and his voice changed somewhat as he continued to speak: "When we were fightin' around here on a regular basis, lots of times the gooks would cut a wire line and then set up an ambush and wait for a wireman to come out and repair it."

He pointed up the road to a large tree that almost looked out of place in an area that had lots of stumps but very few trees. "Two wiremen from battalion got caught by the gooks about two weeks ago. They were out hand-fuckin' a line lookin' for a break in it.

"We found them hangin' from that tree. They had been strung up with comm wire wrapped around their necks like a rope. We found their cocks and balls stuffed in their mouths and shoved down their throats."

Tom Fuhs paused to let that sink in. "Now we've got to send out a grunt with every wire party, to sort of bodyguard them, you know, in case they spot any of the gooks we missed when we mopped up the area. Them fuckers are like lice; you always miss some. Don't get alarmed or nothin' like that. It ain't like we're gonna be attacked by a big bunch'a gooks. You know what I mean?"

I nodded like I knew what Tom Fuhs was talking about. But to tell the truth I didn't know if I was afraid or exhilarated to find out that I hadn't missed out on the war after all.

Since I was, in all probability, going to work with and be responsible for the BD-72 switchboard, I asked Fuhs for more information concerning it. "How often do you have trouble with the BD-72, Tom?"

"Well, like I told you, that switchboard is tougher'n a cob. It works like a charm. All it ever needs is somebody to replace the old batteries in it with six new flashlight batteries once a week. That's all."

"That's all?"

"Yep, that's all," Tom Fuhs said.

I was going to ask more questions, but Tom Fuhs got my attention going in another direction.

"Look, Corporal. I don't want to be scarin' you with war stories or nothin' like that, but we're rapidly gettin' into an area where there might be gook stragglers. So why don't you crank a round in the chamber of your rifle and point that rifle outboard on your side.

"Now if we do get shot at, don't try too hard to aim or anything like that. Just crank off a quick eight rounds in the general direction of where the shots come from, okay?"

I looked in his direction to see if he was pulling my leg or not. He wasn't. What he was doing was constantly swiveling his eyes along the broken road stretched in front of us, as well as back and forth along his side of the jeep.

I wasn't scared or anything. Well, not really scared.

But I must admit Tom Fuhs did have a way with words. He got my attention real quick. I scanned my side of the road. On the far left flank was a built-up area of tents.

"Over there is First Battalion headquarters. Usually that's about as far as I have to go. I make a run there twice a day," Tom Fuhs said.

"Right now we're about a mile from the company area. We came through here about ten days ago. We kicked the gooks in the ass and shoved them out when we were straightening out the lines. It was a big fight. We called it the 'September Push.'"

He looked at me and said, "Take a deep breath."

I inhaled. I knew he had told me to do so for some reason, but I couldn't figure out why. The cold air had a peculiar odor to it, a decayed odor, somewhat pungent, somewhat unclean.

"What you're smellin' is dead gooks. Most of them are underground only a foot or so, anyway," Tom Fuhs said. He looked at me and chuckled. I guess I must have looked startled or something.

"There ain't been no reports of gooks here for a couple of days now. But you can never tell. You gotta keep a lookout. You miss seein' a gook just one time, and that's all she wrote. And I'm gonna tell you true, Corporal, I keep a good lookout. I want to take my ass home with just the right amount of holes in it, if you get what I mean."

I nodded my complete understanding. In essence, Tom Fuhs had summed up my feelings exactly.

"Usually I don't make this run without a shotgun rider, someone in that seat watchin' that side. It's hard sometimes to get someone in the company to ride along, though. Pickin' you up today, I at least got someone to ride shotgun on the way back to the company."

"Maybe I can do it again for you, Tom, providin' my duties with the Four Deuces will let me," I said. Tom Fuhs flashed me a grin and I knew my volunteering mouth had made me another friend.

As we drove on I noticed the landscape looked more and more rugged. It looked like it was right out of a movie set, something made up to be a battlefield. The ground had a churned-up look and seemed to have been both used and abused. Trees, naked now and looking like thick, helpless old men, had been snapped off, sometimes high up and more often lower to the ground. The broken trunks, ringed jaggedly about at the top, looked sore. Those trees that had escaped being snapped off had a tilted look about them, their roots showing. All around, patches of ground had a charred look, as if a forest fire had passed through. It was all so colorless; it carried the dark look of despair.

War machines had rutted the ground with deep tracks of rubber tires and iron treads. The tracks were painted into the ground in a surrealist manner, going in straight lines that suddenly dipped down at right angles, crossing and recrossing each other in a great big mishmash of uncertainty. Larger-than-life footprints trod the ground, some made by running and hurrying, others by plodding, some by walking tiredly around barbed wire.

The ground had been gone over. All souvenirs and mementos of the fight had long since been picked up. Only individual or heaped combat C-ration tins remained, scattered about haphazardly, each of their opened mouths showing a shiny silver cavity that sparkled occasionally as the light of day peered inside, all in direct contrast to the dull olive-green outside coloring.

There were hundreds of thousands of spent rifle and big-bore ammunition casings on the ground, a few here, a dozen there, all thickly piled where action may have been heaviest. Heavy metal ammunition cans and wooden boxes, rusting and warped, lay emptied now, cluttering the land.

Sandbags, torn, holed, and partially emptied, lay awkwardly on each other around scooped-out and shallow holes or deep pits. All the acne pits of war and the good earth seemed ugly and, even now, frightening.

Tom Fuhs didn't need to tell me; I already knew that death had recently been here and that death had been delivered swiftly and surely in all the frightening ways it can be when propelled by gunpowder. It was quite something else to look at photographs of a battleground as opposed to the actual viewing of a battlefield. Sure, I had looked at and even studied at length some of the excellent black-and-white photos taken of Korean battlegrounds, photos like those taken by combat photographer David Douglas Duncan, photos taken up close and personal, photos that seemed so real they almost came alive in your mind, photos so accurately portrayed that, when looking at them, you could almost smell them, could almost feel the gut reaction of the men pictured in them. But no matter how well those photographs portrayed this war and its battlegrounds, they just did not call up the emotions I had now, emotions that ran along and over my backbone, emotions I felt as my eyes—like a Dali-esque mouth—devoured all the scenes around and about me, emotions known as my nose smelled the tainted, fetid, rotten-egg, sick-sweet odor of this place, and as my throat tasted it—all the way to my gut. And I knew full well I could not digest it all without feeling sickened.

My emotions and my senses were working overtime; I could not actually see death, yet I could picture it in that awful landscape. I did not see death as it was popularly conceived, striding relentlessly forward in a long, sweeping black cloak, carrying a scythe in bony fingers. Instead I pictured death in action, and the action was likened to that of the Four Horsemen of the Apocalypse, charging recklessly forward on the backs of wide-eyed steeds with nostrils flared open, with mouths foaming, with heads strongly thrust forward and black manes flying up and out and back, horses with their chests heaving, their legs digging holes into the ground.

"We had a lot of mortar and artillery hit in this area, both theirs and ours. You can see the holes," said Tom Fuhs, pointing with his hand.

"We came through here with the grunts, right on their asses. A couple of tanks made it this far, too," he said, pointing at the deep tracks. He was driving the jeep real slowly now, very carefully moving it along.

"Keep a good look out on your side of the road. If you see any fresh dug-up dirt, holler out quick! It could be a mine or something." If Tom Fuhs didn't have my full attention with his talk of war, I'm telling you he got it with those words. Now that I knew what to look for—freshly dug-up dirt—I kept my eyes glued to the road. He drove on in silence for a minute or two, but mundane things like mines buried in the road just were not going to preoccupy Tom Fuhs very long. He liked to talk, to share the things that made up his life.

"You can bunk with me if you want, Corporal. I'm in a good bunker near the captain's headquarters bunker. There ain't nobody in the bunker but me. It's big enough to hold two guys. The bunker housing the communications setup for the company is close by, too."

"Sure," I said. I was anxious to ask Tom Fuhs about his whiskers, and the fact that he was so dirty, but I didn't have to. The Four Deuces was looking to be my kind of an outfit.

"We don't have much water up on the line, even as far back as we are. Just what can be brought in by water buffalo—you know, the water tanks. We've got a couple of them. But it works a real hardship drivin' them in and out of the company. The gooks think they make good targets.

"It's not that we're on water discipline or anything. But we just don't waste water. And besides, the Funny Gunny and the captain both said it was okay to grow mustaches and beards. The Funny Gunny said that when we got to stinkin' too bad, he'd run us all down to the battalion shower point."

So much for my worries about shined shoes and haircuts, I thought. Now all I had to do was figure out a way to get promoted to buck sergeant.

Tom Fuhs pointed to both sides of the road ahead. It was a desolate-looking spot, all shot up.

"We were fighting here about two weeks ago. One time the gooks were so close to us that we couldn't use the high-angle overhead fire we need with the mortars.

"Maybe I should tell you how the Four Deuce works. That way you can appreciate what the Funny Gunny did."

Tom Fuhs told me the Four Deuce mortar was a long, heavy barrel with lands and grooves inside that turned counterclockwise. The barrel, or tube as it was called, had on its outside base a heavy metal ball, maybe a bit bigger than a tennis ball, that locked into a socket on a heavy, square base plate. Out in front of the tube and attached to it by a sleeve that fit neatly all around the tube were two metal legs that had their own smaller base plates. The telescoping legs could be adjusted by raising or lowering them to gain the exact angles needed on the tube for firing purposes. Aiming stakes, with measured computations marked on them in luminous paint for night firing, were placed about twenty-five feet out and around each gun emplacement.

The Four Deuce, I was told, fired a variety of shells. Each shell, or round, was basically the same in external appearance. Painted bands of different colors circled around each shell, informing the gunners of the shell type. Each heavy shell, close to twenty pounds, measured 4.2 inches in diameter, giving a name to the mortar. Each shell, about fourteen inches long, tapered to a snub point at its impact end and looked sawed off at its firing end. All around the base of each shell was an inch-wide copper band that served a specific purpose after the shell was dropped down the mortar tube.

"I'll tell you that purpose in just a minute," Tom Fuhs said. Continuing, he explained that jutting out of the firing end was an inch-wide, three-inch-long cylinder that had many, many holes spaced equally all around. A special ignition cartridge filled with fine-grain powder was housed inside this cylinder. The cylinder was surrounded with gunpowder increments, twenty-five in all. The increments —often called "charges"—were composed of four very thin wafers of pressed gunpowder. Each increment delivered a specific amount of thrust; maximum thrust was achieved by using all twenty-five increments. The increment wafers were made with a round hole in their center; they fitted around the ignition cartridge cylinder.

"It's up to the Fire Direction Center, the FDC, to compute firing determinations based on information provided by the forward observer, the FO. These computations are relayed by sound-powered telephone to the gun crews. The gun crews place the correct angle and deflection on the mortar tube in order to guarantee a proper flight course for the shell to take to the target," Tom Fuhs explained.

He explained a lot more about the Four Deuces, some of which I could readily understand and grasp, much of which eluded me. Tom Fuhs talked as he drove carefully on the dirt road that had now turned into two deep ruts, almost impossible to get out of, making steering extremely difficult. Still, he was talking a lot with his hands, using them to show how the round was fired, how it reached its apex, and how it plummeted downward. After fully explaining the firing procedures of the Four Deuce, he returned to his previously interrupted story.

"We had just set up our night positions, but there was still lots of daylight left. The FOs were shootin' up a storm. The FDC was workin' about five missions at the same time, usin' their slapsticks and rulers and their angles and makin' all kinds of shootin' determinations for the fire missions going on when, fuck me, here come the gooks," Tom Fuhs said, pointing to where the old gun pits had been and, to the front of the gun pits, toward the area where the gook attack had been launched.

"The fuckin' gooks had busted through the lines, which were, like they always are when you're movin' up, kinda spongy. Anyway, the gooks came through the lines. They came through the 60s and the 81s and they left a lot of hurtin' grunts behind them, too. And, goddamn, here they come right at us, headin' straight for our guns in some kind of a goddamn banzai charge like the Japs used to pull in World War Two. They come right the fuck at us."

I noticed a change in his voice. Tom Fuhs was speaking in a sort of a monotone, yet spitting out the words; he was talking about something only his eyes could see, vividly, realistically, feelingly. Tom Fuhs was all caught up in his recollection and it was like I wasn't even in the jeep with him.

"There was no way we could poop a round straight up in the air to come down on the gooks, what with them bein' only about sixty, seventy-five yards away and comin' on strong, tryin' to shoot our hearts out. And that's when the Funny Gunny took over. He jumps down into one of the gun pits, and he unhooks the tube from the base plate. 'Watch me!' he yells to the other gun crews, like he was holdin' school or something. Then he tells the gunner to drop a round down the tube.

"Goddamn, but the Funny Gunny was something, him standin' asshole deep in high-explosive rounds and holding the tube braced at the bottom, tellin' the gunner to slide a round down the tube.

"We all thought at first that, well, maybe he had cracked or somethin', but the Funny Gunny knew what he was doin'. He felt that round hit the bottom of the tube and ignite. And then he quickly lifts the ass end of the tube right off the deck, leveling the tube at the gooks comin' chargin' in at us, and that fuckin' round goes WHOOSHING out at them in a straight line, its ass end on fire with burning increments and all and, shit, man, it's like the Funny Gunny stops them gooks cold! That fuckin' round didn't explode or nothing, but it wiped out a path about ten feet wide right through about fifteen gooks!

"Jeez! He just stopped them cold. They didn't know what the fuck was comin' off. It was like he had a new weapon or somethin'. And the Funny Gunny, he's actin' like he's shootin' a bazooka or somethin'! BLAM! and out goes another round right through a big bunch of gooks. BLAM! another round goes out! And another! It's like he's got that Four Deuce on automatic!

"The fuckin' Funny Gunny is using Kentucky windage and he's stoppin' the fuckin' gooks right on the spot. He cranks out maybe about five or six rounds, and he's shootin' right into them, knockin' down and wipin' out the gooks in big batches, cranking big holes in their lines.

"And that fuckin' Funny Gunny! He's whoopin' it up, crankin' out round after round. Nobody else can get it down pat like the Funny Gunny, but a couple gunners tried, and one guy knocks out his aiming stake, is all, and another gunner sets his increment bucket on fire and we got them sizzlin' all over the place!

"The thing is that the Funny Gunny bought us some time. The rest of us get to our rifles and carbines and we're bangin' away, crankin' off our own shots, but I shit you not, it was the Funny Gunny who stopped them gooks cold, that old fucker!" And now Tom Fuhs is chuckling to himself, loud enough to let me in on it.

I didn't know how to respond to his story.* But I saw that the glazed look that had sort of come over his eyes was washing away.

"How many gooks did the Funny Gunny kill?"

"I'll tell you straight, Corporal, I really don't know, and I don't think anyone else does either. He must have killed some, there's no doubtin' that." He paused for a moment,

---

*Publisher's Note: Presidio Press/Pocket Books believes that this obviously apocryphal tale must be approached with great caution. To our knowledge, Newton's Second Law of Motion has not been repealed (the recoil would have knocked the gunny into the next county) and the torque produced by the rifling would have made him into a large pinwheel, assuming he could have held it. But, the author tells us, "Marines never lie in telling a combat story."

thinking, and then said, "It wasn't like he was a fuckin' killing machine or nothin' like that. What it was, well, the thing of it was that the Funny Gunny stood his ground when maybe the rest of us was feelin' like it would be a whole hell of a lot safer headin' out of the area. And because the Funny Gunny stood his ground, the rest of us stood our ground, too. He stopped them fuckin' gooks! Make no mistake about that! The Funny Gunny just plain stopped them! And he stopped us, too. He stopped us from buggin' out!

"What he done was give us that couple of seconds we needed to regroup ourselves, to see what it was we were up against. And then, instead of panicking like I think a lot of us was thinkin' about doing whether we realized it or not, we regrouped ourselves and got back into the act. And when we got back into the act, we pushed the gooks right out of the area, right back into the guns of the grunts up on line who had finally got their shit together.

"The only thing I know for sure is that none of those rounds the Funny Gunny cranked off exploded. They didn't have time enough to spin around a couple of times in a counterclockwise way like they're supposed to do to arm themselves. They just plowed through the gooks and then, I guess, they buried themselves in that little hillside out there. Nobody's dug them up. I guess they'll stay there forever," Tom Fuhs said. He was silent for a moment.

I had a question I wanted to ask, a question generated from having read newspaper accounts of the recent Punchbowl action, and of the number of gooks involved. The newspapers, in writing stories of that fight, had used a word, a favorite word, it seemed, to describe the attacking enemy. The newspapers had called them a "horde."

"Tom," I asked, "you've been through it. Tell me, just how many gooks make up a horde?"

Tom Fuhs looked questioningly at me. And then he smiled his rotten-toothed smile: "Well, to be exact, I'd say a whole shitpot full, is how many."

CHAPTER
5

Tom Fuhs negotiated a sharp curve in the rutted road and the jeep growled up a gentle slope that came out onto a flat plain of sorts, the roadway bisecting it. Ahead, on both sides of the roadway, were huge circles of earthworks composed of sandbags packed at least five feet wide and three feet high all around. A tubelike something jutted out at an angle from its position in the middle of each pit; the pit was about ten feet in diameter and about three feet below ground level. I knew without being told that I was looking at Four Deuce mortars; the metal tubes, like noses, seemed to be sniffing out targets beyond the menacing high mountain area to the front. Jutting back from each circular pit was a small rectangular affair mounded over with sandbags; intuitively, I knew that ammunition was stored inside.

Tom Fuhs swept his arm around, encompassing the gun pits, the drop-off in front of them, the bunkers where most of the troops lived that were dug in on the far side of the hill opposite us, and the tangle of rough woods that filled in another drop-off on the right side of the rutted roadway leading to the bunker living area. Everything, raw and ugly, fitted in exactly right together as though it were natural and not man-made.

"This is a good position. It'll be easy to defend unless the gooks get up into those trees. They'd have to have suction cups on their asses to stay in one place up there because of the way the land slopes uphill."

Pointing, he said, "That road goes straight on up to the lines where the grunts are, whatever there is of the road, anyway, because it sort of peters out by the time it gets to the 81s."

He pulled the jeep a bit farther off the road and backed it into a U-shaped buildup of sandbags about four feet high. There was no cover over it.

"This is where I park the jeep. When it rains—or even in the mornings when the dew is heavy—I could never get the jeep up that roadway," he said. He pointed, drawing my attention by his extended forefinger, to the road that led to the edge of the ravine fronting the guns, to the sharp left curve of the road and the way the road sloped downward to bottom out briefly before starting steeply uphill again, ending at the tree line above the main camp of the Four Deuces.

On closer examination, now that I was out of the jeep and standing at the edge of the ravine, I could see dozens of bunkers hidden, camouflaged, along both sides of the sloped cul-de-sac where they were dug into the ground.

Tom Fuhs pointed at the rough-looking mountain covered over with thick brush and rock outcroppings and trees that grew crowded and tall, heavy-limbed, some still holding onto bright-colored leaves. For a moment, just a moment, I thought about my last deer hunting in the Panther Valley back home in Pennsylvania.

Tom Fuhs pointed to the far side where the rutted road entered the wooded area. "The 81-millimeter mortar company has a cleared area, just like this one only not as big, maybe about halfway up the mountain. Beyond them by a couple of hundred yards, but higher up on the mountain, is where the grunts have their trenches. If the trees don't get knocked down when the grunts are fightin' for a hill, they use composition C-3—that's a plastic explosive more powerful than TNT—to clear fields of fire for their weapons. Our FOs are up there in the trenches with the grunts."

I nodded my head trying to understand what he was talking about. I looked around the area again, evaluating it. Someone had done a good job. It wouldn't take but a handful of men to hold off a company using the lay of the land to good advantage. Someone had really picked out a good defensive position for the offensive work of the mortars.

"Come on," said Tom Fuhs. "We've got to pass the FDC bunker on our way up to the skipper's bunker. They're still shootin' a mission. You can look in on them and listen to them, if you want to." He led me down the roadway to a pyramidal tent that was heavily sandbagged all around.

"ON THE WAY!" a staff sergeant inside the tent said into a field telephone as I heard a sharp crack of man-made thunder behind me, the crisp THWAAK! sound of another round being fired. The staff sergeant had a stopwatch in his other hand and I watched him mash down on the knurled knob at the top of it, starting the sweep second hand and then watching it closely. In less than a minute the staff sergeant said, "YOU GOT A SPLASH!"

Tom Fuhs said to me, "When the FDC tells the FO he's got a splash, that means the round will hit the ground in exactly ten seconds. They've got the timing of a shell in the air down to a science.

"That's an important ten seconds if the FO is firing counterbattery fire, that is, if his position is being fired on by gook artillery or mortars. Our FO can keep his head down until he actually knows when his round has hit. And then, if his ass is really in a bind, he can count another five or ten seconds, long enough for black smoke to show where his round has landed.

"Then all the FO needs to do is pop up his head for about a half second in order to spot where his round impacted and determine if he needs to make any adjustments to his firing. If he needs to adjust, he tells the FDC what adjustment is required.

"The reason for all that is when you're getting shit

incoming on you, you just don't want to keep your head up in the air too long."

Motioning with his head as he casually shook it toward the pathway up to the bunker area, Tom Fuhs said, "Come on, Corporal. Let's get up to the command bunker."

The command bunker was large and square shaped, about ten feet on all sides. It was about seven feet high, domed over on top with many layers of sandbags. I could see that part of the bunker, more than half of it, was actually dug right into the side of the mountain. Two windows—Four Deuce ammunition boxes, really—were placed on the bunker side that faced the ravine.

As we walked past the windows, Tom Fuhs called inside, "I've got him, Cap'n. We just got back to camp."

Entry to the bunker was through a door opening that had a camouflage poncho hanging down to keep out the weather. Inside, the walls were reinforced with the metal posts used for stringing barbed wire. Along the back wall and the far side wall were two medical stretchers, the handles braced on wooden ammunition boxes. Stacked neatly in a corner were an M1 rifle, a carbine, a BAR, and a Thompson submachine gun with a round drum. Even though it was daylight outside, a Coleman lantern patterned shadows overhead.

Below the lantern was a field desk, on which sat a small olive drab machine that looked like an adding machine or a very compressed typewriter. A spool of quarter-inch-wide paper threaded its way through the machine, coming out on the side opposite from where a crank handle was located.

The machine was being used by a man seated at the field desk. Technical sergeant stripes were inked on the bill of a winter-issue fake-fur hat that was about two sizes too small for his round head. This had to be the Funny Gunny. His presence dominated the small area inside the bunker.

Muttering and cursing "Decipher, goddamnit!" he punched savagely at the small keyboard with a blunt forefinger and, just as savagely, hauled down repeatedly on the crank handle. With a muted sound—rachetta-whir—the paper tape advanced a fraction of an inch, an alphabetic character imprinted upon it.

He was an older man, someone rapidly closing in on forty

71

years or so. That was old age when compared to most of the rest of the men in the company I had noticed on my way to the command bunker; they were all young, mostly in their teens and early twenties. A thought struck me, nothing profound or anything like that, but it just seemed to me, all of a sudden, that the wars I knew about were usually fought by young men who had very little experience in the business.

Without even knowing him, other than what Tom Fuhs had said on the way up from regiment, I felt pretty good that the Funny Gunny was in the company. He was the kind of man the marines needed. I later learned that the Funny Gunny had, during World War II, been a Mustang, a former enlisted man selected for commissioning as an officer because of his demonstrated leadership potential and military knowledge in specific areas. In order to avoid being "mustered out" when the war ended, the Funny Gunny had turned in his captain's bars and reverted to his former enlisted man status as a staff NCO. Now, a few years later, with a desperate need for fighting men at the beginning of the Korean War, the marines were mighty glad to have the hundreds of men like the Funny Gunny on hand and ready for service.

The Funny Gunny—nobody had the guts to call him that to his face—was a large and florid man. He was thick and heavy in appearance and short in stature, and there is no doubt that he compared unfavorably with other leaner and meaner young men. Like many other older career marines, the Funny Gunny had a false kind of a barrel-like and bravely upheld chest; it was a chest that at any moment might fall down and reveal itself to everyone to be merely a beer belly.

He had a face all rough and angled and pockmarked from what at an earlier age probably had been a severe acne problem. Fine, slender blood vessels, red and blue in color, ran wild trying desperately to disguise the Funny Gunny's slightly canted and off-to-one-side, rather bulbous and battered nose, a nose that looked like it hurt all the time. The W. C. Fields nose satirically complemented mean, little porcine eyes, startling blue eyes that hid behind heavy, black plastic-framed military glasses he used for reading.

72

His face had the saving grace of a crooked smile that showed strong, nubby, misaligned, and very badly stained teeth. It was the kind of face that, no matter if he had just shaved, looked like it needed a shave. He had a five-o'clock-shadow kind of a jaw. Deep jowl lines ran from the corners of his nose to the outside lower edge of his jaw. And he wore that winter-issue fur-lined Mickey Mouse hat on his nearly bald head, the ear pieces sticking almost straight out because the hat was too small.

I never did learn his first name. Like the other men in the Four Deuces, I would call him "Gunny" to his face and "Funny Gunny" when I knew he couldn't hear me. After I got to know him better, I decided flat out that if God had wanted all the men in the Four Deuces to be outstanding marines, then He would have made them all short and fat and rather disheveled—and would have named them all Funny Gunny.

I never did learn the first name of the commanding officer, either. It didn't matter all that much since I would only call him "Captain" or "Sir" or occasionally "Skipper" the entire time I knew him, this in spite of the fact that, when on line in a combat area, most officers prefer you do not call attention to them by addressing them so respectfully or, worse yet, by saluting them.

It wasn't like Captain Massey was standoffish or anything like that; it was just that he was an officer and I was just an enlisted man and I had my own views about the decorum of being or sounding friendly with marines of higher rank. Anyway, that was how he first introduced himself to me when I met him in the command bunker.

"I'm Captain Massey," he said when he stuck out his antiseptically clean hand. He had the hands of an aristocrat —manicured fingernails on long tapered fingers, the back of his hands showing thin blue veins, and the tendons of his fingers very well defined. Truth to tell, I was very much surprised at the strength of his handshake.

Captain Massey presented a direct opposite in appearance to the Funny Gunny, a Mutt and Jeff contrast. The captain was tall, slender, and wore a neat, hairline-thin black mustache. He looked like a dandy. I was very happy to see that the hair around his ears was longer than mine. He wore a neat, clean, herringbone twill type of a dungaree outfit that actually had creases on the front and back of both the trousers and the jacket. Clean-shaven, the captain smelled of expensive aftershave and cologne.

"I'll speak for both Technical Sergeant Boyd, here," the captain said, nodding in the direction of the Funny Gunny, "and myself. We're both awfully glad to have you on board, Corporal Crawford."

The captain motioned with his head again in the direction of the Funny Gunny and said, "The two of us have wrestled with that Haggler cryptographic machine long enough. And try as we might, we just have never succeeded in decoding any of the messages sent to us by either regiment or battalion. Of course, neither Sergeant Boyd nor myself are trained in that particular field of communications. It takes a specialist, so you're a godsend, Corporal Crawford. We surely do need a cryptographer."

I was too surprised to respond in any other way than to smile stupidly and shake his hand. What the hell was going on here? I'm a half-assed switchboard operator who was retraining to be a backroom man and now, all of a sudden, I am being referred to as a cryptographer, whatever the hell that was.

The captain decided I would share a bunker with Tom Fuhs. "Tom, you take Corporal Crawford on down to see Lob Stratton at the supply bunker and get him squared away with all that he will need. Get that extra field desk that the Lob is using for his card games at night, the small portable one, and let the corporal use it for decrypting messages," the captain said to Tom Fuhs.

Then, looking at me again, the captain said, "You might just as well start your work here by breaking these last encipherments we received earlier by radio message. I'm certain they will tell me the coordinates of where we have patrols moving out in front of the lines. I need that information. It's vital! I don't want either my FOs or my gunners shooting at the wrong targets."

The Funny Gunny handed me the small olive drab machine he had been muttering and swearing at, along with message papers that had five-letter code groups on them, ten code groups to the line. The five-lettered code groups appeared to be randomly selected letters of the alphabet. I later found out the code groups were the result of messages being enciphered. The small olive drab machine, called the Haggler, when properly keyed according to daily changing instructions contained in key lists, would decipher these code groups to the meaningful information that the captain said he desperately needed.

I had not uttered a single word after the captain had shaken my hand beyond the mandatory "Hello, sir" expected of me on meeting someone. And here I was being dismissed with the Haggler under my arm and messages needing decryption in my hands. I walked away from the command bunker wondering why the captain had referred to me as a cryptographer, and wondering what the hell he meant when he told me to start decrypting messages.

Naturally I played it cool like a good NCO should. I did not say anything at all when the Funny Gunny handed over the Haggler and the enciphered messages. All I did was give the captain my own version of a lopsided grin, all the while bobbing my head up and down in agreement like I was some kind of simpleton.

Still bobbing my head and still grinning, I backed away from the command bunker, following Tom Fuhs. No sense in showing the captain, and the Funny Gunny, and God and everybody else in the world that I was a dumb shit.

When we had walked a decent interval away from the command bunker, I hissed out to Tom Fuhs, "What the fuck was the captain talking about?"

"I guess he wants you to break those messages, Corporal."

I pondered that statement as we got the gear I was instructed to get from the supply tent. Lob Stratton, the supply chief, a little marine with curling blond hair and a face without whiskers, bitched the whole time, muttering about what the hell was he going to use for a poker table in the late night hours.

I stowed all my gear in the small bunker I would share with Tom Fuhs. Less than half the size of the command bunker, it was just as sturdily built. It soon became crowded inside with my field transport pack, my winter sleeping bag, my rifle and extra bandoliers of ammunition, and the small, portable field desk with the Haggler perched on top.

Tom Fuhs started explaining things to me.

"The captain has been askin' the regimental personnel officer to send him a cryptographer, MOS 2561, ever since our last crypto man got rotated home a couple weeks back."

All of a sudden the light dawned. Now I understood the meaning behind the transposed last two digits of my MOS on my orders. The regimental personnel officer had apparently thought I was a cryptographer, MOS 2561, and so assigned me to the Four Deuces. And Captain Massey thought I could decipher encrypted messages.

"I'm gonna tell you straight, Corporal, the captain and the Funny Gunny have been balls to the walls ever since our last cryptographer, a buck sergeant, left. They've been tryin' to figure out how to work the Haggler. No luck. They've never broken any of the messages that our radio section copies and sends up to them.

"And I'll tell you somethin' else, Corporal. That places this company between a rock and a hard place, us not knowin' who's movin' around in the dark in front of our lines."

Tom Fuhs motioned with his head in the direction of the front lines.

"Now you take Big Dog Ondrak, he's our best FO. You know what an FO does, don't you?"

He grinned his black-toothed grin at me as I admitted by a negative shake of my head that I knew shit from shinola about the Four Deuces.

"Well, an FO is one of our guys who goes up on the lines with the grunts, the infantrymen. Him and his team—a wireman and a radioman—live with the grunts and sleep up in the trench lines in bunkers with them.

"The FO establishes concentrations in front of the company he's assigned to work with. A concentration is the known location, on the map and on the actual ground, of an established reference point. Both the FO and the FDC know exactly where that established point is located, and they give it a name. And the name they assign comes as a result of following a certain pattern," Tom Fuhs said, wrinkling his forehead as if trying to remember the pattern.

His face cleared with remembrance as he continued: "Okay, so when the FO team goes up on the hill, they're all collectively called a certain code name and number. The FDC assigns the code name and number to the FO teams up on line. Like the FO to the extreme left might be called FO One Able and the guy to his right might be called FO Two Baker. You see what I mean?"

I bobbed my head up and down.

"Well, when the FO establishes his concentrations he uses a similar system. He calls the first concentration he establishes in front of his position as One Able, and then One Baker, and on up the line, using his FO number and then a phonetic to designate his concentrations.

"The FO is not restricted to working from just left to right. That ain't the way of it. What the FO does is to spot a prominent landmark in front of his position, like, say, a rock formation or maybe the mouth of a draw.

"Anyway, the FO selects a prominent landmark and then he locates that landmark on his map, according to map coordinates. And then he uses his compass to shoot an azimuth to the landmark. And then he calls the FDC and tells them the map coordinates and the compass reading," Tom Fuhs said. He was drawing a picture of it all on paper, using stick figures and simple lines.

"When the FDC gets this information, they plot it on their charts. The FDC charts aren't maps or anything like that. They're just paper with grid lines on it. The first thing they compute is their own exact location. Then they compute the exact location of the FO. Then they mark in the compass reading, and the map coordinates.

"Are you still with me on this?" Tom Fuhs asked.

I nodded affirmative and he continued.

"The FDC men then use their charts and graphs and calipers, and all the other stuff they have, and come up with the right answers as to how many increments are needed and what setting should be placed on the guns, and then they pass this information on to the gun pits.

"And then the gunners do their thing, and next thing you

know a round is on its way. The FO spots the round landing, and he gives any corrections he has to, like adding yardage or going to either the right or the left or whatever correction is necessary to get the round on target.

"Usually an FO will be on target within a matter of a round or two. Everyone of them say they use the Comanche system to get on target. They just plain sneak up on it with their rounds," he said, giving me a chance to laugh at his joke with him.

Somehow I felt that Tom Fuhs had given me a long answer to a short question, so that I would know a lot of things the next time around. I think he was trying to save me embarrassment. I was grateful for his consideration, suddenly realizing there was a whole lot more to Tom Fuhs than just his loquaciousness.

"Well, like I was sayin' about the Big Dog," Tom Fuhs went on. "He's our best FO, but, well, there have been some times when he was, maybe, a little too quick to call in shots. Sometimes, maybe, he would shoot first and ask questions later. The only thing I can say is that maybe that's a good thing when you're up on lines and you're just shootin' a rifle, but it plays hell when you're shootin' the Four Deuce. With a rifle you gotta be right on target; with the Four Deuce you only need to be near your target and shrapnel will get it for you."

I noted that Tom Fuhs had a little bit of hesitancy explaining that last bit of information. I was going to question him about it, but he started talking again, knocking the question right out of my mind.

"So now you know why the captain needs a cryptographer. Right now either him or the Funny Gunny has got to go up to the 81s and sort of root out the information from them about where the patrols are going to be located. And that's embarrassing to them."

I took a deep breath and, in the closeness of the bunker with Tom Fuhs nearby, I was quick to exhale and while doing so I blurted out, "Tom, I'm not a cryptographer. My MOS is 2516, not 2561. All I am is a backroom telephone central repairman trainee. The last two digits of my MOS must've been transposed by some dumb clerk when they were cuttin' orders.

"I don't know dip-shit about a Haggler. I never saw one before in my life. Shit, I never even heard of one before today."

Tom Fuhs thought that over for a moment or two. During that long moment the silence in the bunker was too deep to interrupt with words. Tom Fuhs sighed and looked sad faced at me.

"I think you're in a world of shit, Corporal."

I sighed, too, and looked at him, grim-faced. "Yeah," I said, "I think so, too. What do you think I ought to do about it?"

"I don't know. You're the NCO. NCOs are supposed to come up with the right answers to problems like this. Do you think you could learn how to use the Haggler?"

"Shit, Tom! What the fuck do you think? If the captain and the Funny Gunny with all their experience in the marines, if they can't break any messages on the Haggler, then how the fuck do you think I'm gonna do on it? I'm gonna have about as much luck as a monkey tryin' to fuck a football.

"Besides, I don't have any idea at all how the Haggler works. Do you have any ideas how it works? And stop callin' me corporal. My name is Crawford. Call me Crawford, okay?"

"Okay, if that's the way you want it, Crawford it is. Now, about the Haggler, I don't know exactly how it works. But I've seen the captain and the Funny Gunny take this little pick and mess around with these cogs and wires up here under the lid in the back of the Haggler. See, they open this book of instructions. Then they sort of pick around at them cogs," he said. He had a loose-leaf notebook opened on the field desk. The plastic cover had a red slash printed diagonally across it. In the middle of the red slash, large, bold, black letters spelled SECRET.

Damn, I thought, saying the words out loud for Tom Fuhs, "All I have is a confidential clearance. This is my out, Tom. I've got no business messing around with secret key lists!"

79

That didn't matter at all to Tom Fuhs.

"No one cares about that, Crawford. They put that on so we'll try harder to keep it from the gooks. What the hell, I'll bet most of them gooks can't even read English. Besides, if the captain and the Funny Gunny couldn't understand those instructions, fat chance a goddamn gook is gonna have tryin' to make heads or tails outta it. And anyway, that secret stuff doesn't apply to me and you, at least not right now. Don't forget, it was the captain and the Funny Gunny that gave us this stuff."

I couldn't argue against that kind of logic.

The Haggler was sitting atop and in the exact middle of the field desk. I opened the hinged back and looked at the cogs inside. It was still daylight, but inside the bunker it was dark. Tom Fuhs lighted two small, stubby candles, placing each one in a previously prepared dry rations can that had half a side cut away. Although the silvery inside of the cans reflected the light brightly, there were still shadows to contend with inside the Haggler.

I took the small pick—something like a dentist's pick but with a flattened end instead of a pointed one—and poked among the wires. I pulled out some of the wires and reaffixed others in the small slots on wheels that were attached to the shank of the handle.

I shut the cover. I was not certain what I had done with all that picking, or even what I had hoped to accomplish. I reached for one of the coded messages that I had brought from the command bunker.

I closed my eyes and mentally tried to recall what it was I had seen the Funny Gunny doing moments earlier in the command bunker. The Funny Gunny had the forefinger of one hand pointing at a five-letter code group. He had punched a letter—perhaps the first letter of a code group—on the Haggler and then had pulled down on the handle. I could both feel and hear the cogs and gears mesh inside the Haggler as they whirled and whirred.

Rachetta-whir, the Haggler said, popping out an alphabetical character stamped on the white tape which advanced a fraction of an inch.

"Damn!" Tom Fuhs said, excitedly. "You got it workin'!" He pointed at the just-printed alphabetical character.

According to what I had read in the instructions of the key lists, the Haggler had the capability of turning the meaningless five-letter code groups into intelligent messages, providing, of course, that the coding machine was set up properly in accordance with existing codes, and that the cogs and wires were placed in a specifically prescribed sequence, according to the keylist.

But I did not have the training, the knowledge, or the skill to use the keying material provided to me. By relying on haphazard, hit-or-miss methods in setting up decipherment procedures, I could have spent a lifetime using the Haggler without even the faintest hope of decrypting a message.

Still, I felt I had to try. And I did try. Oh, Lord, did I try. I worked that Haggler and that first message I had been given for nearly six straight hours. The net result of my work was long strands of confettilike tape streaming endlessly from the Haggler with meaningless garble imprinted on its surface.

Each time I punched the keyboard and pulled down the handle, the Haggler seemed to come alive, momentarily, speaking a single hyphenated word of its own language prior to spitting out a printed alphabetical character. The Haggler spoke in its mechanical language the only word it knew. With a spinning of cogs and wheels, the Haggler would sound out, very distinctly, rachetta-whir!

I was no typist, but that was quite all right, for the keyboard of the Haggler had only twenty-four characters; there was no J or Z. The Haggler did not look too much like a typewriter, either; it was too blocky, too square. I tried remembering and then tried copying the movements the Funny Gunny had made earlier. I stabbed at the keyboard with my left index finger; my right hand, in an almost reflexive movement, then hauled down on the handle. And each time there was a rachetta-whir sound and an alphabetical character was printed.

Tom Fuhs tried to read whatever was printed on the white tape. We went through at least three spools of white tape during the course of the afternoon. After using up the first spool of white tape, the two of us figured out how to replace the tape in the Haggler, a minor victory. We continued to fill the bunker with used white tape.

Late in the day we experienced a certain thrill of victory. Right there in the middle of a long length of meaningless alphabetical characters marching endlessly along one after the other in single file were two words that could quite easily be read. The two words—"it came"—filled Tom Fuhs and me with a tremendous pride of accomplishment.

"Goddamn, Tom! Look there! Look at those two words! Don't you shit me, buddy! We're onto something! For just a couple of seconds there we were using the Haggler just right." And then I asked, "Do you have any idea of what we were doing that was right?"

"Shit, no, Corporal," Tom Fuhs said, still trying to remember to call me by my last name. "Those words just sort of jumped right out there on the tape. Do you think they mean anything special? Do you want to show them to the Funny Gunny, or what?"

I thought about that for a moment. I wanted to share this small victory with someone in command, to let those in charge over me know that I had been working at the job to which I had been assigned, but then I thought, Naw, there's got to be more than that to this message.

I said aloud to Tom Fuhs, "I'm gonna tell you true, Tom. I think we ought to get more than just those two words to show the Funny Gunny. Let's just keep crankin' on the Haggler, okay?"

The sun was low in the winter sky and day was coming on toward dusk when Tom Fuhs said he had to make another run to battalion.

"Do you want to come along as my shotgun rider, Corporal? There's no way I can shoot back if I'm drivin'. You'd be doin' the same thing like you did this mornin', just keepin' an eye out for trouble. I wouldn't ask, but it's a big pain in the ass to get someone to ride shotgun for me."

Riding shotgun seemed to be the least I could do for Tom Fuhs. I readily agreed. The Funny Gunny okayed the two of us making the run to battalion. I made some points when I told the Funny Gunny I would volunteer on a permanent basis as shotgun rider for Tom Fuhs. The Funny Gunny liked that.

"That's good, Corporal Crawford. The captain likes men who volunteer. He goes to bat for them when the time comes around for him to do so.

"You're gettin' off to a good start in this outfit. I could hear you workin' over in the bunker with Tom Fuhs. You were stayin' right on the job. And that's good, too. Did you get anything done on those messages yet?"

I was going to answer negatively, but Tom Fuhs burst right out: "Shit, yeah, Gunny. We started bustin' a message, but had to stop because of the run. We'll get the rest of it done when we get back."

CHAPTER
6

I stayed quiet until we got to the jeep. "Why the fuck did you hafta say we could bust those decryptions, Tom? Shit! Two words don't make a message. Now my ass really is in a sling."

"Don't worry, Corporal. We'll do somethin' when we get back here. But right now, let's get this show on the road. It'll be like it was this morning, only I think we're gonna hafta make part of the run back here in the dark.

"Remember, if anyone fires at us, you just crank off a couple rounds in his general direction. Aimin' ain't gonna help any with the way the jeep bounces around.

"And don't fuck around with any of them silly password games. You just shoot and I'll drive like hell!"

He pointed to a couple of ragged holes turning rusty that were in the side of the jeep on his side. "I got these about two weeks ago when me and the captain and the Funny Gunny came up here on a quick reconnaissance before the rest of the company. It was right after the Punchbowl fighting stopped being so serious, but there were still a lot of gooks around.

"Well, anyway that Funny Gunny might look like some

kind of a clown, but don't let him fool ya. When the shootin' started and the jeep gets these hits, the Funny Gunny sort of reared right up in that back seat there like some kind of an angry bear, and he cranks off just two shots from his M1—and I'm not shittin' you now—he nails him two fuckin' gooks!

"You gotta understand that I'm drivin' this jeep like a bat outta hell, bouncin' around and all, tryin' my best to haul ass outta here, so I don't actually see the gooks go down, but the captain did. The captain whoops out, 'You got the fuckers, Gunny!' and the Funny Gunny said, 'Well, I hope so. I sure as shit was shootin' at them!'"

I was impressed. But with a name like Funny Gunny, well, that didn't sound like a killer marine. It just didn't have the right ring to it. But getting two gooks, that was something to write home about.

I asked Tom Fuhs why, if the narrow, rutty dirt road between the company and battalion was so hairy and all, it was necessary to go back and forth twice a day, once each morning and evening.

"A couple of reasons is why. Mail call is one of them. Battalion gets mail in at different times every day, whenever a run is made from regiment. So I go after the mail, mainly. While I'm there I check in at the adjutant's office for any orders that might've come in. And then I go down to the battalion laundry a couple of times a week. As you might have noticed, the captain likes his dungarees clean, starched, and pressed. He's particular that way."

I was waiting in the jeep while Tom Fuhs was checking on the mail when I saw my friend Sergeant Posty come out of a nearby tent. I hollered over to him. I had lost track of Posty on the deck of the USS *Marine Lynx*. We shook hands and exchanged news of the past two days. I was trying to make a big thing out of my being assigned to the Four Deuces, and not back in the rear with the gear.

"What the fuck's a Four Deuce?" Posty asked.

So I told him. At least I told him all that I could remember of what Tom Fuhs had said to me. It didn't sound so hot chewed over a second time.

Trying another tack to impress my hometown friend, I

told Posty I had been busy all afternoon trying to decode a message on the Haggler. I casually mentioned breaking two words—"it came"—but Posty wasn't too impressed with that, either.

"What the hell, Crawford. You're not a cryptographer. Why are you working out on the Haggler?"

So I told Posty about the MOS screwup. I also told him my ass was in a sling if I couldn't break those messages for the captain.

Posty gave me a big smile.

"Your worries are over, my friend," Posty said to me.

I knew that Posty was a communicator of some kind but I had no idea just what it was he did. Posty told me that he worked in the battalion message center. Part of his job was dealing with classified messages.

"We mimeograph all those classified messages for distribution. Come on, we'll go over to the message center now and I'll introduce you around. Then, if you come down here twice a day, you can pick up the clear-text copies of all the enciphered messages that are sent out to the Four Deuces. How does that sound?"

My salvation took less than five minutes' time. The battalion cryptographic center personnel were most accommodating. I talked with the crypto chief.

"Shit, yeah, Corporal Crawford. I'll put your name on the distribution list. That way any time you are in the area you can come by here and pick up any traffic we have for your mortar company. It will be typed in plain English, typed out and run off on properly marked paper.

"The only reason we send those messages out by radio, really, is for training purposes. Most of those radiomen don't even know how to pronounce the phonetic alphabet, much less be able to write it down so it can be read." He snickered, and so did I, enjoying a laugh at the expense of a few radiomen sitting nearby, all of whom were giving us the finger.

"What was the name of the last cryptographer up there at the Four Deuces? He was a buck sergeant. I think he rotated home recently.

"He would always come in here. A funny kind of a guy.

He'd copy down the deciphered messages—the clear-text copy—in his little yellow message center book. Do you want to do that? Or do you want me to put you on the distribution list so you can pick up these typed-out copies?"

I opted for picking up the typed-out copies, those mimeographed on clean white paper that had the proper marking on it showing proper classification. I figured anything good enough for the battalion staff was good enough for my captain.

I was given four messages on clean sheets of paper. Each message had a diagonal stripe on it, going from the upper left-hand corner to the lower right-hand corner. A yellow stripe indicated confidential material; a red stripe indicated secret material; a blue stripe indicated the material was top secret.

The messages were neatly reproduced without smudge marks. I was provided with a large manila envelope to protect the paper en route. I kept on thanking the cryptographer—a staff sergeant—who had saved my ass.

"No sweat, Corporal. I've put you on the distribution list. You can pick up any messages we have for the Four Deuces any time you stop by here," the staff sergeant said, smiling.

And I smiled, too. I smiled a great big shit-eating grin of a smile. There was absolutely no doubt about it; us marine corps NCOs knew how to help each other out. Life in a combat zone was terrific!

I was still smiling as I waited in the jeep for Tom Fuhs to finish his business at battalion. As he got into the jeep I cut him in on the scoop, on what had happened. I was so goddamned happy I could've shit marine corps emblems.

"Son of a bitch!" Captain Massey cried out, enunciating each word distinctly, a short time later.

I went directly to the command bunker after Tom Fuhs and I arrived back in the Four Deuce compound. I shook the camouflage poncho that covered the entranceway to the bunker. Responding to the challenge of the Funny Gunny, I simply said my rank and last name, then handed in the clean, mimeographed, classified-marked messages.

Then I heard the captain swear loudly and distinctly,

something I had been told his manners and bearing would not normally permit him to do.

"Look at this, Gunny!" the captain said, excitedly, thrusting the messages at the Funny Gunny. Then he looked at me. "You are all right, Corporal Crawford! My last cryptographer, a buck sergeant, was a good man. He brought me my deciphered messages every day. But his messages were written in a scrabbled hand on those little yellow message center pads and I could just barely read them. I worried a lot of times if I had read his writing correctly.

"But, you, Corporal Crawford. You have really distinguished yourself. And this just your first day here at the Four Deuces. You keep up this good work, you hear?"

Being dismissed, I backed away from the command bunker again, this time into the darkness of a Korean night. I felt like a Western Union delivery boy who had done a good job.

The Funny Gunny followed me out into the darkness. As he was coming out of the bunker, I could see that he had a tight smile on his face.

"You're a good man, Corporal Crawford. I heard you bustin' ass all afternoon down in the bunker with Tom Fuhs. Both me and the captain appreciate people who work hard. You just took a big worry off his back. And that's good."

The Funny Gunny told me to take a seat on some nearby sandbags. He sat down, too. He started to talk, telling me of the situation in the 1st Marine Division in Korea at that point in time. He said he was going to give me his standard orientation lecture.

"Back in June, when we were straightening out our lines, one of our objectives was this sheer line of mountains," he motioned with his hand, "the mountains we are in right now. From our location last June 20, we looked down into this area. As you know, it's a deep, almost circular valley. All the mountains located here are of about the same height." He paused to light a cigarette, shielding the flaring match by hunching his shoulders down over its flame. He offered me a light from the burning end, cautioning me to keep my cigarette between my cupped hands, to draw on it carefully.

"We occupied part of this mountain area; the gooks owned the rest. Not much has changed over the past couple of months. Somebody in charge of naming things called this area the Punchbowl, and the name stuck." The Funny Gunny motioned over his shoulder with one hand. "Up there a couple hundred more yards is what we call 'being on line.' When the grunt marines got to that spot, they set to work laying lots of apron and concertina barbed wire. They brought in yobos of the Korean Service Corps to dig trenches and gun emplacements into the military crest of the hills we would occupy. And then they mined every inch of the mountain—except for one pathway up located in the rear—with every killing device we had."

The Funny Gunny butted out his cigarette and fieldstripped it, rolling the remaining bit of paper in a small ball, which he flipped away. I was struck with the incongruity of his being so neat in a combat area. But then, I figured, once you learn something the marine way, you just naturally keep on doing it the marine way.

"Trench warfare," the Funny Gunny said. "It's like we were going to fight World War One all over again, only this time in the mountains and not on flat land.

"There's you in a trench, with the long, steep, downward slope of the mountainside in front of you and every foot of it covered with barbed wire and the whole of it mined so a gnat couldn't get through without blowing his ass away. And then there's another long, upward slope of mountain to where the gooks are in their own trench line.

"It's a stalemate, that's what it is. We ain't trying to get any more land, and we sure as hell don't want to give up any. In this kind of a waiting game, people, careless people mostly, get killed every day."

The Funny Gunny was silent for a long moment, and then he said, "Your draft landed at Sochiri, right? You came in on an amphibious landing above the Thirty-eighth Parallel?"

I gave him an affirmative nod and then, just as suddenly, realized the Funny Gunny couldn't see my bobbing head so I croaked out a "yessir" to him.

"We came in loaded and looking for bear," I told him. "They gave us live ammunition and everything. And then after we had landed and all, they told us it was a practice landing. What in the world did they want to do that for? Give us live ammunition and make-believe like we were really landing against the North Koreans? Somebody could've gotten hurt," I said, remembering how I tried to line up my sights on two asshole marine truck drivers.

"That's a good question, Corporal Crawford. Let me see if I can't give you a good answer," the Funny Gunny said, settling himself better on the sandbags.

"A couple of weeks ago, late in August, it was pretty much decided the marines would be given the job of making an amphibious flanking attack on the east coast. Our boss, Major General G. C. Thomas, sure wanted the chance to make that landing.

"But—and this makes a long story short—the amphibious flanking attack idea ended up being shit-canned. Marine planners, however, figured you people on the Thirteenth Draft—since you would have been involved in the amphibious landing anyway, and since you already were on a ship at sea that had landing craft aboard it—well, they figured you might just as well get the practice even if it wasn't the real thing. I guess they didn't tell you it was for practice in order to have you all in the right frame of mind for it, if you know what I mean."

I muttered an "uh-huh."

The Funny Gunny continued: "As for the rest of us, instead of hitting the gooks with an amphibious attack, the First Marine Division was told to get ready to fight for the rest of the Punchbowl. And that's what we have been doing.

"Our zone of attack came right through some of the most rugged terrain fought in during this war. We found ourselves asshole deep in gooks, fighting in an area dominated by steep, heavily wooded mountains. Roads, even trails, were almost nonexistent. And everywhere—looking right down our throats—were gooks and chinks who had all summer long to dig in. And let me tell you, them fuckers knew how to dig in. They fought us, and they fought us hard, for every hilltop and bunker."

The Funny Gunny paused for a long moment. I thought

he had finished talking. But he continued, "I'd guess the fighting we did here over the past month has been about as difficult—taking into account both the terrain and the fierce enemy resistance—as any battle in the war so far. Just nine days ago, on September 21, the First Marine Regiment went up Hill 854.

"That's the hill up there in front of us. And I'm going to tell you now, getting it was a bitch! We did some fighting, all right, both the grunts going up that son-of-a-bitching hill and us who were behind them, backing them up. There were enough gooks to go around for all of us to get a piece of the action. And there still are a lot of gooks out in front of us, moving around in that fluid area called 'no-man's-land.' It is not ours and not theirs; it sits there between us, fought over every day."

The Funny Gunny paused to light another cigarette. "So now you know, Corporal, why it's so important for the captain to have good information on who and what is out in front of us. Him and me are going to depend on you getting us those messages so that we can read them.

"You did a good job today. I don't know how you did it, and I don't care how, either. The point is that you did the job you were asked to do. And that's all that really matters, that really counts in a war, men doing their jobs."

The Funny Gunny paused a moment or two, as if taking the time to form his words. "The gooks, now. The ones we're fighting. They're doing their jobs, too. And don't you forget it.

"Don't just hate your enemy, Corporal Crawford. Try to know your enemy. Or at least try to understand your enemy. He's over there doing the same damn thing that we're trying to do over here and that is to fight this war the best way we know how.

"We didn't know a whole hell of a lot about what the Russians and their partners the Chinese were doing in North Korea. And I guess we didn't know because we just plain didn't give a damn one way or the other.

"I'll tell you this as the gospel truth, we sure as shit didn't know—at least until the gooks came barreling across the

91

parallel in June 1950—that the Soviets up north had built the most powerful military force in Asia, aside from their own.

"So that's who you're fighting. A highly trained North Korean army and not just a bunch of asshole gooks. I'm telling you now that if you want to whip their ass, then you better make up your mind that you'll be fighting a trained army, a Russian- and Chinese-trained army, and you better fight them with all the skill you have because if you don't, you're gonna get your ass kicked and someone is gonna take down your name and tell your folks back home what a great marine you were."

The Funny Gunny finished his cigarette, and then said, "Okay, Corporal. I'm finished with my lecture. We'll sit down again a time or two and talk some more. Right now you go get some sack time."

For the second time, a senior staff NCO had taken the time to notice me, to talk with me one-on-one, to teach me. Tired as I was I didn't want the moment to end. I had enjoyed the camaraderie between us, the way this man, a technical sergeant, took the time to talk to me, to inform me, to let me be at ease in his presence. It was almost like talking to an older brother. I wanted to say something that would reassure the Funny Gunny he could count on me. And I knew when I tried to express myself in this way, well, I knew I was going to fuck it up. Still, I blurted it out: "Gunny, thanks for talkin' to me, and not talkin' down at me. I'm new here, you know that. And to tell you the truth, I think I'm a little bit scared, if you know what I mean. It's not like I'm scared of the gooks, or nothin' like that, or scared of the dark. I think I'm scared I might not do my job right. So I'm glad I done it right today. I'll bust my ass for you and the captain, doin' the job you assigned me today. And that's all I got to say."

I thought the Funny Gunny might laugh at me or something. He didn't. Instead he said to me, in a quiet voice, "Well, that's good, Corporal. I think you're going to do just fine in the Four Deuces. You got a good attitude, and that's important.

"And as far as being scared is concerned, well, I think it

all boils down to the fact that in a war, any war, there's just a lot of scared men on one side doing their damnedest to kill a lot of scared men on the other side. All of us are scared. Or at least we ought to be."

I was promoted to buck sergeant three weeks later.

Tom Fuhs and I had just returned to the Four Deuces from making the morning run to battalion. I had three clean sheets of neatly typed and mimeographed classified messages. The Funny Gunny took the messages from me, handed them inside the bunker to the captain, and then told me he wanted to speak to me, privately. We walked a short distance away from the command bunker area.

"The captain wants to talk with you this morning, Corporal Crawford. And in order for you to make the best possible impression on him, maybe you ought to find some soap, and maybe a razor blade to scrape across your face. See if you can't find some clean dungarees, too. Lob Stratton down at the supply tent can fix you up with what you need. You go and get cleaned up and then come back here to see me, understand?"

So what was there to understand? My bubble was about to get busted. I shook my head, thinking, That's the start of it. You get to cleaning up just a bit and pretty soon they start looking to see if you have a fresh haircut and stuff like that. Thank God for the mud! Maybe it would keep the captain from demanding shiny boots.

Now that I had been told to change my dungarees, I realized that I had been living in them since the morning when I had disembarked from the USS *Marine Lynx*. That was just a bit more than three weeks ago. Not only had I not changed my dungarees, I had continuously worked and slept in them. As far as personal hygiene was concerned, I had to admit I had not really washed all that good, not up under my armpits, that's for sure. Okay, maybe I had given my hands and face a token wash, a quick once over lightly before I ate my rations. I mean, no one likes to be a consummate crud.

Having been ordered to clean up and all that, I thought it in my own best interests to take a whore's bath, using my helmet as a basin. I took off the camouflage cover, removed

93

the helmet liner, filled the helmet halfway with water, and then heated everything by using heat tablets, which were hard to come by. That was another reason why frontline marines were so dirty. During the cold days of October, who wanted to strip to the waist and wash with cold water?

So we would take a dry-ration can, remove the lid, and punch holes in the sides for oxygen to flow through freely. Then we dropped a heat tablet to the bottom of the can and lighted it with a match. The heat tablet would burn the alcohol that soaked the tightly packed cotton-wool batting with a hot, very hot, translucent blue-yellow flickering flame. All a man had to do then was balance a partially filled helmet on the can and in minutes he had hot water for washing and shaving.

Gingerly I dipped my last clean handkerchief into the hot water and used a small sliver of soap to work up a lather. It felt pretty good to wash my face and neck. It felt so good I took off my utility jacket, the brown wool winter shirt under it, and the really dirty white skivvy shirt that was next to my skin. I washed under my arms. I shuddered a little putting my smelly undershirt back on again; I attributed the shiver to the cool winter day.

I lathered my face with shaving cream and scraped off what little beard and mustache I had accumulated. I was very fair haired. I would have given almost anything to have been able to grow a heavy black beard. I doused myself liberally with the contents of a small bottle of Ice Blue Aqua Velva aftershave lotion, figuring that if I wasn't clean, I might at least smell clean.

I put on the dungarees I had managed to scrounge from supply chief Lob Stratton. I didn't have a comb, so I ran my fingers through my hair and put my utility cap back on again, then hurried back to the command bunker.

"Well," the captain said as he came out of his command bunker. He was holding a sheet of crisp, heavy white bond paper in his hands. "You smell good today, Corporal Crawford."

"Thank you, sir," I said, mentally chalking one up for Aqua Velva.

"The purpose of this meeting, Corporal Crawford, is to

94

say you bring me fresh, clean pieces of paper daily, every morning and evening, all neat, carefully typed and mimeographed, never smudged, and all marked correctly as to their classification. Those pieces of paper give me the information I need to utilize the mortars of this company properly to good and full advantage," the captain said, motioning with his hand in the direction of the gun pits.

"Today I thought it would be a nice gesture to give you a clean piece of paper, all neat and carefully typed and without smudges," the captain smiled, gesturing with the crisp white paper he held in his hand.

"This is a promotion warrant to the rank of sergeant. Company Gunnery Sergeant Boyd and I feel that you have earned it. You have earned it because daily—armed with the coordinates and other complementary information you bring here in the form of neatly typed messages—I now have a high degree of confidence in firing the company mortars knowing that I will not accidentally fire into our own troops.

"Corporal Crawford, you have done a good job. Since the job you are doing actually calls for the rank of sergeant in our Table of Organization, I see no reason why you should not be a sergeant."

Sergeant! The man said "Sergeant"! I couldn't believe what I had just heard. I had spent forever as a Pfc in the marines and now, with less than six months' time in grade as a corporal, this neat and clean man is promoting me to sergeant. Damn! How far up the NCO ladder would I go if I really put my heart and soul into the game? Everything was within my grasp! The sky was the limit! There was no end in sight for me!

Maybe, I thought, looking at the captain, just maybe I might even get myself a commission. And, maybe, I thought, if I got myself a commission and kept on doing things the marine corps way, why maybe, just maybe, I would be promoted to captain. Me! A mustang captain!

Captain Massey was reading quickly from the promotion warrant. His fine, even white teeth—no yellow stains there—seemed to sparkle with each word.

"To all who shall see these presents, greetings: Know ye,

95

that reposing special trust and confidence in the fidelity and abilities of Charles S. Crawford, 1092787, I do appoint him a sergeant—temporary—in the United States Marine Corps, to rank as such from the twenty-fifth day of October, nineteen hundred and fifty-one. . . ."

I listened carefully as the captain precisely, articulately, read about how I was to carefully and diligently discharge my duties by doing and performing all manner of things thereunto pertaining.

The captain read out loud about how personnel of lesser grades were expected to render obedience to my appropriate orders, and how I was to observe and follow such orders and directions as may be given me by my superiors.

The captain finished reading. I was duly impressed with myself. I remembered what I had told the last man who had promoted me: Nobody was going to take away my corporal stripes. I resolved again that nobody was going to take any of these three stripes, either.

I extended my hand to receive the warrant that Captain Massey was holding out to me. I had washed my hands minutes earlier, sure, but there was still a lot of grit and grime in the creases of my skin, and farther up on my wrist where the water had not quite reached there was a definite demarcation line between the clean and the not so clean. I had a lot of washed-up but not washed-out dirt under my ragged, chewed-off fingernails.

As my semiclean or, if you want, my semidirty hands touched the promotion warrant, the captain, his eyes widening, suddenly whipped it back and away from me.

Anxiously I watched as the captain eyeballed first my extended hand, and then my face, and then my uniform.

I knew it! There always had to be some kind of a catch: If they give you something, it's because they want something. Now comes the shit about how NCOs are expected to be clean at all times, are expected to have their boots shined, and, I guess, are expected to have white-side-walled haircuts.

But that didn't seem to be on the captain's mind.

"Usually you are much dirtier than this, Corporal . . . that is, Sergeant Crawford. Now I am not diminishing any

96

efforts on your part—and I really do appreciate the fact that you have tried to dignify this ceremony by washing, even under these most trying circumstances—but, and it just dawned on me right now, how do you manage to keep the messages you deliver to me in such a clean and pristine state, knowing the normal condition of your hands most of the time?

"And, having said that, how do you manage to type these messages and reproduce them on mimeograph paper, when I know for certain that we do not have a decent typewriter, much less a mimeograph machine, in the company? Or do we have this type of office equipment, Sergeant Boyd?" the captain asked, looking at the Funny Gunny, who was shaking his head negatively.

Without hesitation I quickly explained the MOS fuck-up and how Tom Fuhs and I worked the Haggler every day for six, maybe seven hours. With a certain amount of pride I brought out from my utility jacket pocket a ragged piece of tape, showing it to the captain, telling him that on my very first day working as a cryptographer I had actually decrypted the two words "it came." I told him how I had volunteered to ride shotgun for Tom Fuhs, twice daily, and how I picked up the clean-text messages at the battalion crypto center. Most importantly, I told him I had made the decision on my own part, opting for the clean, white paper (marked appropriately with a correct classification slash) instead of writing it down in the message center book as the man before me had done.

That little piece of information raised the captain's eyebrows a bit. He pursed his lips as I leveled with him.

"Oh, well," the captain shrugged. "I did read this promotion warrant all the way through to you, Corporal . . . that is, Sergeant Crawford. And I did mean it when I commended you for the way you have provided me with the information I need daily for the guns.

"The company gunnery sergeant and I agree that you gave me what I wanted and needed. I must agree to the basic and main principle of what marines believe: Get the job done; get it done any way that it can be done, but get it done.

"And you did take the initiative, Sergeant Crawford,

didn't you. You brought back clean, white paper appropriately marked, and that was quite a step ahead of my last cryptographer who, by the way, I also promoted to the rank of sergeant."

The captain didn't falter, but he did hold onto my promotion warrant just a bit longer. Then he smiled his sparkling white-toothed smile, and he handed me my promotion warrant.

"By rights, Sergeant Crawford, I should have you transferred back to battalion or even regimental command primarily because of your telephone central repairman trainee MOS. Somehow, though, I really do not think you would want to go back there, would you?"

I didn't speak out, but I vigorously shook my head in agreement with him.

"I like your style. I have another communicator, Big Dog Ondrak, who trained to become a forward observer for me. He, too, was a former wireman. The Big Dog volunteered to be a forward observer, the job he is now doing. Did you know that?" the captain asked.

I didn't say anything. I was too busy nodding my head in complete agreement with whatever the captain was saying. I figured as long as he talked about the Big Dog, and about volunteering, and stuff like that, why, then I had a better-than-even chance of holding onto the three stripes I had just been given.

"I always need forward observers, did you know that, Corporal . . . er, Sergeant Crawford? I sure wish I had another one. The Big Dog surely does need a break up on the front lines. . . ."

I could see where the captain was headed.

I beat him to it.

I volunteered to become an FO. I wanted to be certain that I could keep my buck sergeant stripes. Volunteering to be an FO seemed to be the way I could be certain.

I was scheduled to go up on the hill the following day. I was excited about it; I knew that October 21, 1952, would always be a red-letter day for me. I had been in Korea for less than a month, and now I had my chance to fight, really fight, in a war.

I hurried back to the bunker I shared with Tom Fuhs. I wanted to share my excitement with him.

Apparently he didn't understand my excitement. He just shook his head and sort of gave me a sad smile. I guess he figured he would have a tough time finding someone else to ride shotgun with him every day as he drove back and forth to battalion on the mail run.

I had it all figured out and I tried to explain it to Tom Fuhs. I told him it was definitely to my advantage to be an FO. I told him that when I got up there on the front lines then surely nobody would give a big rat's ass about whether or not I had on clean clothes or even how long I wore my hair. I figured my friend Tom Fuhs would certainly be able to understand that.

BOOK II

Yellow Legs and Mickey Mouse Boots

CHAPTER
7

I saw Hill 854 right after I had gotten out of the commanding officer's jeep. With Captain Massey's approval, Tom Fuhs had driven me up the tight and narrow path through a living forest of brambles and tall trees. We drove beyond the forward edge of the Four Deuces and the 81mm mortar company. I was his shotgun rider going up. But I would stay on the hill; Tom would return to the Four Deuces alone.

We had tried to talk, but the low, grinding growl of the vehicle nosing continuously upward in four-wheel drive had made talk an impossibility. Tom Fuhs had to pay close attention to the track as he carefully inched the jeep forward. The vehicle still slipped from side to side as he negotiated the gradually narrowing, ever-rising track. The sound of the powerful engine reverberated back eerily from the grim woods closing in on us; trees reached out into the pathway with treacherous-looking, long, leafless fingers, clutching in a strange, threatening way.

Dismounting, I said my thanks to Tom Fuhs. It was little enough to say, yet it seemed sufficient at the time. Tom and the Funny Gunny were both due to rotate home in a few weeks, during late November. I hoped we would get the chance to talk again. But for the moment, my thanks said it all, and Tom Fuhs knew it.

I slid out of the jeep, grabbed the packed Willie Peter bag that was strapped to a backpack—new items that had replaced my field transport pack—and watched Tom Fuhs negotiate a turnaround point in the pathway.

"Don't you forget what the Funny Gunny told you," Tom Fuhs said. Then, with a wave of his hand, he headed downhill. I sure felt lonely at that moment.

Earlier, I had talked with the Funny Gunny. He had told me to watch my step. He meant his words both literally and figuratively. As a result, that was the way I first saw Hill 854, at boot-tip level, watching my step. As I climbed the ragged trail going uphill, a trail marked with bits and pieces of inch-wide, yellow, clothlike tape held in place on the ground with four-inch-long metal stakes, my eyes were on the mud-mired path. I was looking for what the Funny Gunny had earlier described as loose or newly dug earth. I also had my eyes peeled for trip wires.

"Loose dirt, or newly dug-up dirt, most always means something has been placed below it. You really don't want to step on it and find out the hard way what might be down below," the Funny Gunny had told me.

"Boot mines," he said, describing them to me, "were wooden boxes the size of a cigar box with up to five pounds of black powder inside. Pressure contact sets off the boot mine. You step on the lid, it presses down on a firing pin, and when the smoke clears, you're missing your foot and most of your shin bone. A year later you can hobble around on your crutches. It's a whole lot better not to step anywhere near freshly dug-up dirt on a trail or a path, you hear me?" I had heard him.

The Funny Gunny told me to constantly keep my eyes on the ground looking for trip wires. "They're hard to see, but they're sure worth looking for. They aren't but a cunt's hair thick, and there's no color to the wire. It blends in with the ground. But you can spot the wire if you look for it four to six inches off the ground, pulled tight and tied off to the trip release of a Bouncing Betty, or a grenade, or a detonator of some kind.

"You'll never tell anyone what a Bouncing Betty sounds like; it'll take your head off. A Bouncing Betty is a shell that's propelled upward, detonating about six feet above the ground. It's definitely a killer.

"Maybe you can live if you trip a boot mine, one that has only black powder in a wooden box. But you'll live with a mangled body that'll hurt forever." The Funny Gunny definitely was broadcasting on my wavelength.

"When a boot mine goes off, it's just an ugly, small, muffled explosion. Right away, whether you've heard it before or not, you'll recognize the sound of a blasting boot mine as being the ugliest sound of all the noises of war. You just don't want to hear it close up," the Funny Gunny said.

He told me that if I was at all uncertain about a path or a trail, and the telltale signs to look for on it, that I should just set my ass down. "You need to look first, of course, to see just where you're going to park it. And then you wait until someone comes down the hill or goes up that path ahead of you. That way the other guy takes all the chances and you get to take home the family jewels."

As far as the rest of the action was concerned, the Funny Gunny told me to live by a couple of rules: "Keep a tight sphincter muscle, and keep your head down when there's incoming fire."

So I waited at the bottom of Hill 854 until I saw some grunts coming down the mountain. They all nodded their heads in greeting as they passed me, and as the last man stepped away I heard him mutter, "Chicken shit!" Maybe so, but they were my gonads me and the Funny Gunny had been discussing earlier.

Marines did not refer to their front lines as being on mountains; instead, using a misnomer, they called the mountains "hills" simply because it was an easier reference term. On military maps, Hill 854 was noted as being exactly 854 meters above sea level. Hill 854 was located almost in the middle of the main line of resistance assigned to the 1st Marine Regiment.

Hill 854 was an ugly mountain, spotted here and there with huge acne-pitted holes bitten into its face—a face that had nothing higher on it than jagged stumps of trees blasted off at ground level and looking like overnight whiskers trying to make a comeback. Hill 854 was a mountain bristling with the scattered refuse of a stagnant war poking through snow, which lay like hastily applied shaving cream patted smooth or formed into wavy ridges.

The zigzag pathway leading to the trench lines was extremely narrow and slippery with mud. At its steepest slopes, wooden ammunition boxes were dug in as steps. The wet, warped wood, combined with slick mud, made these steps perilous. I might have sprained either one or both of my ankles a dozen times over had I not been wearing calf-high leggings, the famous "yellow legs" of the Marine Corps.

Piss and moan as we might, marines had still not been issued the black, smooth-leather, ankle-high boots the army was issuing its combat soldiers. Marine grunts still had only their pale yellow canvas leggings, which fit like a pair of spats over boondockers. Form-fitting, the leggings hugged the ankle and lower leg up to a few inches below the knee and were tied at the outer side with strong round laces woven through metal eyelets. Supple, they really did support a man's ankles and lower calf muscles.

The yellow legs had another value, too. Earlier, during the fighting at Pusan, then later during the Inchon landing, and more recently during the August and September Punchbowl fighting, both the Chinese and the North Korean People's Army (NKPA) developed an aversion to fighting troops with yellow legs. To this point in time, in Korea, the Marine Corps had not lost any battle in which they had become engaged. Marine grunts had, in fact, "kicked ass and taken names" every time they had come in contact with an enemy force. Sure, the marine grunts had sustained high casualty rates, but they had inflicted an even higher casualty rate on the gooks, many times in the three-to-one, four-to-one, five-to-one category. And the marine grunts always achieved their objectives—when they stemmed the retreating tide at Pusan as the newly arrived 1st Provisional Marine Brigade, when they came in over the mudflats at Inchon to take Seoul back from the NKPA, when they slugged their way up to and then down from the frozen Chosin Reservoir, and when they beat back numerically stronger guerrilla forces earlier in 1952.

Prisoners told interrogators that the Chinese and North Korean troops just did not want to fight the marines. They said their leaders, when planning assaults, tried to bypass any outfit wearing yellow leggings, if it were possible to do so. When I had been told that, I felt lucky to have the yellow leggings.

Now, climbing up Hill 854, the self-satisfaction and well-being I had felt on my promotion to buck sergeant was fizzling flat as I realized I had very little knowledge about a whole lot of things that might become very important to me. Admittedly, I had led a very sheltered marine corps life so far. I knew a lot about operating the Quantico switchboard, a little about telephone central backroom repair, and that just about summed it all up.

I knew zilch about how to use a Haggler, and the only thing I really knew about being an FO was that I would be calling in shots while I was up on the front line.

If I had anything going for me at all, it was that I was far too naive about everything to be afraid. I was just too new to the business of war. In the back of my mind I figured fear would come along soon enough, clutching and grabbing and all-encompassing. When that happened I would have to deal with it. But for right now, all I had to do was learn a few things, do a few things. I didn't know exactly what it was I would need to learn, what it was I would have to do.

So far I just happened to be lucky enough to have someone like the Funny Gunny on hand to cut me in on the scoop, to tell me a few things. He decided on the name I would use when I was up on the hill: "If you want to go home with all the parts you brought with you to Korea, then you practice what I've been talking to you about. You start by being cautious. That's going to be your hill name; you're going to be FO Eight and your call sign will be Cautious." And he made recommendations concerning the type of weapon I should carry, since FOs had their choice of weapons. He suggested I carry a .45-caliber automatic pistol: "It's a comfort weapon, that's all it is. It'll make you feel safer having it in your sleeping bunker or when you're standing watch."

He also suggested I carry some weapon that I could use to spray the area if the need arose for me to do so. In spite of its weight—and the Funny Gunny's grim look—I selected a heavy Thompson submachine gun with round ammunition drums.

"This will be my spray gun," I said.

The Funny Gunny rolled his eyes upward and shrugged his shoulders. Lob Stratton snickered. I didn't care, I felt secure holding the tommy gun.

Lob Stratton warned me of the weight I would be carrying with the tommy gun—an extra eighteen pounds when you included the round metal drumlike magazine that held thirty .45-caliber rounds and that snapped in place underneath, at about the halfway point of the weapon.

The Lob urged me to take a tanker's "grease gun," with its straight ammunition magazine, telling me the wire-framed weapon was much lighter and did the same job of delivering a fast load of heavy, man-killing hunks of lead very quickly and with a great deal of inaccuracy once the trigger was pulled.

But words could not stop my selection. I wanted both the .45-caliber automatic pistol and the tommy gun. Lob Stratton provided me with two extra boxes—fifty rounds to the box—of ammunition for the weapons and eight more pounds to carry. The tommy gun was macho enough for anyone's image. I needed something to bolster mine.

While the tommy gun may have enlarged my ego, I soon found out it was both difficult and awkward to carry. The round ammunition drum dug into my side with every step. The streamlined front hand guard and the heavy stock created an out-of-balance situation, causing the weapon to become extremely difficult to carry at sling arms.

"You need to remember one thing," the Funny Gunny said. "You're the Four Deuce FO. You have a special job to do. The Big Dog will teach you how to do it. The job of the

FO is to kill gooks with mortar rounds. The job of the grunts in the company you will be attached to is to kill gooks with their rifles, their grenades, and their machine guns. Don't get so carried away with that tommy gun that you forget to do what you're being sent up on the hill to do."

At the command bunker Captain Massey looked me over. "Except for needing a shave, you look just like the rest of my FOs," the captain said. He gave me a pair of binoculars and a map case.

"These are the tools of your trade, Sergeant Crawford. Big Dog Ondrak will stay on the hill with you until you learn how to use them. Learn from him. He knows the business," the captain said. He wished me luck.

The Funny Gunny walked me over to where Tom Fuhs was waiting by the jeep.

Somehow, during the brief time earlier when he was explaining all that I needed to know, the Funny Gunny lost his droll, troll-like, comical look, his two-sizes-too-small Mickey Mouse winter hat with its earflaps sticking straight out notwithstanding. Okay, sure, all the outward appearances were still there. But for me he was an entirely different person. He cared. I knew that he honest-to-God cared about me, just as he cared about Tom Fuhs, and Lob Stratton, and the Big Dog, and the captain, and everyone else in the Four Deuces. It was his job to care about all of us, to look out for all of us, to protect all of us the best way he knew how. That was when I looked at the Funny Gunny and, although I should have said more, simply said, "Thanks, Gunny, for everything."

All of which was why I was looking down at my boot tips, keeping an eye out for freshly dug dirt and trip wires on the muddy steps going steeply up Hill 854.

I made it to the top without incident. I was puffed, and I had worked up a sweat. I sort of slid into the trench line on the reverse slope of Hill 854, dug in as it was on the military crest of the hill. That position was located such that, even if a man was standing upright, there was still the backdrop of the hill behind to prevent him from being silhouetted against the skyline and becoming an easy target.

My lungs burned as they pulled in deep draughts of cold air. My shaking legs told me I had just climbed the steepest goddamn mountain in Korea.

I rested a moment in the trench line. I was amazed at the silence. The only noise being made was coming from me. I greedily sucked air in and then exhaled it in heavy streams of vapor. The climb had bushed me.

Out of the corner of my eye I saw a grunt moving toward me, hunkered over in the purposely irregularly dug trench line. The grunt was wearing both a helmet and an upper-body flak jacket—mine were both in my backpack—and he was carrying an M1 rifle. Even on this side of Hill 854, the grunt was hunched over, taking as much advantage of the trench line as he could get. We sort of faced each other as he maneuvered to pass me.

"Where do I find Sergeant Ondrak?" I asked the grunt.

"Beats the shit out of me. He ain't in Item Company, is he?"

"He's attached here. He's the Four Deuce FO."

"Oh, shit! You mean the Big Dog, don't you? Damn, I never knew his last name. Everybody in Item Company just calls him the Big Dog. He's probably up at the FO bunker. Do you know where that is?"

"Nope. I've never been on the hill before. I'm the new Four Deuce FO. I'm gonna relieve him."

"Well, hell, pardner. Welcome aboard, as the skipper here would say. I sure hope you're as good callin' shots as the Big Dog is. He can put a round right in your back pocket, that's how good the Big Dog is. Come on, follow me. I'll take you to the FO bunker."

I muttered a "thanks" to his back as the grunt took a turn in the trench line and then angled up to a cut that seemed to go directly across the top of the mountain, bisecting it. The grunt got down on his hands and knees and snaked his way over the crest of the mountain, using a shallow trench that was about eighteen inches deep. I watched as he sloshed through a slick half inch of mud and I thought to myself, that shit ain't for me.

So I heaved myself into the shallow trench line, stood

upright, pushed out my chest to sort of fit the packboard a bit better on my back, and, as I walked, I raised my right arm high up, reaching over with my left hand to catch the strap of my tommy gun, which had slid down to the elbow area of my right arm. I curled my right hand, fisted it, and pulled it up and back, adjusting the gun strap on my shoulder as I did so.

I heard what sounded like bees buzzing past me, and then, from a distance, distinctly heard five or six low-sounding pops. I remembered thinking at that time, since I was allergic to the poison of bees and wasps and would swell up around my eyes, nose, and mouth when bitten anyplace at all on my body, Shit! Just my luck to get stung by a bee!

I dug my boondockers into the slippery bottom of the trench, first one and then the other, and sort of sauntered on toward a deeper, wider trench line that had sandbags on the shoulder of the far side and many, many fighting holes dug facing the gook positions. The grunt was already in the trench line. He was looking back at me and he was wearing this big, dumb-looking grin.

"I'll be a sonofabitch! You fuckin' Four Deuce FOs just don't give a big rat's ass, do you?"

I sort of shrugged my shoulders, settling my backpack. I had no idea what he was talking about, so I nonchalantly gave him a sort of tight-lipped smile.

Inadvertently, ignorance notwithstanding, I made a name for myself right then. I was to learn that five grunts of Item Company had been shot digging that shallow communications trench across the mountain. Painstakingly, the grunts had lain on their bellies and scooped at the shallow trench line with entrenching tools. When it was deep enough to slide and hunker across in sort of relative safety, they just stopped digging it.

The grunt who was leading me to Big Dog Ondrak thought I had walked across upright on purpose, not in ignorance. Moreover, he thought I was giving the gooks on Hill 1052—which loomed menacingly to the right front and was about a quarter of a mile away—the Italian "fuck you" salute, hitting my right elbow with a cupped hand, bouncing up my right forearm. And, of course, it was bullets from a heavy machine gun, not bees, that I had heard buzzing past my head.

Big Dog Ondrak was a tall drink of water with half-hooded eyes on a very lean, very Polish-looking face. One of his front teeth was broken and showed on a slant as he talked. He was very, very dirty and he needed a shave in the worst kind of way. He was drinking coffee from a canteen cup and he was slouched against the sandbagged wall of the FO bunker, which protected him against incoming small-arms fire. His helmet, with its dirty green-side-out camouflage cover and chin straps dangling, was cocked rakishly at an angle over his tired-looking face. He had been watching the whole affair through half-closed eyes.

"You just ain't too cautious, Cautious," the Big Dog said, shaking hands with me and offering me some of his coffee. Much later I was told that after the Big Dog had returned to the company area, he had told the Funny Gunny that I "had given the gooks the bird."

Right now the Big Dog waved me on into the FO bunker. It did not take him too long to show me where he had registered his concentrations in the area to the front of Item Company, or how to use the maps and binoculars I had brought to the hill. Surprisingly enough, I learned quickly, mimicking his actions. Even more surprising, I found out that my ability to make distance judgments on far locations was still with me. I could no more explain it that day to the Big Dog than I could earlier to my friend Posty on our drive across country.

"How can you figure the yardage distance between an exploding round and your target so quickly?"

"I don't know, Big Dog. All I can say is that I just look at it and right away I know what it is."

"Well, we've called enough shots in and you've made the right corrections too many times for it to be just luck. Maybe you just naturally have the knack for it, Cautious. Come on," he said then, leaving the FO bunker and going out into the trench line.

The trench line was deep and wide enough to accommodate two grunts passing each other, providing they both sidled along with their backs to the trench walls. About five feet deep, the walls of the trench were smooth, not rough, as I had imagined they would be. The smoothness, I found out, was from our clothing continually brushing up against the walls as we moved. Sandbags were placed carefully, interlacing with each other, on both edges of the trench. On the chest-high parapet side, facing outboard, individual and crew-served fighting holes were placed about every fifteen feet. The trench angled off to the left or right at each fighting hole. The Big Dog said the kinks in the trench line kept any gooks who might get into the trench from shooting down the whole length of it. I noted that most of the crew-served fighting holes were covered with thick layers of sandbags, supported by either logs or metal stakes, and that, like the FO firing bunker, they looked out to the entire area to the front.

The Big Dog hollered his name at a bunker entranceway and, shaking the covering poncho, entered and motioned me to follow. By its size I recognized it to be the command bunker. The Big Dog introduced me to the Item Company skipper and his first sergeant. He made a big production out of telling them I had given the gooks the "fuck-you" sign as I leisurely walked across the shallow communications trench.

"I think you got yourself a winner, Captain. Cautious here just ain't afraid of nothing. And from the way he used the Four Deuce this afternoon, I think he's gonna do okay calling in shots for you," the Big Dog said.

By this time I was almost believing that earlier I had purposely given the gooks the arm. I needed something to establish myself and this was tailor made for me.

The courtesy call to the Item Company skipper complete, the Big Dog led the way back to his sleeping bunker where I stowed my gear. I would share the bunker with him that night. We returned to the FO bunker. As the Funny Gunny had given me advice, so did the Big Dog.

"You want to keep your head down, Cautious. There's a whole lot of grunts up here being paid to keep their heads up, seein' where to shoot and what to shoot when things get hot. But there's only one of you. And you're the guy calling in the Four Deuces. So don't be a hero. Keep your head and ass down when you're calling shots."

The Big Dog had another bit of information for me.

"Once you get a 'splash' from FDC, it means your round will land in ten seconds' time. I can tell you right now that you'll develop a feeling about firing shots. It's like you have invisible antennae, feeling, feeling, willing yourself to hear and know the sound of your own rounds landing.

"And when you develop this—well, it's sort of like a sixth sense or intuition—then no matter what's going on, you're just gonna know, you're gonna feel your round impacting, exploding.

"You wait and see. No matter how many rounds are being fired, incoming or outgoing mail, you're gonna be able to tell which exploding round is yours. You're just gonna know. You're gonna be able to define that one particular sound from everything else.

"And when you feel your round go off, well, you just keep your head down a couple seconds longer—especially if you're shootin' counterbattery fire—and then bring your head up quick for a look in the direction of where you expected your round to land. Look for a quick puff of dark, salt-and-pepper-colored smoke."

The Big Dog told me to develop my abilities, and then to trust my abilities.

The Big Dog and I were looking out the aperture of the FO bunker at the area occupied by the enemy. Like any command post bunker, the FO bunker had heavy timbers overlaid with sandbags for a roof. The aperture from which we looked out was about eight inches high and about six feet wide, with an overhang of timbers and sandbags. We had a panoramic view of the war zone in front of our lines. Battlefields that surround troops dug into trench lines, if fought over very long, quickly wear threadbare. Homes and buildings, if there are any, are quickly leveled and turned to rubble. Because of trenches and bunkers and fighting holes, the contours of the ground are disturbed, changing from serene to ugly.

The Big Dog and I were looking through the aperture, our

arms resting on it, binoculars to our eyes. He was explaining the Comanche system of firing the Four Deuce.

"That's when you sneak right up on your target, Cautious. You select a concentration to work from, one that's already been established with FDC, and you make your corrections from it, going farther out or closer in, going either left or right. Then you call for your first round and put it out there in front of you.

"Once the first round is in the area of the target, that's when you use the Comanche system. You just sneak right up on it."

Big Dog Ondrak pulled on his cigarette, inhaling deeply and then pushing out all the smoke.

"Let me tell you something, Cautious. A lot of FOs fuck around and use a lot of ammunition getting in on their target. That's for shit. Anybody who uses more than three rounds to get on his target, well, they ought not to be calling shots, it's as simple as that.

"These grunts up here, they want you to be shootin' gooks, not just rearranging the landscape. They want you to get on target right away. They want you killin' gooks. You better understand that right now. You're going to be calling in shots that kill people. And the people you're going to kill are gooks who are doin' their damnedest to try to kill you and those grunts.

"You think about that for a minute and if you can't hack it, you say so right now and then get your ass down off this hill and I'll just stay up here a while longer."

The Big Dog couldn't have made it plainer. Like it or not, I faced the reality that I was in an FO bunker in Korea and I was there for one purpose only; I was there to blow the shit out of gooks.

Up to this moment the Big Dog had been telling me what I needed to know to be a Four Deuce FO. Now his voice softened. I had to move closer to hear. I looked at his eyes and they seemed to be focused on something far, far out in front of the lines.

"That's a killing field you're looking at out there, Cautious," Big Dog Ondrak seemed to whisper.

115

"If you see anything moving out there—and I mean anything—and nobody has checked in with you and you know that Item Company doesn't have any patrols out or anything and the goddamned patrol leaders are always supposed to, well, shit, they're supposed to check in with you before they go out, why then, when you see somebody moving out there, then you go right ahead and blow the shit out of them," the Big Dog blurted out, hurrying his words, spitting them out as if they had a bad taste.

Again the Big Dog was silent and I knew intuitively that he didn't want me to say anything.

More slowly now, the Big Dog said, his eyes looking straight out in front, "You just keep on firin' and firin' until whatever it is that was moving out there ain't moving no more." Again he whispered his words low, so very, very low, so low I had to lean forward and listen hard to hear the Big Dog say, "And then you count the bodies."

The Big Dog was satisfied with my performance as an FO. The following day he went down off the hill. Late that same day one of the grunts told me that a patrol had been out in front of Item Company some ten days earlier. "It was a reconnaissance patrol from the company next to us over there on the left side of the line. It was a patrol from George Company. And the fuckin' George Company patrol leader—a brand new second lieutenant—didn't even check in with our company commander or the first sergeant or anybody and so no one here in our trenches knew shit about the patrol."

I was told a light machine gun started firing first, joined in by one or two BARs, and then individual marksmen with M1s. That was when the Big Dog called in his shots. Immediately after firing had ceased, the Big Dog was in high cotton, calling down to FDC that he had at least three confirmed kills. And he was right. George Company confirmed the three kills—a grunt lieutenant, a buck sergeant, and a corporal.

I had already been introduced to my wireman, Pfc Bill Bixby, whose job was to keep my land line open for use

116

between the EE-8 and the company switchboard, and my radioman, Cpl. Soupy Campbell—everyone named Campbell is automatically called Soupy—who operated the huge, ungainly SCR-300 radio. Both men would be with me in the FO bunker in the event of a firefight. I would pass my orders to the FDC through the telephone. Since this was a practice, I wanted to do my own talking with the FDC, to become acquainted with their procedures. I turned the generator handle on the EE-8 field telephone to generate enough electricity to signal the Four Deuce company field switchboard.

I damned near shit a brick when I heard a male voice answer me: "Windbreak, operator." I just was not expecting to hear a male voice. Shit, I thought, I have come full circle. I wanted to leave Quantico because I thought marines were fighting a war in Korea, not answering telephones. And that code name: Windbreak! It sounded like someone was going to fart, or something.

I asked for the FDC and identified myself and asked for a fire mission to adjust concentrations. The Funny Gunny was right; it took less than two minutes to have a round on the way. And I was right, too; I was right on target. I impressed the hell out of myself and my radioman and wireman as I fired the Four Deuces for the next half hour. I just knew what corrections to call in to FDC. I would watch a round go off, explode with first a lightning flash and then a roar followed by a ball of black smoke billowing up, and I just knew the right correction to make to bring it to whatever target I wanted to hit. I was like someone playing golf for the very first time, using the wrong club and whacking away without finesse or skill or knowledge, and getting a hole in one.

Visibility was excellent. The day was cool and there were no heat shimmers to distort the view. It was crisp, cold, and perfect. And, as it happened so many times on such days, I could see the black dot of the mortar shell plummeting down on target, exploding on contact with the ground, shattering and scattering and digging into whatever was below it at impact point. Late that same afternoon, one of

Item Company's grunts spotted some gooks digging a trench line—a huge trench line—on Hill 1052. One of our machine guns banged away at the entrenched gooks, but the gooks were too deep. They kept on throwing out shovelful after shovelful of dirt. The dirt thrown out was almost a taunt as it came flying up and over the lip of the trench line.

"Can you do it, Cautious?"

"I'm sure as shit gonna try."

I figured an adjustment from the nearest concentration I had in the area and, after informing my FDC of the adjustment to make, said that I wanted one HE round. Everyone in Item Company saw a gook come cartwheeling through the air after my round hit.

It was my first confirmed kill. It was the first of eighty-five confirmed kills I would chalk up over the next ten months' time. That night when writing my almost daily letter to my wife, Joann, a letter that would be sent whenever there was opportunity for a mail call, I told her about what had happened. I was not as exultant with having done my job just right as perhaps I had the right to be. I wrote, instead, that I was twenty-one years old, a buck sergeant in the Marine Corps, and had just found out I was good at killing people at long distance. That realization did not make me happy, nor did it make me unhappy. It just did not do anything. And I wondered about that. I asked around later that afternoon, trying to find out how other people felt the first time they realized they had actually killed a gook. Some of the grunts said they felt guilty but couldn't give me any reason for their guilt; it was, after all, their job to kill gooks. Other grunts said that, because of their religious beliefs, they were afraid after they knew for certain they had killed a gook, but they couldn't explain their fear. Some grunts said they found it exciting, the knowledge they had just killed someone.

I thought about what the grunts had told me. I reasoned that their view, my view, any view on the subject of killing gooks was not limited to any specific emotion. Those who felt guilt, or shame, or fear told me they probably felt that way because of their background and education, and because of it perhaps they could more reasonably examine their emotions, their principles.

As for those grunts who said they felt excited about having killed a gook . . . well, I figured maybe I ought to stick close to them if the gooks ever did get into the trenches.

CHAPTER
8

I had been up on line for about three weeks, and with the passing of each winter's day of late October and early November, everything still seemed new and strange to me. They weren't bad days; I spent them getting used to the idea of being nervous and uncertain about everything. I was always on edge. I don't think I was scared or anything like that, but maybe I was. Or maybe it was just because I was so ignorant, so uncertain, about so very many things.

Some of my uncertainty came from the fact that I was just plain dumb about almost everything that was going on about me. Red, the 81mm FO, an older guy who was a World War II veteran, right away took the time to tell me about what was going on as we stood duty in the FO bunker. We shared a sleeping bunker and the same watch hours.

Red was a big favorite with the grunts. They would see him and wave, getting his attention, and then they would yell out, sort of cadencelike, "Hey, Red! Red! Red on the head, like a dirty dog's dick!" and that would tickle everyone and we would all laugh, Red included. He sure had a good disposition. He just never got mad at anyone. Red told me he wanted to be a schoolteacher when he returned home to his family. I could tell you straight-out that Red would make a good teacher. After Big Dog Ondrak went down to the company area, Red took time to teach me the fine points on how to shoot mortars. He had been shooting mortars at the gooks long enough, almost a year. When Item Company was due to be relieved off line at the end of the month, Red would have finished his year in Korea and would rotate home. He had a nice-looking wife and two kids, both girls. He had showed me pictures of his family. Red was sure anxious to get home to them; he never took chances as long as he was up on the hill.

Red was the guy who first told me about the "whirly-birds," the "eggbeaters," the "windmills." At first I didn't have any idea what in the world he was talking about and so he told me about the big Sikorsky helicopters the marines were using in Korea. To be completely honest, up until the time when Red first mentioned them, I hadn't even the slightest idea what a helicopter was or what it did, and so Red explained their use to me. Red told me he had been at Quantico, Virginia, during the early months of 1948 when a new concept for the execution of an amphibious assault was being tested.

"This new concept is years ahead of its time," Red said. "The concept calls for helicopters to be used to fly marines into a battle area, just like landing craft are now being used during the amphibious assault." The concept, he said, "calls for aircraft carriers to be used as transports for both the helicopters and the marine grunts who would be brought to the battle area in them."

This was the theory of vertical envelopment. More recently, Red told me, just about the time I had come up on the hill a whole battalion of men—about a thousand marine grunts —had been lifted. It was a big operation. About a dozen Sikorsky HRS-1s made more than 150 round-trips in a little more than six hours' time. And not one casualty. "If they would have had to climb that mountain they'd have lost five or six men, if only to broken or sprained arms and legs from falling down. It happens all the time that way," Red said. "And those North Korean gooks never fired one shot at them, can you imagine that?"

Red had the latest skinny—the absolute truth—concerning the on-again off-again peace talks. "A month or so ago, about this same time in September, the word was going around that the communists had never intended to make peace, but had been stalling in order to protect their buildup in forces, probably for another big offensive.

"As their strength increased, prospects of peace dwindled, and as the mouths of the Reds got wider, their voices got louder. They claimed a United Nations night-flying plane had attacked the Kaesong truce site and threatened the city—can you imagine it?—by dropping an illumination flare above it. That was just one of the ways they disrupted the peace talks. They're acting like little kids, always arguing about what's right and what's wrong about even the smallest thing. They got pissed last week when our negotiators sat in seats that faced south; they walked out of the meeting. Someone told me it was because only victors sat in seats that faced south.

"More recently they rejected Matt Ridgway's suggestion to move the peace talks from Kaesong to Songhyon, a town that is more equally situated between the demarcation lines, being about eight miles closer to our lines. They came back with a counterproposal and said why not hold the peace talks at Panmunjon, a small village just a mile away from Songhyon. I'll bet they crapped in their britches when Matt Ridgway agreed on Panmunjon. Anyway, that's where the peace talks are gonna take place from now on."

Red talked to me about the Punchbowl, pointing out and showing me how the name described the way the huge mountains of the area circled, forming a bowl. As I looked through my binoculars, I saw an extremely rugged area, an area dominated by precipitous, heavily wooded mountains, an area of wide paths and few roads.

"Some of the toughest jobs are usually assigned by the simplest of commands," Red said. "Back when we started the September Push, the command was, 'Straighten out the main line of resistance.'"

Red told me the fighting in the Punchbowl area was termed a battle by Headquarters, Marine Corps. "That means you already have a battle star for your Korean Service Ribbon."

I mentioned I really hadn't been in a battle yet.

Red shook me up when he said, "Don't worry about it. You'll be in one before too long. Right now we've sort of stagnated. We got all the high ground we need, except maybe we should'a gone over there and gotten Hill 1052. The North Koreans over there are lookin' right down our throat."

The North Korean defensive positions were just a couple hundred yards away as the crow flies or, as Red more aptly put it, "as a recoilless rifle fires."

Red told me about how good the North Koreans were when using mortars or artillery. "Don't ever give them a target of opportunity. They'll get you every time." Red said the communists used more than one FO when they could when calling in mortar or artillery fire. "They use the principle of triangulation. They get three different compass readings, and where the lines cross, that's where they put their rounds. It's as simple as that."

After every fire mission I called, Red told me I would need to inform my FDC of the extent of damage I inflicted, and that would include an estimated count of enemy dead and wounded as well as any materiel damage observed.

"All FOs have KIAs and WIAs on their personal tote boards. Now that you're actively involved in this war, you'll be adding numbers to your tote board. It's easy to kill, Cautious, with a shell that has a twenty-five-yard killing diameter."

Red smiled, kind of sadly I thought, and then said, "This war is going to turn you into a magician. You're going to be able to turn gook bodies into pencil marks on your personal tote board."

Red pointed out the deep ravines and steep mountainsides of Hill 854. He showed me acres and acres of barbed wire. "It's all heavily mined and booby-trapped. It won't be easy for them to come up our hill, if that makes you feel a little bit safer. Just watch out for their bullets, mortars, and artillery."

October, then, saw the beginning of a new type of warfare for the Marine Corps, that of vertical envelopment using helicopters. October also saw the other end of the warfare stick as well, that of fighting a war in trenches. The marines were firmly in place, facing north all along the Punchbowl mountains; the trench and bunker warfare stage of the Korean War, likened to warfare of World War I in that it was fought from trenches, began in earnest.

I was firing daily, mostly at targets of opportunity. I hadn't called in any short rounds, yet. A short round was any shot computed by the FDC that fell on or behind our lines. There was always some goofy reason why the round was called in short. Usually it was because the FO had read his map incorrectly. Sometimes it was because the communicator bungled and gave the wrong map coordinates to the FDC. It was a heart-stopping situation when an FO realized he had provided his FDC with bum information. When that happened, well, that was when the FO screamed out "Fire in the hole! Fire in the hole!" That was when the FO wanted everyone to get his ass in a bunker.

I was established now, an FO with kills to his record. On the tote board in the Four Deuce FDC, I was credited with an even dozen confirmed kills. They were not "guesstimated" kills where, after you have fired a mission, you suggest to FDC what you might have accomplished with your shooting. My kills were confirmed by the artillery observer, 1st Lt. John Francis McLaughlin, or by the grunts of Item Company who saw the bodies flying like rag dolls to hit the ground like sacks of shit.

Let me tell you about those kills, those confirmed kills. They were distant kills and they were not at all hard to take, not at all hard to live with. And the reason was because I didn't have to see them up close; I didn't have to step in their clotted blood or smell their stinking guts spilled out on the ground or look at their eyes popping out of their sockets or smell the shit in their trousers—the very last thing they did in this life, stink up my nose. Those dead gooks killed by Four Deuce mortar fire represented just one dozen pencil marks on the tote board back in FDC behind my name. Being an FO made it easy to kill gooks. It was easy to kill

124

gooks when a mortar was used. It was easy to kill at a distance.

The grunts, other marines both officers and men, made it even easier by teaching me to call the enemy the tasteless name of "gook." You call somebody, anybody, a gook and you dehumanize him. And it is not very hard at all to kill those you have dehumanized. You can live with it.

Call them gooks and you don't think they must hurt, too, when they are cut and gouged and maimed by shrapnel with razor-sharp cutting edges blown into them from an exploding mortar shell.

That mortar round exploding out there, the one just called, the one just going off, hell, it's way out there. It's a puff of black smoke if it's an HE round or it's a puff of billowing white smoke if it's a white phosphorus round. If you try hard, really hard, you can feel it impacting and exploding, but you can't see the results of it going off, can't actually feel it exploding with a horrendous roar.

All you can do is whoop it up when your round goes off and you are on target and you can see little figures in their padded winter clothing who aren't people, real people, lying all around where you have fired your round.

Being an FO is like getting to play an arcade game, trying to knock down something, and you don't have to put any quarters in a slot. All you have to do is speak into a telephone handset or a radio handset and say the magic words: "Fire mission!"

CHAPTER
9

This passive trench and bunker warfare stage was at first a welcome relief. Like the rest of the division, Item Company grunts no longer had to continually contest and then wrest mountainous land masses from the enemy.

And then, almost as suddenly as it had become a welcome relief, this style of warfare turned both monotonous and boring. The actual business of having nothing to do but stand guard, the necessity of having to be constantly alert to what the North Koreans were up to on their mountain, of having at the very minimum one-fourth of the grunts on duty in their fighting holes at all times, frequently needing 50 percent of them on watch, and even when at night grunt runners hurried to all the sleeping bunkers awakening everyone, telling us in stage whispers in the dark to get up, that we were in a balls-to-the-walls situation, well, even so, it got to be, after a few weeks, both a boring and a monotonous routine.

Grunts of Item Company, and that included me, found out the hard way that when monotony sets in, troops tend to become careless. And when you become careless, you fuck up.

I remembered that the Funny Gunny had told me that you seldom get the chance to fuck up a second time in a combat situation. He was right. The Funny Gunny was almost always right about things like that. But, thinking back on things, I figured sometimes a man could fuck up just by being in the wrong place at the right time. And sometimes a man could fuck up because he was just trying to do something decent for somebody.

When the shit hit the fan on the marine corps birthday— November 10, 1951—it wasn't too easy to separate all the events that happened. It was late on that marine corps birthday when I talked over the events of the day with Cpl. Albert Truelove.

Albert Truelove was a rarity in the marines; he was a naturalized citizen whose family had come from Armenia. His religion was Judaism, and so everyone called Albert Truelove the Armenian Jew.

Albert Truelove was a cook with the Four Deuces who had earlier been detached to an independent assignment with battalion. When that assignment was finished, Albert Truelove volunteered for still one more job, and that was when I got to know him.

Right away we both agreed on those two morale boosters —hot food and hot coffee. Any grunt up on the lines living in a bunker dug into the side of the trench line on one of those freezing Korean mountains and having nothing to eat but cold C rations would definitely tell you the straight skinny—that anything hot and edible and drinkable and not coming out of a C-ration can was definitely a morale booster.

It wasn't as if the food in the C rations—except, of course, the "deadly three"—was all that bad. It was just that far too often a grunt either couldn't take the time or wouldn't take the time to heat up the rations. Sometimes it just was too much trouble to go around trying to scrounge the use of one of the small, portable gasoline stoves, to pump it up and then light it up if it could be primed just right and if you had the white gas it needed, just to be able to heat the C rations or maybe boil some water for a hot cup of

127

the instant coffee that came packed in small envelopes with the rations.

Everyone lost weight eating C rations even though the government said the food was enriched, whatever that meant. Up on the lines when a grunt got hungry enough he would open a can of the wet rations, like maybe a can of ham and lima beans, which was considered to be one of the good rations even though we called them "ham and motherfuckers." Anyway, the grunt would choke and gag down as much of the salty ham chunks as he could after scraping off as much of the congealed white fat as possible, the fat that was all over and in between the ham chunks and the lima beans. And then—after eating all the ham and without ever having touched a lima bean or any of the fat—the grunt would throw the can and whatever was left in it as far out into that contested land mass in front of his position as he could. I don't believe this really happened, but there were grunts in Item Company who swore that it did: One of the grunts was said to have thrown a can of the deadly three rations out in front of the lines just as it was getting on toward dark when zing, there came the can flying back into the trenches and a gook was yelling out, "Keep your fuckin' rations, Yankee bastard!"

It was late in October when volunteer cooks and messmen set up a coffee and hot soup kitchen at the base of Hill 854. Everyone thought they had picked a good spot for their kitchen; it was in a small, naturally formed pocket protected on three sides by rugged trees growing straight up with huge, round, granitelike boulders at their base. Someone in battalion agreed that one way to combat monotonous hill duty would be to provide the grunts with their morale boosters at least twice a day.

Cooks and messmen volunteered to man the galleys, which were set up behind the letter company up on the line. Item Company ended up with a bunch of gung ho cooks and bakers who, divided into teams for day-on day-off duty, did their level best trying to outdo each other in cooking up something hot and tasty. Using field cooking stoves and ovens, thick metal pots, heavy black frying pans, and one hell of a lot of ingenuity, those volunteer cooks and mess-men made the smell of their cooking something that beat the best of all that was good about the outdoors in the fall of the year. Using foodstuffs provided them by battalion supply, they would cook up a meal in the morning and another again in the late afternoon.

The Item Company first sergeant paired off his grunts and gave instructions: "Wunna you guys goes down the hill in the mornin' for hot chow. Ya get some chow an' ya eat it. And then ya bring hot chow back to yer buddy. And then later on in the day, yer buddy goes down the hill to eat chow, and he brings back food for you." That way, the first sergeant said, everybody would get two good meals daily. It sure as hell beat opening up C rations with a John Wayne can opener. That day late in October when the hot chow line got started, we all thought it would be worth whatever it might cost.

When the stoves and ovens got heated up that first morning—and it was a cold one, too, with the temperature in the low twenties and small chance of it getting too much warmer any time soon—the company first sergeant passed the word, and the word was: "Now you people listen up! Don't bunch up! I don't wanna see more'n a couple of you goin' down the hill at any one time. And spread out down there when ya get yer food!"

It didn't take the grunts long to work out a schedule so that everyone had an opportunity to go through the hot chow line every day, fill up his mess kit and canteen with hot chow and hot coffee, stuff his field jacket pockets with bread or rolls, and then head back up the hill.

I said hot food and I meant it. The bakers and cooks baked bread and rolls and made hot vegetable soup on their gas-operated ovens and stoves. Everything went into the vegetable soup. I can remember eating long strands of spaghetti, macaroni, string beans, peas, corn, onions, toma-toes, and potatoes. There were beef chunks, ham chunks, cut-up morsels of chicken or turkey; it all went into the soup and in the thick Brunswick stews. There was plenty of seasoning—salt and pepper, thyme, oregano, you name it.

On those cold autumn days, the hot, highly seasoned and spiced, thick and delicious soups and stews were about the best things we had going for us.

There weren't a lot of fresh vegetables, so the cooks and messmen opened gallon jars of sweet or dill pickles or green olives.

I couldn't believe the taste of the homemade bread and rolls, with butter melting all over, with maybe some sugar and cinnamon and hot, plump, moist raisins inside. Those warm, yeasty-tasting rolls, still kind of doughy on the inside and flaky and deep golden brown on the outside—eating them was heaven on a cold day.

To keep the metal mess kits clean, the cooks fired up their immersion burners and stuck them in GI cans filled with hot water and soap, and just plain hot water for rinsing, positioning the GI cans off to one side of the chow line. There was still another GI can filled with hot water where a grunt could dip out some and fill a small Korean-made brass basin and then use soap, washcloths, and towels—provided daily by the cooks and messmen—and wash up or maybe take a whore's bath. Razors and shaving cream and small mirrors were available.

After a few weeks of living in a dirt bunker, of traveling around in trench lines, I welcomed the thought of washing and even shaving. I would even have been happy to have someone give me a white-side-walled haircut.

All of us grunts knew the cooks and messmen were knocking themselves out for us, working long and hard hours. We got to know them pretty well, and we liked them, we liked their spunk. The Item Company skipper told them they were just as much a part of his company as any of the rest of us. When he called them a "bunch of grunts," well you bet those cooks and bakers and messmen liked that.

I guess all of us grunts up on Hill 854 looked forward to the big shoot-out that someone thought up concerning the massed blanket of fire missions on that particular marine corps birthday. The Division G-3, the Operations and Planning section, had sent out the word to all hands that exactly at noontime, 1200, every weapon in the division would be fired at the enemy for one minute, a "mad minute."

Every weapon, every hand-held pistol or automatic, every carbine, M1, BAR, every light or heavy machine gun, even the heavy .50-caliber machine guns we had mounted on tripods in some sniper bunkers, all of our mortars, the 60s, 81s, Four Deuces, all of our rockets, the racks of 3.5mm and even the bazookas, all our 105mm and 155mm artillery pieces, the 8-in. self-propelled guns, even our aircraft overhead loaded with bullets and bombs of all sizes and napalm pods, and, yes, even the ships at sea would get in on the act.

The mad minute was called T.O.T.—time on target—fire. Such fire was always delivered as a surprise of devastating proportions. Big guns and all available mortars would be aimed at one specific target, with the firing of each gun timed so that all rounds impacted simultaneously on the target. I had never before been involved in a T.O.T. fire mission. I was told it was great to watch. "You wait and see. We'll blow up the whole fuckin' hill!" a grunt told me. All I could figure was that it must be devastating to live through if you were the target. I wondered how the enemy on Hill 1052 would react to the T.O.T. firing.

Over the past few weeks I had swapped an occasional round with the North Koreans when they had potshotted at a grunt who had stayed too long in one spot, making a target of opportunity out of himself. The Koreans could never resist shooting at such a target, just the way I couldn't resist shooting when I saw a shovelful of dirt being tossed in the air, up and over the side of their big trench line.

The way I looked at it was that there wasn't anything malicious about the kind of shooting the enemy and I traded off with each other. After all, we were just a couple of FOs trying to earn our pay. I had never experienced, never been under a concentrated mortar or artillery attack. I had been told that such an experience—when the rounds just kept on coming in, impacting and exploding—was sometimes so fierce that all a man wanted to do was to set his ass on the deck and reach up and pull his helmet all the way down.

One of the main reasons for shooting a T.O.T. at Hill

1052 was that the enemy soldiers there had been sighted daily digging on an enormous trench. The trench, covered over daily with heavy timbers and sandbags, ran from the bottom of the hill straight as an arrow up to the top. John Francis McLaughlin and I had shot at the ugly sandbagged scar, hitting it time and again, but our rounds did no apparent damage. In digging such a trench line right in front of our faces, they were thumbing their noses at us. Hill 1052 was too far away, over far too exposed and dangerous ground, for us to use patrols against the trench line. Besides, it would have taken all the C-3 explosives a fifty-man work party could carry to do a job on that trench.

A day or two earlier, Division G-3 had taken a look at the trench and spelled it all out for us. "We've seen this kind of thing before. Those gooks are gonna take that trench line right to the top of Hill 1052 and I wouldn't want to be in your shoes when they get up there. What they're doing is building a protected trench line big enough and wide enough to move field artillery up to the top. When they get up to that higher elevation, they're gonna look down your throats over here and you people just won't have a chance to move," the G-3 major had said. He stood out among all the rest of us. He was wearing new utilities and had on the gold oak leaves of rank. He smelled clean. On departing the hill, he told us he would be back: "I'm going to fix up a surprise for them."

No wonder we hadn't been getting any prolonged mortar or artillery attacks. The gooks were saving their rounds. They were waiting to give us their big Sunday punch. They would do it, too, unless we could give them a helluva punch first. The G-3 major had set things up for us.

The trench line, and the big guns on the battleship USS *New Jersey,* were the subject of conversation when John Francis McLaughlin and I were called to the Item Company commander's bunker that marine corps birthday morning.

"Which one of you can direct naval gunfire?" was the blunt way the question was asked.

I stayed quiet, waiting for John Francis McLaughlin to answer. I was learning how to shoot the Four Deuce pretty well, but I had no idea what was involved in shooting naval gunfire. The only thing I knew about naval gunfire was from watching movies about World War II invasions.

John Francis McLaughlin spoke right up. "I'd have to shoot those guns the same way I do my artillery. I'd have to first shoot a long shot and then a short shot, and then let my FDC calibrate just how the third shot should be called based on the information I provided them from the first two rounds. Is that the kind of shooting you have in mind, Skipper?"

"Nope," the company commander said. He leaned forward a bit, as if to take us more closely in his confidence. "That major from G-3 who was up here the other day. He's got the USS *New Jersey* on tap at noontime. It's all been planned as part of the birthday shoot-out. The battleship has sixteen-inch shells, and she can hit that mountain, I've been told.

"Anyway, the navy observer who was being sent here to call in the shots fell and broke his leg getting out of a jeep at division this morning. So I need somebody here who can take his place calling in heavy weapon shots . . . the big stuff, sixteen-inch guns.

"The battleship will be on station close inland for about thirty minutes. She'll be in position to shoot at exactly 1130." Looking at John Francis McLaughlin, the company commander said, "John, we just don't have the time for you to shoot your long and short rounds. The navy has already informed me they have computed what is needed to hit Hill 1052. They'll put their first round on the hill, right out there where we can spot it. What I want to do is put all those big fucking rounds—those one-ton shells—right into that gook trench line. I want to put those fucking gooks right out of the trench-digging business."

We both knew what he was talking about and understood why the Item Company commander didn't want to let the opportunity sail away of directing sixteen-inch gunfire from the battleship. He wanted to get rid of that trench line. He looked from John Francis McLaughlin to me.

"Okay, Sergeant. The job is yours. Use your Four Deuce

Comanche system and sneak right up on that trench line. I need this job done. I don't want any of my men killed by gook fire coming here direct from that mountain."

I was a bit startled to hear the company commander putting that job on me. But why not? I had all the confidence in the world and, I think, most of its ignorance, too. Again I let my alligator mouth overload my hummingbird ass.

"Yes, sir, Skipper. If the navy can hit the hill, I'll get those shells into that trench line," I said. As I spoke I noticed the black, bushy eyebrows of John Francis McLaughlin shoot right up to the peak of his Mickey Mouse cap. He didn't say anything until we were out in the trench line heading to the FO bunker.

"Can you do it?"

"I think so, providing the navy lets me shoot their guns the way I shoot my mortars. The skipper thinks I can do it. If I can, I'll be makin' a lot of points with him."

John Francis McLaughlin got tickled over that. "You know, Cautious, you're a fucking brownnoser. Right now you've got your nose so far up the skipper's ass that you're in great danger, because if the skipper farts, he's gonna blow your brains out."

I was still smiling when I told my bunker buddy, Red, and John Francis McLaughlin that I was going down the hill for some hot chow. Red and I were chow partners. There was plenty of time for me to get down to the chow line, have something hot to eat, bring back hot food for Red, and still be ready way ahead of time to shoot the navy guns. I checked the path downhill. There was one grunt on it, heading down. He was nearly at the bottom. I figured enough people had traveled over the path and that it was safe enough for me to go downhill. I remembered the Funny Gunny's lesson. And then, for some reason, I shivered. I got goose bumps all up and down my back, even though the day was relatively warm. Back home, if I had shivered like that for no reason, my mother would have said it was because someone was walking on graves in the graveyard; my mother believed that a quick shiver, like the one I just had for no apparent reason, was a premonition of bad luck. Right now, with having to shoot the big navy guns and all, I didn't need any of that kind of hokey. I put all those thoughts behind me. With a leap, I was over the sandbags and on my way downhill.

The cooks and messmen had done themselves proud. Their specialty for the marine corps birthday breakfast was big, hot, yeasty-tasting golden brown doughnuts all dusted over with either grainy brown sugar or snow white confectioners' sugar. I quickly gulped down a couple of them, drowning them in hot black coffee. I could never eat a doughnut without thinking of a sign, written in Old English, posted in a bakery window in Wilkes-Barre, Pennsylvania: "As you travel on through life, brother, whatever be your goal, keep your eyes upon the doughnut, and not upon the hole." Smelling those doughnuts now, eating them, I couldn't help but think about that sign, wondering at its significance, if any.

I went back through the hot chow line a second time. I gobbled down a cup of hot and delicious vegetable soup and some hot rolls. I had still another cup of coffee, and two more doughnuts. Sitting with my back against the trunk of a tall tree, metal canteen cup in hand, I again felt quite anxious. I had this strange feeling, a shivery kind of feeling; I couldn't explain it better than that. I tried to rationalize away the feeling. Maybe, I thought, I had really put my ass in a sling telling the Item Company skipper that I could shoot those big navy guns.

The noise of a lot of men all talking at the same time, grab-assing around, interrupted my thoughts. I was startled as I looked around and saw there were thirty or more grunts—far too many men—in and near the chow line, and that didn't include me and maybe the dozen or more cooks and messmen.

I got up quickly and rinsed out my mess kit and canteen cup. I went back through the mess line another time, filling up my mess kit with food to take back to Red.

"How'd ja like them doughnuts, pardner. I made 'em," a smiling, dirty-looking cook asked me. He was a young kid, lots younger than me. He had on a really filthy gray apron, tied high up on his chest, and he had his dungaree jacket sleeves rolled up, flour and white confectioners' sugar all over his hands and arms.

"I'm gonna give it to you straight, pardner. They were the best goddamned doughnuts I've ever eaten. You guys sure do one helluva job down here."

That kind of a response brought out a bigger smile on the kid's face. He was standing on an outcropping of hard granitelike rock. He proudly told me he was in charge of cooking the doughnuts. Behind him I saw a field stove, fed by gasoline, and on top of the burners was a big vat of bubbling hot shortening with doughnuts in it turning over and over. In front of the kid, on the serving line, was a large shallow pan partially filled with big, golden brown doughnuts, all covered with sugar. In front of the doughnuts was a hastily made sign: "Eat as many as you want, and take some with you. The Cook."

The kid leaned over the doughnuts and pointed to the sign. "That's me. I'm the cook. I just made buck sergeant about a week ago. Why don'tcha take a couple more of those doughnuts. I'll be cookin' up plenty more."

That young kid, that new buck sergeant, knew how to make my day. I stuffed a couple more doughnuts into the pockets of my field jacket.

"You guys deserve some kind of a medal, comin' up here and bustin' ass cookin' for us. And don't think us grunts don't appreciate it," I said. In a moment the two of us had struck that instant rapport that so often is found between a couple of young men trying their best to be marines, no questions asked, no reward expected, just a grin and an understanding.

But I still had that uncomfortable feeling down my spine. I picked up my mess gear, called out my thanks again, told the cook to watch out for his ass, and then headed out of the area. All I wanted to do was get up the hill and into the relative safety of the trench line. I hustled to the base of Hill 854.

Six men were on the path coming down the hill. The grunts were well spaced-out on the path. They were following the rules; no one was bunching up and they were keeping their irregular pace coming downhill, moving in a jerky descent and by doing so keeping any gook observer just a bit off the mark from zeroing in a shot.

I didn't want to get on the path with that many men on it already. I stopped at the base of the hill, close to the side of the trail. Behind me was a steep slope pockmarked with broken trees that led down to a gully and a narrow but quick-moving stream of icy water. I was breathing fast for no apparent reason. I was almost hyperventilating. There was no physical exertion in what I had just done, but suddenly I was both out of breath and scared. It was as if I were suddenly in a glass shell. I was alone. My ears were ringing. I could hear nothing except that ringing. My lips were dry. I had a sour, disgusting, greasy taste of doughnuts in my mouth and, oddly enough, for some unknown reason, I felt ashamed. All at once I realized I was very much afraid of death. And, just as suddenly, I knew that we all had a death coming to us. I heard the noise of jeeps pulling into the hot chow area. I looked quickly in that direction and saw three jeeps drive in and park. I thought, "Uh, oh. This is some bad shit!"

Just then the last of the grunts who had been coming down the hill passed me, every one of them smiling and looking at me and saying out loud "Chicken shit!" and all of them heading for the huddled mass of grunts in and around the chow line.

I wanted to yell at them, the way the Funny Gunny would have yelled at them, "Hey, you dumb fuckers! Spread it out! One round could get you all!" But then I thought, shit, no, I can't yell that. I figured I hadn't been a buck sergeant long enough to take that kind of initiative, to do something like that. So I didn't do anything. I didn't yell out because I didn't have the balls to yell out. I was afraid that everybody would just ignore me. So I didn't do anything. I just knew I wanted to get my own ass out of the area. I wanted to get back to the safety of the frontline trenches and bunkers. I wanted to get away from the area of the trail at the bottom of the hill and the embankment behind me that went down to the war-torn wooded area with all of its trees snapped off, with all the jagged stumps thrusting up.

I looked back one more time because I thought I heard someone yell my name. Damn! Standing there by one of the jeeps were Tom Fuhs and the Funny Gunny. Tom Fuhs was yelling at me and the Funny Gunny had just raised his hand. I could see the Funny Gunny was holding some white envelopes in his hand.

At that exact moment the first of a dozen mortar rounds lobbed in by the gooks exploded high overhead, showering silvery metal shards into the troops below. Each round was fused with a variable-timed (VT) fuse; the rounds were set to explode at treetop level. A VT shell sends out an electronic signal that strikes an object and then instantaneously bounces back to the receiver of the exploding timer in the nose of the shell. The gooks had set their VT fuses to go off at treetop level, maximizing the lethality of the shrapnel with chunks of tree limbs.

Tom Fuhs and the Funny Gunny were right under the first of the exploding shells. Shrapnel, in large and small lacerating sizes, slammed downward; jagged hunks of tree limbs competed for space to pierce deeply.

The fucking gooks were right on target. Every shell exploded almost as if it had been put in place by hand. Those goddamn fucking gooks never missed a target of opportunity.

I don't know whether or not I had the presence of mind to jump down into the gulley area behind me or whether concussion knocked me off the side of the trail. I was rolling downhill toward the stream of water when a VT shell exploded almost directly overhead. I curled close to the base of one of those jagged tree trunks and I can remember pulling down on the chin straps of my helmet, wanting to get as much cover over me as possible. I was scared shitless as those ragged hunks of shrapnel and wood beat into the ground all around me, thunking down, and then I was knocked flat on my gut when something pounded into the small of my back.

I tried moving. The small of my back ached. I felt like I had been beaten with a club. I reached behind, stretching my fingers to feel my back and afraid of what I might find. I thanked God all the while that I had worn my flak jacket. I moved my fingers under the overlapping layers of the light plastic sewed inside the tough green nylon of the flak jacket. I knew something had hit me in the back. I was praying I wouldn't feel blood. I was dry. There was nothing sticking out of the flesh of my back.

I scrambled up the embankment, digging in and climbing my way up to the trail. I didn't give a shit about trip lines or boot mines or anything. I got to the top and ran to where I had last seen Tom Fuhs and the Funny Gunny.

I looked down at them and started to cry. They had probably been the first ones to be killed. Their bodies were riddled with small and large holes. The Funny Gunny still clutched two envelopes in his hand. They were letters addressed to me from my wife. Gently I removed the letters from his still-warm hand and I was so sorry, so very, very sorry.

That young kid, that young buck sergeant cook in charge of the doughnuts, was screaming and screaming. The vat of hot shortening had emptied all over his back and was already starting to congeal in the cold air. He was lucky, so very lucky to have a big hole right in the middle of his gut, right in the middle of that dirty gray apron that was turning wetly red. The kid cried out, over and over again, his fingers moving over the dirty apron, "But where is the hole? Where is the hole?" And then he just died.

I looked around at a nightmare scene. Someone was trying to tie a tourniquet around the stumps of another man's legs, on a guy who was on his back on the driver's seat of a jeep, his arms wrapped around the steering wheel and the back of the seat. The guy didn't have any legs, just stumps, neatly severed at the crotch area, and the blood was shooting out from those double stumps, and the tourniquet kept slipping off first one leg and then the other. The guy with no legs was wearing a brand new green field jacket; it was not one bit dirty, it was brand new. On his clean camouflage helmet cover he had a gold oak leaf attached. There were two more gold oak leaves on the shoulder straps of his clean field jacket. The G-3 major's face was dead white and his mouth was drawn back, his lips were drawn tight, and I could see he was in terrible shock or pain or both. He was mouthing the words of a Hail Mary, but he didn't utter a sound. His eyes closed, his mouth fell open, and he stopped breathing.

All the while I kept looking at him and thinking, You dumb fuck. Nobody wears the insignia of their rank up on the hill. What the fuck did you want, a salute or something? And then all of a sudden I was saluting him, saying good-bye the best way I knew how, even if I didn't know his name, just that he had been a G-3 major.

I knew for sure that four men had been killed: Tom Fuhs and the Funny Gunny, that young buck sergeant who had insisted that I take more doughnuts, and the major wearing all those new clothes. I wasn't doing anything, I was just standing in the middle of all that blood and those cut-up bodies. I wasn't even helping anyone. I was just standing there hoping that I wouldn't throw up or something. My back was aching, and the ache was so hard I was feeling queasy. I hoped I wouldn't do anything dumb, like puke or shit my pants.

I started to move out of the area, slowly, walking around everybody who had only minor wounds and who were helping those with bad cuts. I saw three more bodies. I looked at them and recognized grunts of Item Company. I didn't know their names but I knew their positions in the trench line. They lay crumpled on the ground like paper bags, blown up and popped and then discarded, no longer of value. One of the grunts was that young kid I had talked to the first day when I had come up on the hill looking for the Big Dog, and I thought he didn't know the Big Dog's name, either. And then I thought this is wrong, to die and not have someone know your name.

I guess it was partly because I knew I couldn't help Tom Fuhs or the Funny Gunny, or maybe it was because I was shit-scared that the gooks might throw in some more VT, but anyway I moved on out of the area of the hot chow line. I didn't look back either. I just kept on saying good-bye to Tom Fuhs and the Funny Gunny over and over in my mind. I just plain walked away from all those guys who had earned their medals the hard way; the living and the dead would all get their Purple Hearts, a nice medal and all that, but the

140

kind of a medal that was a dime a dozen in Korea. A man didn't have to do anything notable to earn a Purple Heart either, just get wounded or killed. I didn't run. I didn't even walk fast. I didn't gawk or look around at what had happened, but it was all registering itself in my brain.

I climbed back up the hill, my back throbbing with every step. The throbs seemed like they were in time to a counted cadence of a march out of hell. I had just found out what an exploding mortar shell did to people.

CHAPTER
10

Someone had reached the trench line before me. The word on what happened at the chow line had already been passed to the skipper of Item Company. He was in the trench line looking down the hill. There was nothing he could see. All the carnage was out of sight around the draw at the bottom of the hill.

"Was it bad?"

"It was bad, Skipper, real bad."

"How many dead?"

"I saw at least seven, Skipper. Three of them were your guys, but I don't know their names. I knew two others; they were from my outfit, the Four Deuces. And a young cook got killed. And that major from G-3 who was up here the other day."

The Item Company skipper sort of pursed his lips before he spoke. "Go and get ready to shoot those fuckers."

He said it softly.

I just nodded my head at him. There wasn't a whole lot more I could say. I went to the FO bunker and told my radioman and wireman what had happened to the Funny

Gunny and Tom Fuhs. Then I telephoned the company to let Captain Massey know what had happened. He would send some Four Deuce men to retrieve the two bodies. He sounded distraught and distant. He told me to be careful.

John Francis McLaughlin and Red had listened in on my conversation. Neither asked a whole lot of questions. Both had grim looks on their faces. They had been in the FO bunker when the VT had been lobbed in over the mess hall area. Neither had sighted any smoke from out in front, although both said they had heard the sharp cough that artillery makes, and both were feeling guilty that they had not been able to shoot back, to retaliate. The two of them just nodded their thanks when I stuck my hands in my field jacket pockets and brought out the doughnuts I had put there. Those fucking doughnuts. They weren't even broken. Banged up some, sure, but still whole and still with sugar on them. John Francis McLaughlin and Red just took the doughnuts and ate them. I put my eyes to the BC-scope and studied the trench line going up Hill 1052, mentally computing distances. I kept my eyes on the scope for a long, long time.

The first shell from the USS *New Jersey* took more than two minutes' time to splash; when it did it was right on schedule and right on Hill 1052, biting out a gaping hole of tremendous size. I was surprised at two things—that the battleship, firing from such a distance, and on choppy seas to boot, had actually hit Hill 1052 in an area where we could see the round go off, and I was surprised at the size of the hole the sixteen-inch shell had left in the side of the mountain. I heard the shell coming in from a long way out. It had like a chugging, pulsing sound that built up in crescendo to where it was really roaring just before it smashed into the mountain. Even as far away as we were in our trenches from where the sixteen-inch shell impacted, I could feel Hill 1052 shudder and then quickly I felt our mountain shudder as well.

Someone had once told me that a sixteen-inch shell costs as much as a Cadillac. I don't know about the cost of the shell, but I could see that it left a hole wide enough and deep enough to park two Cadillacs side by side in it.

143

My eyes were glued to the BC-scope. I could hear people muttering in the FO bunker. There were more than just us FOs and our communicators in there. But Hill 1052 had my attention. I said to my radioman: "Soupy, tell navy to come left about 750 yards and drop about 500 yards. Tell them I'm going to try to put one in the trench line at the bottom of the hill and then work my way up the hill."

The second shell was close, but it was still not on the trench line. It was close, but not on target.

"Tell them up about 30 yards, and left about 25 yards." I heard Soupy mutter into his radio handset. He listened for a moment and then said to me, "Cautious, those navy guys said enough of this 'about' shit. They said for you to be more exact."

Well, fuck me, I thought. I knew I had an audience in the FO bunker so I played it up for them. I said to Soupy, "What do they want me to do? Go out on that mountain with a yardstick and give them corrections in feet?"

Soupy muttered something into his handset, and then he listened. "Cautious, they said they would even take a correction in inches if you had the balls to go out and measure it. They said they'll deliver their rounds exactly where you say. They said they ain't trying to hassle you or nothing like that, just that they can deliver, but you gotta tell them where to deliver."

I was a little pissed. I had already dropped in two shots and was still not on target and those navy guys were giving me the red-ass. Soupy was still talking: "They said they could shoot the hair off a gnat's ass without hurtin' the gnat if you could give them the right dope."

I could hear a couple of guffaws from the people in the bunker, and I got a little bit more pissed off. So I really computed my next shot. Then I added some "Kentucky windage," the kind that Red had told me about, by taking into allowance certain elevation contour discrepancies printed on the maps we were using. These maps had been copied from those the Japanese had made during World War II. The maps were accurate to some degree, but there were still some flaws, mostly in elevation contour lines.

Someone like Red, an FO who used the maps daily, would readily note the flaws on the maps, especially in the areas where he was shooting his mortars. Using Red's Kentucky windage, I gave my next correction to the navy in yards, then feet, and then, jokingly, in inches.

The next sixteen-inch shell impacted directly on top of the gooks' trench line, about fifty feet up from the bottom of the mountain, knocking timbers and sandbags to hell and gone. Everybody in the FO bunker gave out with a goddamn cheer like I had just made the winning shot in a high school basketball game.

I worked my way up the mountain with the next twelve shots. I hit the trench line ten times and had two very close misses. Those of us who had binoculars saw at least four gooks flying up in the air and, remembering Tom Fuhs and the Funny Gunny, I muttered to myself, "Well, that's two apiece for both of you."

The USS *New Jersey* steamed out of range at 1155, five minutes before the division T.O.T. started firing with every weapon on line aimed at the enemy.

Campbell had been keeping the battleship posted on the hits they scored. He said to me, "Those navy guys said 'good shooting' to you, Cautious."

Someone in the bunker standing next to Soupy said, "It was good shooting, Sergeant."

"You're damn right it was, considerin' I wasn't usin' my own Four Deuces," I said, quite unabashedly.

"Maybe you can do it again for me. Those four dead men out there, they help make up for my major. He was killed coming here this morning. He had his legs blown off."

I turned toward the man talking and nearly shit a brick when I saw two small silver stars on his collar tabs. I just nodded my head.

"I know how you feel, sir," I said, never mind the fact that grunts could call officers by their first name in a combat area. "I had two friends killed this morning, too."

Major General Gerald C. Thomas, the head honcho of the 1st Marine Division, the man who had made the arrangements to have every weapon in the division fired in a "mad

145

minute" T.O.T. at high noon, observed with a tight, grim smile on his face as the earthshaking volley of fire rounds struck the front lines of the enemy.

Hill 1052 was still shrouded in dust and smoke when, satisfied, General Thomas departed the FO bunker, his small retinue of officers following close behind.

CHAPTER
11

Just about the time I was thinking of myself as some kind of hotshot, Albert Truelove burst my bubble. The Armenian Jew poked his helmeted head inside the FO bunker and said, "Hey, Cautious. How about givin' me a hand, will you?"

Outside in the trench and near the opening to the sleeping bunker I shared with Red, the 81mm FO, were bags of flour and sugar and cans of shortening that Albert Truelove had conned some grunts into bringing up the hill.

"Let's get this stuff inside your bunker," Albert Truelove said, pushing aside the poncho hanging down across the entranceway.

"What the hell do you have there, Albert? That bunker ain't a fuckin' mess tent."

Albert Truelove looked me right in the eye and gave me one of his Armenian Jew smiles. "Well, Cautious. It just so happens I've got a lot of Armenian Jew cousins up on this hill, and they all like doughnuts. And some of those cousins didn't get any doughnuts this morning. Never mind the fact that some guys comin' through the chow line walked away with a dozen or more in their field jacket pockets. I'm here.

I'm a cook. And I've got everything I need to make doughnuts.

"And just to get it straight, a lot of those cooks and bakers serving chow earlier today, well, they were my friends. There was this young kid, just made buck sergeant. He joined the marines when he was sixteen years old, convincing God and country he was eighteen. He's dead now, before he got to be old enough to buy a beer. Well, he was an Armenian Jew cousin, you see. Cooking doughnuts today was his idea. He wanted to make sure everybody up here on the hill got plenty of them to eat.

"I'll tell it to you straight, Cautious. I'm gonna see to it every grunt up here on the hill gets plenty of doughnuts today. I've got everything I need except a bunker. I figured I knew you well enough that you would let me use yours."

How could Albert Truelove get by with saying that he figured he knew me; I had seen Albert Truelove in the Four Deuces a couple times, sure, but as far as I could recollect I had talked with him only one time and that was just to comment on the weather.

Albert Truelove cooked his doughnuts in oil heated in a steel helmet, heated over a small, portable, gasoline-fueled stove. There wasn't too much shape to his doughnuts; mostly they were just round balls, but they were awfully good.

He told me how he had been a baker—following the trade of his father—in a New York City short-order restaurant his father owned. We talked for a long time, long after all the dough had been used up making doughnuts, long after the cooking oil had cooled and had been emptied out, the pot again assuming its real role as a helmet.

Albert Truelove told me about his family. "Way back before my father brought me and the rest of my family— I've got seven older brothers and two older sisters—well, back in the old country before my father brought us all to the United States from Armenia, we had the last name of Etchmiadzin," Albert Truelove said.

"When my father was on Ellis Island—at least according to what he told me later on when I got old enough to understand what he was talking about—he said that he

148

looked up and could see the Statue of Liberty and he figured it would be nice for all of us to have a new last name to go with our new country."

In the Armenian tongue, Albert Truelove said, Etchmiadzin, in addition to meaning "the Holy One descended," could also be translated quite literally to mean "True love."

"And so my father changed our name. And now look at me, Cautious. I'm the Doughnut King of Hill 854. Not bad for an Armenian Jew who doesn't know shit from shinola."

The way Tom Fuhs and I had filled a whole bunker full of tape from a Haggler crypto device, the way the Funny Gunny could fill a whole company of marines full of respect for themselves and others, that's the way Albert Truelove filled Hill 854 with the smell and taste of hot doughnuts. The grunts coming to the bunker doorway called Albert Truelove "the Doughnut King of Hill 854."

"You know, Cautious, Tom Fuhs talked the Funny Gunny into riding shotgun for him this morning. Tom wanted you to have the letters he had picked up from battalion. He said the letters were from your wife, and that you loved her very much, and so he didn't want you to have to wait for your mail," Albert Truelove said.

I had just lighted up a stale-tasting C-ration cigarette. I had forgotten all about the letters even though I had felt them against my body all day long, for I had shoved them under my undershirt to keep them safe. I looked at the letters now, the envelopes brown with the smear of dried blood.

I started coughing from the cigarette smoke, coughing so hard tears came into my eyes. I went outside and stood in the trench line during the darkening hours of that marine corps birthday for a long, long time. I knew I had made a good friend in the Armenian Jew, but I just wanted to be by myself for a little while.

CHAPTER
12

On the evening of the Marine Corps' birthday, after Albert Truelove and I had cleaned up the sleeping bunker, we realized it was too small to accommodate me and Red and the Armenian Jew. Since John Francis McLaughlin slept in the FO bunker, and since it was roomy enough, I asked him if Albert Truelove and I could sleep there with him.

John Francis McLaughlin slept nightly in the FO bunker because, he said, he wanted to be available at all times to shoot artillery whenever it became necessary. Let me be honest with you, John Francis McLaughlin had a kind of quirk, his own peculiarity. And it was this that was reason enough for none of the rest of us to want to share a bunker with him. Water was the main reason for his peculiarity.

We were on strict water rationing up on the hill; everyone received two canteens per day. The water was brought up to the Item Company commander's bunker every night by Korean "chiggy bearers." I don't know where that name came from or how it originated; it was just what we called the Korean labor force. Mostly they were older men. They wore a mixture of baggy Oriental trousers and jackets and rubber shoes coupled with whatever GI uniform parts they either found or scrounged. They were all short and husky and seemed strong as hell and I guess they were, too, because each man could bring up two filled five-gallon cans of water by himself. You couldn't hear them coming up the hill—they were that silent—but you could smell them about fifty yards away; they all had terrible body odor and bad garlic breath. They seemed dumb as mules, but maybe that was because they couldn't understand what we were saying to them or about them. I'm not sure I trusted them, but they sure could scramble up a hill loaded down with water, ammunition, and C rations.

John Francis McLaughlin used his two daily canteens of water strictly for drinking purposes. He had one redeeming virtue in that he kept his teeth sparkling clean, brushing them four or five times daily; what water he didn't use for drinking was used for brushing his teeth. He did not use any water for washing, none at all. That was why no one on the hill wanted to share a bunker with John Francis McLaughlin. Albert Truelove found out about this peculiarity—and took care of it—the night he stayed up on Hill 854. Albert Truelove had a knack for doing nice things like that.

It was late that night when we were getting ready to sack out. Three of us were arranging our fart sacks on the dirt floor of the FO bunker. Usually two FOs stood bunker watch from 2300 to 0200 and then again from 0400 to 0630. These were the dangerous hours. It had been pretty well determined from previous experience that if the enemy were going to hit your lines, it generally would be from late evening, around 2000, to sometime after midnight, or from very early morning, around 0300, to just before dawn. The North Koreans were excellent night fighters. A grunt would never know when they were coming until all at once they were in the trench fighting with him.

In Korea, for the most part, the night belonged to the enemy. At night they played their psychological games on us. They would creep as close as they could in the utter blackness of the stygian Korean night and then, to the blaring sound of discordant bugles or shrill, ear-piercing whistles, they would be in your trench line. When the whistles and bugles blew, the shit flew, and it was everybody up and into a fighting hole.

There were some dark nights that turned out to be not so dark after all. Tonight was to be one of those nights, a dark-of-the-moon night turned blue-gray.

John Francis McLaughlin, Albert Truelove, and I were leaning against the parapet of the FO bunker when suddenly the contested area between the hill masses was almost magically diffused in a bluish gray light. It was a light almost like the false dawn that comes with a cold winter day. From points of origin well to the rear of the front line, sharp, swift, pencil-thin shafts of blue-gray light shot out, seeking out and then striking overhead clouds. The light then reflected downward, diffused now and spreading wide, illuminating the no-man's-land in front of Item Company in an artificial moonlight that really did hold back the night. It wasn't the kind of light you would get from turning on an overhead light in a darkened room, and it wasn't the light of dawn. It was sort of an in-between blue-gray eerie color that lighted our immediate front, a light that was good enough to see anything out front that was standing, creeping, or crawling.

Huge floodlights—like those used at airfields—were mounted on flatbed trucks that were moved in position, one behind the other, forming a line on roads located to the rear. Using information provided by air tower control units, marine engineers knew just how to adjust the shafts of light to reflect off overhead clouds so as to gain the maximum downward reflection for use in lighting up the area to the front of the lines. The artificial light was all to our advantage; we could see the gooks as they approached our lines, but they could not see us in our fighting holes. There was no doubt about it, the artificial light took the heat out of a hot spot.

It was well after midnight when John Francis McLaughlin said, "I'm sure glad we have the lights tonight. Too bad we had to pay such a heavy price for them."

Because of the artificial light, the chances of a probe in force were diminished to nearly nothing. We knew we would all be able to get some sleep when our watch was finished. It was at that time, when John Francis McLaughlin was preparing to get ready for sleep, that his peculiarity manifested itself.

I've told you that John Francis McLaughlin didn't wash at all. He really was very, very dirty. He had a gag-a-maggot dirty smell about him.

Everything John Francis McLaughlin was wearing was filthy, and had a ground-in shiny, dirty look. Both a sweet and a sour odor emanated from him. I later found out that he had a large supply of quite expensive deodorants and colognes which he used lavishly. It was easy to both locate and identify John Francis McLaughlin on even the darkest of nights.

John Francis McLaughlin had given the Armenian Jew the word on our sleeping arrangements. "We usually sleep with our heads pointed toward the bunker door opening. The reasons for that are multiple. If anyone needs us during the night, they just stick their heads in and start talking. And they don't need to speak but just above a whisper.

"The second reason is probably just as important: In the event we get a hit on the bunker roof and it caves in on us, whoever is digging us out can get to our heads and shoulders first.

"And, finally, with our heads pointing toward the entranceway, we get the benefit of any fresh air coming in and, believe me, when you get zippered into one of these fart sacks, you're gonna find out a man needs all the fresh air he can get."

Albert Truelove nodded his understanding. "Where do you guys hang up your clothes?"

"We don't hang up our clothes, Albert," I said. "We wear our clothes. Maybe, if you want, you could roll up your heavy field jacket or parka and use it for a pillow. But mostly all we do is take off our boondockers and just crawl right inside the fart sack."

I nodded in the direction of John Francis McLaughlin. "He sometimes even takes his socks off. Sometimes."

"You're right, Cautious. And tonight is a testing night. I haven't tested for about a week or so," John Francis McLaughlin said. He rooted around on top of his sleeping bag until he was in a sitting position. He leaned over at the

153

waist and pulled an incredibly evil-smelling winter wool sock from his left foot. He eyed the far end of the bunker, drew his arm back, whirled the sock around in the air a time or two, and then released the sock, throwing it as hard as he could at the far wall.

Thwock!

I swear the sock made that kind of sound hitting the far dirt wall. And for just the slightest instant the sock seemed to cling to the dirt wall. Then, with an audible plop, the sock fell. John Francis McLaughlin reached for the sock, shook it out, so to speak, and pulled it back on his foot again.

"Not tonight, Cautious. Maybe not even tomorrow night. But soon. You can bet your ass it's gonna be soon," John Francis McLaughlin said. He crawled into his sleeping bag and was almost instantaneously asleep, snoring lightly. God, how I envied him the way he could go to sleep.

Wide-eyed, Albert Truelove had just witnessed the peculiarity that made John Francis McLaughlin a name up on Hill 854.

"He was lookin' for his indicator, Albert," I said.

"What the fuck is an indicator, Cautious?"

"Well, some time back, John Francis McLaughlin told me that the night his sock stuck to that dirt wall he would, well, he would quit, he would walk right off the hill the next day. He said he told the Item Company commander he was going to stick with his job as an FO until he was dirty enough on the outside to fit the dirtiness he felt on the inside.

"When his sock sticks to that dirt wall, he said he was going to call his outfit and tell his boss that he was long overdue at being relieved up on the hill," I explained.

"Hell, Cautious, why doesn't he just wash up or something? I mean he might be an officer and a gentleman and all that stuff, but he sure does stink."

I nodded my head, shadows flaring on the wall from the small, already guttering candle we had lighted.

"Things are different up on the hill, Albert. Look around. There aren't any conveniences. There's no running water; the only water we get are two canteens each day, and you learn to make it last.

"We've got a shithouse on the other side of the hill. It's a

154

tent fly fastened on four poles stuck in the ground above a piece of plywood that has four holes cut in it, with the plywood on sandbags and settin' over a hole dug in the ground. The gooks keep their eye on that shitter. They'll throw a round of VT over it if there's more than one guy sitting on it, takin' a crap. Up on the hill, even taking a crap can be detrimental to your health.

"We've got piss tubes dug in the trenches, all facing outboard. The gooks even have the piss tubes zeroed in with their mortars. When you're up on the hill you can't even take a leak without putting yourself in jeopardy.

"You saw those chiggy bearers come up earlier, that Korean labor force bringing up rations and those cans of water and the ammunition, just the bare essentials needed for living and killing. Don't think they're all good gooks. Personally I think half those chiggy bearers are North Koreans. Someone sure as hell is telling those gooks on Hill 1052 all our secrets.

"Maybe they don't have to tell them anything, though. Those gooks over there are looking right down our throats. We might have knocked out their trench line, but they still have their FOs, and anything that moves or just plain stands still long enough on this hill is fair game for them. You know how well they can shoot. They just don't miss a worthwhile target.

"So what we have, Albert, is a situation where we've got plenty of everything we really need, so long as we don't misuse it. The skipper has figured out just how much water we really need daily, how much food, and how much ammunition. We don't have anything to waste, except maybe some of those deadly three C rations."

Albert Truelove nodded his head in agreement while I lighted a cigarette.

I could see Albert Truelove was listening. I took a drag from my cigarette and then snubbed it out, sailing the butt up toward the front of the FO bunker.

"Listen to me talk, Albert, and I've been up on the hill only a couple weeks now. I'm the new guy on the hill and I'm talking like I run the place. But I'll tell you what, Albert, you learn fast up on the hill. It's a different world when you're sittin' up here. Makes you think about things differently."

I knew this was the first time Albert Truelove had ever been up on the lines with nothing between him and the North Koreans except the thickness of his flak jacket. Back behind the lines at the Four Deuces, even if it was only a half mile or so, well, that distance made all the difference in a life-style in Korea.

"John Francis McLaughlin can't go down off the hill. Neither can I, or Red, unless we're wounded or unless the company sends up a relief for us for some reason or other, like the way I had to relieve the Big Dog, and you know why he had to get down off the hill.

"So, in order to keep his sanity, John Francis McLaughlin lets himself get disgustingly dirty because there just isn't anything he can do about it even if he wanted to be clean. He invented this game with his sock. Hell, everybody's on his side. They know about him throwin' his sock at the dirt wall.

"Back in his own outfit his gun commander told him that if his sock ever does stick on that dirt wall, he'll send another man up on the hill as a replacement. So now maybe you can understand.

"You know, Albert, John Francis McLaughlin comes from a very wealthy Boston family. His family is rich, with a big house, big cars, servants, and all that stuff. I guess when he thinks about what he came from and compares it to what he has now, maybe throwing his sock at the dirt wall is one way of saying that it really is okay for him to be a complete crud. It's the way he keeps going, day after day up on the hill, without cracking up."

Neither Albert Truelove nor I talked for a bit after that. I don't know why I had been defending John Francis McLaughlin; he didn't need me making excuses for him.

"Cautious?" Albert Truelove said, breaking the silence.

"Yeah, Albert."

"You know what I thought there for a minute, right after he threw his sock and it hit the wall of the bunker and made that god-awful noise?"

"No, Albert. Did you think he was crazy or something?"

"No, nothin' like that."

"Well, what then, what did you think?"

"Well, when he threw that sock and it made that noise when it hit the wall, well, you know, shit . . . for a moment I thought the goddamn thing was really going to stick."

The candle was long out by this time. Yet Albert Truelove and I were not quite tired enough to sleep. We talked about a lot of things. Perhaps the fact that it was so dark in the bunker while we talked, so dark that we couldn't see each other, might well have had a lot to do with the way we talked and what we talked about, our families, our hopes, and our desires.

The Doughnut King of Hill 854 departed his kingdom early the following morning, heading downhill at an erratic pace like Red had advised him, heading back to his regular duty being an assistant belly robber.

Two nights later the whole mountain heard John Francis McLaughlin yelling in the FO bunker. A couple of us, me and Red and some grunts, ran up to the bunker. There, on the dirt wall at the foot of his sleeping bag, hanging without visible support, was the filthy sock of John Francis McLaughlin. It hung on the dirt wall like some kind of a poor man's crucifix.

John Francis McLaughlin was ecstatic. Wild-eyed, he repeated over and over again: "I prayed for this to happen. I prayed for this to happen. I couldn't have lasted much longer. I couldn't have, and so I really prayed for this to happen."

We made a passageway for the Item Company commander to pass by us and enter the FO bunker. He took one look at wild-eyed, evil-smelling John Francis McLaughlin—a man who was almost beside himself muttering "I prayed for this to happen"—and then he looked at the dirty sock hanging on the wall.

"Well, John, I'm going to hate to lose you. But an agreement is an agreement. I'm calling your boss and telling him to send me a replacement for you. You've been up here long enough. You can go down the hill at first light."

John Francis McLaughlin put together the few things he would take off the hill with him. He came around and said his good-byes to me and Red and to the grunts who had bunkers nearby. Then he went out to sit near the trench line, near the path that led downhill. He waited in lonely silence for the dawn of a bright clean day.

I told Red that I would stand the night watch in the FO bunker. With the aid of a flashlight I examined the phenomenon of the hanging sock very carefully. Just barely seen on extremely close examination were about a half-dozen small slivers of wood sticking out of the dirt wall by about an eighth of an inch and angled upward. Whoever had put them there must have had infinite patience and maybe a heart of gold instead of one shaped like a marine corps emblem.

I felt obligated to have a talk with Albert Truelove at the earliest possible moment.

CHAPTER
13

Men talk during the long hours they spend on guard duty and so did Red and I. While on watch in the FO bunker, I found out that Red had fought in the Okinawan campaign during World War II.

"Not too many people remember that the capture of Okinawa, and islands adjacent to it, was called Operation Iceberg," Red told me. "I was part of the Fifth Marines back then. We came ashore at the Yontan airfield on 'Love Day,' April 1, 1945, which as you already know is April Fool's Day. And if all that doesn't impress you, then let me dazzle you with the little-known fact that the landing started and finished on Easter Sunday."

Red told me he took advantage of the GI Bill and went to college. "It took me a little while to decide on my major. I finally settled on philosophy and religion, figuring that if I wasn't good enough to be a minister, then maybe I could teach thought or reasoning at a small high school somewhere in New Jersey. That's where I'm from, you know, Madison, New Jersey."

It was Red who told me that a philosopher, at an earlier time, defined civilized man as being "someone who remem-

bered his yesterdays and who dreamed of his tomorrows."
According to Red's philosophy, man was civilized only
when he could make friends, and then hold on to them. I
never disputed his words. But events of the Korean War
knocked the essence of those two philosophical thoughts
right on their individual asses.

Red had a lot to tell me and I was like a sponge, soaking
up his words. "The most effective politics are backed by
steel, mostly in the form of bullets and guns, and don't you
forget that, Cautious." And then, conversely, he said, "The
moment someone starts shooting, when someone tries to
kill you, that's the moment when all political views, no
matter how profound they might actually be, become irrele-
vant. When someone pulls a trigger, your choices are
suddenly gone. You have no other choice but to respond . . .
somehow, someway, doing the best you can with what you
have, to try to kill the other guy. And the only justification
for your action—political or moral or anything else that it
might be—is your own survival. And don't you forget that,
either!"

He was quiet for a long moment. We were both on duty in
the FO bunker. At night, standing watch, everything, every
sight or sound, was magnified way out of proportion. Even
the sound of Red's ticking wristwatch, turning seconds into
minutes into hours, had a Big Ben quality.

And then Red said, "There's no other time than now and
there's no other place than right here; this place, this war,
that's all there is, and you only have to do one thing and
that's to go on living in the best way you can . . . and try to
help your buddies do the same thing."

Red would have made a great teacher. I found out that
Red, Tom Fuhs, and the Funny Gunny had all been on the
same draft coming to Korea. That being the case, Red was,
in the vernacular of the time, "short," which meant that he
had just a little bit longer to go on his one-year combat tour.
I can honestly say that I do not remember Red's full name;
maybe I never knew it.

Red and I shared the same sleeping bunker, one that had
two entranceways. We shared rations, information from
home, everything, right up to the day when Red got his

orders to go home, right up to the moment when Red got his chance to go down Hill 854 for the last time, a happy man knowing that he had pulled all the time on line that he was ever going to pull.

I remember my first night on the hill. The two of us, using lung power, inflated our rubber air mattresses and placed them on the deck of our sleeping bunker. Next, we unrolled our winter sleeping bags. When the two of us got into the small bunker it would be a tight fit all the way around. The sleeping bunker, dug in diagonally on a corner juncture of the trench line, was designed so one entrance was at our head and the other at our feet. Ponchos had been affixed as doors to the entranceways. Hanging down, the ponchos rustled noisily when moved.

Getting ready for sleep, I removed my .45 automatic from its holster. I jacked a round into the chamber and then let the hammer down slowly. I pushed the safety on and placed the weapon within reach of my hand. This was my "comfort" weapon, a powerful stopping weapon, one that would be easy to use in the limited confines of the bunker. Red had a communicator's flashlight, the type that had a right-angled neck. We would use it if a light was needed. We got ourselves settled in and extinguished the small candle in its C-ration can holder. The moment the bunker was utterly dark—pitch-black dark—I heard the poncho at our feet being rattled noisily.

"What the hell's that, Red?" I whispered.

"Nothing. It's just a bunker rat, Cautious. Don't worry about it," Red said.

A rat! A fucking bunker rat! And I shouldn't worry? Who was shittin' who around here?

"Will that fucker come in here, Red?"

"Yep. But don't worry, we don't have any opened food cans in the bunker. The rat will just sniff around some and then pass right on through. Besides, there's not a whole hell of a lot you can do about it, Cautious."

No open food cans? If there was no available food around, that fucking rat might just start in on me. And there was a whole hell of a lot I could do about that! I could shoot that fucking rat! And that's what I told Red.

161

"Bullshit, Red. I can shoot that fuckin' rat."

"I really don't think you should do that, Cautious."

"Why not, Red?"

"Well, Cautious, I guess I could explain all night long why you shouldn't shoot at a bunker rat, but you wouldn't be satisfied until you've had your try at it. Tell me, how good are you with that .45 automatic?"

"I shot expert during infantry training, Red."

"That's good enough for me. Only thing is, on my side of the bunker, down at the bottom, those two things stickin' up are my feet. Try not to shoot any toes, okay? A missing toe might be hard to explain when I got home."

"Okay, Red," I said, groping for my .45 automatic.

"Just wait a moment until I get ready, Cautious."

I could hear Red moving around on his side. I had already raised myself to a sitting position, sitting a bit unsteadily on my bunched-up sleeping bag and air mattress. I held the .45 automatic straight out in front of me with both arms extended; because of the close confines of the bunker, my elbows drooped downward. It wasn't the steadiest position in the world, but what the hell! Red told me he had extended the flashlight and was ready. By this time the noisy rattling at our feet had abated. Still, I could sense the bunker rat had already entered and was waiting just inside the poncho.

"Now!" Red said, turning on the flashlight.

Centered in the flashlight beam was a really big fucking rat, one about half the size of a house cat. A really big fucker!

Blaaaaaammmm! went the .45 automatic. The recoil kicked my forearms back so hard I smacked the middle of my forehead with the front sight blade and immediately raised a knot there the size of a walnut. I was knocked flat on my back. The concussion of the .45 automatic being fired in that confined space caused a small avalanche of dirt to cascade down from the top of the bunker. My eyes crossed and I thought I would go deaf from the noise of the weapon.

I turned my dirty face toward Red. Wisely, knowing beforehand what was going to happen, Red had pulled his field jacket over both his head and the opening of his sleeping bag. He had also packed his ears with moistened toilet tissue.

Red pointed the flashlight beam toward the bunker entranceway. The poncho—with a big hole in its center—was still hanging down. There was no sign of the bunker rat.

"What did I tell you, Cautious? A man just cannot hardly ever hit those fuckers. So there isn't a whole lot of sense shootin' at them, wouldn't you agree with me?"

Red taught me still another lesson. He told me I had to learn to be "a prick with ears." I had heard that comment before, but only associated it with barracks vulgarity.

"When you're a prick with ears—and don't you ever forget that's exactly what you're expected to be as an FO—it means that while you can listen with sympathy all day long to somebody's troubles, you'll still have the guts to call your shots right in on top of his head if that's what it takes to kill gooks. And you can bet your ass, my young friend, that at some time or another the gooks are going to get in that close to you . . . and you're gonna have to do it, you're gonna hafta yell 'Fire in the hole!' and let people know there are mortar shells coming in on your position."

Red pointed out to where the grunts were in their fighting holes. "Those grunts, they're realists. They've already assumed that you're a prick with ears. They've got their job to do, and they know you've got yours."

Red was tall and skinny. He was about six feet tall. Okay, so maybe that really isn't too tall, but to me—standing only about five feet eight inches in my boondockers—that's tall. Skinny? Maybe Red weighed in at about one-sixty-five pounds. On his rawboned frame, that weight looked like nothing but skin and bones. He told me he had topped two hundred when he left the States.

"You've got to understand, Cautious, that for the past year I've been on a steady diet of the deadly three C rations. A man can stay alive eating them, but he ain't gonna get fat."

Anything hot to drink was welcome. The small packets of instant coffee, vile and bitter tasting as the coffee seemed to be, were always welcome. The cocoa disks were something altogether different. The round, half-inch-thick disks came wrapped in cellophane marked with directions: "Crumble cocoa within the cellophane wrapper. Dissolve contents in hot water. Add powdered milk and sugar if desired."

A cocoa disk was impossible to crumble inside the cellophane wrapper with your fingers; it was impossible to crumble even when you placed it on a rock and smashed down on it with the butt plate of an M1. It was impossible to melt the cocoa in boiling-hot water. You could boil away most of a canteen full of water and the cocoa disk at the bottom would still be intact; maybe the water would be colored a shit-brindle-brown, but that would be the extent of it. Those cocoa disks had the longest lives in Korea.

Red said he recalled just one time when he had ever gained anything from the cement-hard cocoa disks. "We had just come north of the Thirty-eighth Parallel in the vicinity of the Pyongyang-Kumwha-Chorwon triangle during late July and into August in a piss-poorly run air interdiction operation that the marines called Operation Strangle. Most of the operation dealt with using air power delivering air strikes. This area—and I got to know it pretty good because I was shooting a lot then—was called the Iron Triangle, or at least that was the army's name for it. This was a very strategic position primarily due to the fact that from where we were situated, way over in the east corner, we could fire on part of the rail line from Seoul to Chorwon. It was important that we kicked the gooks out of the hills near there, and I guess we did, but I don't think we did as good a job there as was expected.

"For two days we had the Twenty-seventh British Commonwealth Brigade on line tied in on our right-hand side. Surprisingly enough, there were mostly Australians in that outfit.

"I had to go over to their lines and set up some concentrations just in case they needed some help. Anyway, I'm sitting down to eat with some of the Aussies and I break out this cocoa disk. I was going to throw it away. I'm tellin' you, Cautious, they went ape-shit over that cocoa disk. This older-looking Australian—I later found out he was the battalion sergeant major—kept hollering out: 'Cow-cow! The bloody Yanks have cow-cow! Why, the bloody Queen doesn't even have cow-cow!'

"You've got to understand me, Cautious; I've never been one to take advantage of a situation, but this one was tailor

164

made. I happened to know that the Australians got a rum ration every day, and the man who issued out the rum is the guy who's breathin' heavy over that cocoa disk.

"So we strike up a deal. I tell him I'll give him ten cocoa disks for a fifth of rum. He agrees right on the spot, but he sort of hedges on when we can complete the deal. He said it would have to be done the following day, at noontime, just before his outfit moved out again. I said that was okay by me. I had to collect the cocoa, and I had to come back to his area in case they needed mortar fire when they jumped off."

Red said that he passed the word when he returned to the company he was then attached to, and very, very quickly he had about two hundred cocoa disks, which he packed into a knapsack.

"Right on time the next day the Australian sergeant major showed up. He had a dozen bottles of rum. I wasn't a cheap charlie so I gave him all the cocoa disks I had, far more than he had bargained for, and each of us thinking we got the better of the other guy.

"Well, when the sergeant major counted the cocoa and saw that he had the best of the bargain, he looked like he had something he wanted to say to me. Instead, he just shook his head and said, 'You're a decent, trusting Yank, and you're okay in my books, Matey.' And then he shoved off, back to his own war.

"Actually, Cautious, I was feelin' pretty cheap about the swap, myself, until I found out he had watered down the rum. Still, it wasn't a bad deal after all. Nobody wanted those cocoa disks except that Australian sergeant major. Sometimes I think about it and I laugh when I imagine him trying to make cocoa out of those disks. I'll bet he's still singing the blues," Red said.

Talk about singing the blues. Red surely could do that. He carried his guitar with him everywhere, slung right across his back. A lot of times he would strum his guitar and sing, sometimes at dusk coming on toward dark. We would all quiet down and listen. One time, after a brief flurry of incoming mortar fire when Red had to hit the deck, he discovered his guitar had picked up a piece of shrapnel. The guitar had saved Red from getting an extra hole in his body.

Red said that that was the closest he had ever come to getting hit. "I've been shot at and missed, shit at and hit, and I'm telling you, Cautious, all I want to do is to be able to climb over that parapet leading to the trail going downhill, and I want to do it without having any more holes in me than the ones I had when I climbed up the hill," Red said to me.

Red had certain peculiarities. His really big peculiarity, which actually had a lot of good sense behind it, had to do with plain, ordinary string. Red always had a piece of string on him, figuratively and literally.

Red never carried anything in the pockets of his dungarees, either the jacket or the trouser pockets, except pieces of string. What Red would do—and I'm telling you the truth—is poke a small hole or two somewhere in his jacket or trousers and then tie a small piece of cotton string to his dungarees. He would take the other end of the string and tie it to whatever it was that he wanted to carry around with him.

I mean, shit, you had to see him to believe him. There was Red walking all around the trench lines with his helmet on his head, his guitar on his back, and he had those pieces of string hanging down all over him, with maybe a John Wayne can opener tied to one string, or a small pocketknife to another string, or a Korean Iddy-wah spoon, or maybe a pencil, or even the stub of a candle to yet another string. You name it and Red probably had it tied onto his clothes with a piece of string.

No one on the hill thought that was dumb or anything like that. It was Red's way and that was okay with the rest of us. Anyway, it sure did beat trying to figure out what Red had that you might like to borrow. With Red it was a case of if you couldn't see it, he didn't have it.

The two of us fired a couple of missions together, me shooting farther out and Red shooting closer in, and we made a pretty good team.

I was a couple of years younger than Red, but it didn't much seem to matter. Somehow, in a really short time, a bond developed between us. I soon realized that Red was about the best friend I had in Korea.

Red taught me a lot of things, important things, fundamental things. He kept repeating one specific bit of advice time and again, as if the repetition would give it weight. Red said, "Keep moving. Don't ever give them a target to shoot at, because them fuckers just don't miss!"

We would talk about our wives and kids and Red would say cornball things like "You gotta play it square with your wife and kids, no matter what. They're the important things in your life." And Red would always say, "Take the time to tell your wife and your kids that you love them. It's important that they know that." Red could get by saying things like that because we all knew that he meant them, he really did.

Talk like that always led to pacts, to promises about how we would keep in touch with each other after we both got home from Korea. I was supposed to visit Red at his New Jersey home and he and his wife and kids were supposed to visit me in Pennsylvania. I liked that idea fine.

Red sort of took me under his wing, so to speak, a lot like the way the Funny Gunny had done. I felt good in his company, and I felt more worthwhile about myself. Maybe that's what friendship is all about.

I remember clearly the day when his outfit telephoned and gave him the good news. Good news was getting the word on the exact day and hour of your departure from the Land of the Morning Calm. Red and I were in the FO bunker looking out over that terribly lonesome mass of torn-up, blown-up, fucked-up, metal-infested terrain that always existed between two opposing and warring outfits and that got its name during World War I; we were looking for targets in no-man's-land. Red and I were in the FO bunker for a specific purpose that day. We were both looking for a newly placed enemy mortar that had already raised hell with Item Company grunts. The gooks had already lobbed in three rounds, getting flesh and blood with each of them.

Red was the man who had told me how good the North Koreans were at calling in their shots, about how they used triangulation.

"I'm telling you, Cautious. Those three grunts this morning, well, I asked around and found out all they were doing

167

was just standing in one spot, having a cigarette and just shooting the shit with their buddies. Every one of them, mind you. They thought they were safe from small-arms fire, from flat trajectory fire. Maybe they were, but nobody's safe from the plunging-down fire of a mortar."

Red was a bit pissed off. He always got pissed off when some grunt got killed or wounded because he stayed too long in one spot on the hill.

There was no compromising with Red: He always felt he had let the grunts of Item Company down when he couldn't spot the location of the enemy mortar position and fire counterbattery fire at it, knocking it out. Red took to heart his job of spotting enemy mortars and silencing them. He was constantly using the sound-powered telephone, talking to the grunts who had fighting holes facing into the hill mass out front, asking them to report any telltale evidence of smoke rings. In turn, the grunts told Red they could hear the Korean mortar being fired, sort of muffled, but no one had spotted any smoke. We all concluded they were using Chinese smokeless powder.

Forward observers earn their pay when incoming rounds are being fired, regardless of how few or how many come into our lines. Sometimes you could be in the middle of a shoot-out and sometimes it would be strictly a one-on-one situation, like the one we were experiencing now. During the day the FO looked for the shimmering white cloud rising up after a mortar round had been fired; in the dark of night an FO looked for the flash of bright white-orangish light from the burning gas of the increments.

The Chinese invented gunpowder. They developed it to a fine degree, and came up with a smokeless type of gunpowder, the kind that was giving us fits. If there was no smoke, there was no way to spot just where the mortar was located in defilade. They would use their smokeless gunpowder as long as they had it, and then would resort to using the U.S. ammunition they had captured by the truckload up around the Chosin Reservoir about a year before.

That was the way of things when Red's FO telephone started ringing. He picked it up, identified himself, listened carefully with a "Golly, gee!" kind of a smile spreading across his face, and then put the telephone back into the leather carrying case.

"I'm going home, Cautious! Great God almighty, my orders are in, and I'm singing my sayonara song as of this minute," Red said to me. He was talking around the world's biggest shit-eating grin.

Red motioned his head toward the parapet of the FO bunker. "That gook out there; he's all yours, Cautious. Get the fucker for me, okay?"

I nodded. "When you leavin', Red?"

"Momentarily, Cautious. And that means like right the fuck now. Watch me! I'm haulin' my ass out of here."

It sure didn't take him long to duck into the sleeping bunker and get what little stuff he had in there. He put his guitar across his back and he was ready to go off the hill.

I walked through the trench line with him to the Item Company commander's bunker where Red checked out, shaking hands with the skipper and the first sergeant. And then Red and I were standing in the trench line behind the hill, where a man had to jump the parapet to start his way downhill. Red had made it, just like he wanted to do; he was going to jump the parapet leading to the path down the hill and he didn't have any more holes in him at that moment than he did when he came up the hill.

We lighted up cigarettes, and we didn't say anything for a minute or two. I guess we really didn't have anything more to say. I mean, what the hell is there to talk about to a guy who has pulled his twelve months in Korea, mostly on the line, and is heading home, and you still have about ten more months to go on your tour?

Red dropped his cigarette on the deck of the trench and ground it out with the toe of his boondocker.

"Take care of yourself, Cautious. Keep a low profile and always keep moving. You know how the gooks shoot at things they can't miss. Don't give them a stationary target," Red said, repeating his sage advice to me a final time. I nodded my head at him and pulled hard on my cigarette. It tasted lousy.

"Remember, if they can't see you, they won't shoot at you. And if they can see you, then remember that a moving target is the hardest of all to hit," Red said.

I nodded my head again. Red was the expert. Here he was going home, carrying along a personal citation or two attributing commendably to his skill and courage and devotion to duty.

Red looked at me and it seemed he wanted to say something and then decided against it. Instead he pursed his lips, and then he gripped the sandbag. He looked me in the eye and gave me a grin and a thumbs-up sign, and then he was gone, already five steps down the path. Red was on his way home.

The lucky bastard.

Briefly I watched Red follow the twisting downward trail through the mine fields that surrounded our position. He was doing what he always said to do, sort of taking his time, watching where he would put his feet, moving downward continuously but at an erratic, jerky pace. He knew it took about thirty seconds for the gooks to put a round on any specific spot on the trail.

When he was about halfway down the hill Red stopped. I put my binoculars to my eyes and I could see him plain as day. He had this big shit-eating grin all over his face. I watched him untie his small pocketknife from its string on the front of his utility jacket. I watched him open the blade of the knife; he was making quite a production out of it, showing off a bit because he knew he had an audience in all of the grunts still up on the hill. And then Red was cutting off first one item from his dungarees, and then a second item. As he cut an item from his clothing, Red hauled his hand back and threw the item as far from him as he could. He was standing there and was heaving the bits of his life on the hill in Korea way out and away from himself, far away from himself. And up on the hill, all of the grunts, all of Red's friends, gave out with a cheer every time he cut off an item from his clothing and threw it away. Red was giving his final performance for the troops up on the hill; he was giving them something to write home about.

I heard two things in rapid succession, one after the other.

I heard the phlegmatic cough of the gook mortar, and it seemed strange to me that I should be able to hear it so distinctly on this side of the hill; and I heard one of the grunts yell out, "Hey, you fuckin' FOs! I see their smoke!"

The grunt ran up to me and said, "Come on, I've got 'em spotted!"

I hurried through the trench line after him, yelling for my radioman to get his radio and come after me.

I could see the shimmering halo of white smoke. Those fucking gooks had placed their mortar to our rear, behind our lines! No wonder we couldn't spot them; we had always looked out in front of our lines.

I quickly made an evaluation and called it back to my radioman who, in turn, informed the Four Deuce FDC. I was going to be right on target the first shot; I knew deep inside me that I would be right on target. That's what Red had asked me to do; he had asked me to get them fuckers and I was going to do it for him.

And then, out of the corner of my left eye, I caught a glimpse of quicksilver. It was the round the North Koreans had fired. It had reached its apex, and had curved, and now it was coming down, down, down.

I raced quickly back to where I had been standing in the trench line watching Red throw away his hill life. I yelled at the top of my lungs: "Fire in the hole, Red! For God's sake, fire in the hole!"

CHAPTER
14

Grunts from the 5th Marine Regiment, like ghostly wraiths, quietly climbed the back of Hill 854, two and three men at a time that freezing night of November 17, a week before Thanksgiving Day. The grunts relieving Item Company had come out of reserve, out of Camp Tripoli, a safe area located well to the rear. They had been trucked to about a mile behind the lines about midnight that Monday and had moved silently—following a Judas goat grunt from Item Company—to fighting hole positions in the trench lines. I've got to hand it to them, those grunts of the 5th Marines had good discipline. Other than the muttered curses thrown when a man slipped or stumbled, the only words, whispered hoarsely by staff NCOs, were, "Don't bunch up!" As each replacement moved into a fighting hole in the trench line, Item Company grunts would clue them in, provide them with pertinent information, give them most of the available ammunition, wish the relieving grunt a lot of luck, and then quickly depart the area, going down the hill. Item Company grouped together at the truck site.

My relief had come up a day earlier. I showed him where I had my concentrations and we fired a few rounds. He was a corporal, an Old Salt. There wasn't much I could tell him, and so I didn't try. I was all business. I guess I wasn't very friendly. I needed a friend but, somehow, I felt jinxed.

I was one of the first men to go down off the hill, and I was glad to leave it behind me. Halfway down I said a special prayer as I passed the spot where, just two nights earlier, I had helped pick up pieces of Red. The round the gooks had thrown in earlier that day had exploded very close to Red, ripping and tearing his body. His radioman and wireman and I had come down the hill that night, long after Red had been killed. We wanted to come down right away, but we remembered what Red had said about not bunching up or staying in one spot for too long. So we waited, and while we waited, his body, what there was of it, lay under a cold sun. The three of us worked fast, putting pieces of Red into the dark green lightweight outer shell of a winter sleeping bag. I was glad we had waited and I was glad it was dark, with just enough artificial light from the searchlight to see by. I didn't look at Red and I didn't think about Red. I just held my breath and I tried to keep from gagging and puking as I handled pieces of a uniformed body that had been mangled. The three of us just choked and retched and dry-heaved and kept wiping our hands with dirt from the ground. The exploding round had mangled Red's legs, blowing the left leg off just above his yellow legging. We couldn't find either that foot or his right arm from the elbow down.

Red's body, inside the fart sack cover, sagged in the middle. His body scraped, bumping on the wooden ammunition box steps as we carried him down the hill. And there we waited, smoking nervously and not talking, at almost the exact spot where I had been blown off the trail about two weeks earlier. We waited for a graves registration team to show up. I had found Red's small pocketknife. I asked his radioman and his wireman if it would be okay with them if I kept it for a while. I said that someday, maybe, I would visit his wife and give it to her. Maybe.

When I passed the site of what had earlier been the hot chow line, I said good-bye to the memory of that young buck sergeant, the young kid who had cooked up those delicious doughnuts. Farther on down the trail I stopped for the

173

smallest of moments to say good-bye to Tom Fuhs and the Funny Gunny. I knew I would never pass this way again, except in memory. I said my good-byes silently, more in my mind than with my lips. I wondered about the words Red had said to me, that a man was civilized when he remembered his yesterdays and dreamed of his tomorrows, who could make friends and then hold on to them. Right then, as far as I was concerned, I was through remembering my yesterdays, and I sure didn't want to dream anything about what my tomorrows might hold. I thought about Red again and I knew that dreams of tomorrow do not always come true. I guessed it was okay, though, to hold on to a friend, if only in memory.

Hurry up and wait. It was an old military game. At the truck site, those of us first off the hill stamped our feet on the iron-hard frozen ground, swinging one foot out and then quickly bringing it banging back into the other, constantly kicking our booted feet together, trying to keep circulation moving inside them. No one talked. No one even smoked a cigarette. With towels acting as scarves and wrapped around our necks and lower faces, with hands holding on to sleeping bags draped over our heads and hanging down our backs, it was too much of an effort to smoke that cold night. Like cattle going to slaughter, we waited patiently. A nose count indicated all of Item Company had come down off the hill. We finally loaded on the trucks around 0200 and trundled south, heading to Camp Tripoli and a month of rest some thirty miles behind the lines.

It was bitter cold. We sat on the wooden seats on both sides of the truck, the wind whipping in through the slatted sides, biting our backs and dancing frigidly on the truck bed. One of the truck drivers, now seated behind his wheel, the doors to the cab pulled shut and the truck heater going full blast, had earlier said that it was expected to drop below zero.

At first that was okay with me. I needed the cold. I needed it to get so cold that all I would be able to think about would be the cold. I looked up, checking out the stars. For some vague reason I looked for the Southern Cross. I tried to recall, or to guess, really, the names of the formations, the ones I had been taught in grade school or the Boy Scouts so very, very long ago. I looked for the Big Dipper, and then the Little Dipper. One of them, I thought, had the North Star at the end of its ladle. I knew I was not normally a sensitive person and so I wondered about the thoughts I was having, the thoughts about Red, and Tom Fuhs, and the Funny Gunny, and that young kid buck sergeant, the baker. At that moment, the moment of seeing the stars so bright in the sky and not being able to identify any of them, I saw a certain beauty, a beauty that was hundreds of thousands of light-years away in a blue-black infinity, a beauty that was so clean, so clear, that all at once I knew peace, and I knew that while I would always remember the men who were my friends, the remembrance would never haunt me.

The truck moved slowly, at about five miles per hour, under blackout conditions. Even so, between the truck's forward movement and the wind, which was picking up some, the cold was worse by far than anything I had ever felt before. The cold knifed in, slicing through all the layers of clothing I was wearing, cutting into my legs and butt where the layered clothing seemed as though it would not, could not, turn the cold away. Then the cold went directly down to my feet, and no amount of tapping one foot and then the other on the metal deck of the truck seemed to help at all.

I sat numbly on the wooden truck seat, a mirror image of the others, my gloved hands thrust up under my armpits, neck pulled down into my shoulders, my head tilted forward, glazed eyes staring at my knees. I shivered constantly, first with a tenseness that was all at once in my back and my stomach, all suddenly tightening and just as quickly relaxing with a shuddering of my entire body. The shudder started at my tight, now-turning-raw throat and worked down to my cold butt and then, moments later, started all over again.

I tried to focus my mind on the fact that being in reserve meant there would be time to rest and relax, time to eat and drink without hurry, without gulping down food and coffee, time to sit around mess tables and play cards with the Mickey Mouse funny money the paymaster gave out once each month, the blue-pink-green bills that represented nickels, dimes, quarters, halves, and dollars, money that didn't feel right, that didn't even fold right. Being in reserve would be a time not to worry. But trying to get there, trying not to freeze to death in the back of that comfortless motor transport truck, I would have gladly given up my reserve time for the relief provided by the protection of a frontline bunker. As I had earlier welcomed the cold, now I just wanted to be warm again and out of the cold.

And then, suddenly, in the cold light of a new, blue day, the truck driver yelled that the camp on the left side of the road was where the Four Deuces were located.

No one dismounts gracefully from the ass end of a marine corps truck on a freezing cold Korean morning after having ridden in the truck for four hours. My eyes were just barely open when I stood up, very stiffly, my legs and feet stinging as blood moved sluggishly through cramped vessels. I staggered as best I could on wooden legs and block-ice feet toward the tailgate, bouncing from side to side off all those packed-in frozen bodies. I lifted my right leg, dangled it over, and straddled the tailgate for a moment, my foot seeking out the U-shaped metal step that normally was welded on the truck, an aid to dismounting. Shit! At this most inopportune moment I found out this fucking truck didn't have a metal step. I lost my balance and toppled over the tailgate. I crunched—my arms, legs, asshole, and appetite—right on that rock-hard roadway. Somebody heaved my Willie Peter bag over the end of the truck and it hit me just as I was raising myself up. Then Soupy Campbell fell off the end of the truck, followed by Billy Baxter, both showing about as much dexterity as I had shown. With a whump, their Willie Peter bags followed them. We stood in the roadway trying to collect our thoughts, our balance, and our gear as the truck grumbled away.

I don't know why—and there is no logical way for me to explain it—but watching that truck move off and not seeing anybody, not one of those grunts from Item Company, look back or even raise a hand in a farewell gesture, well, it sort of got to me. That truck just drove out of my life carrying a cold cargo of nameless grunts whom I had brushed against briefly, and that was all she wrote on that subject. Well, what the fuck, nobody in Item Company owed me anything.

I had a burned-out gasoline smell in my nose and a lousy taste in my mouth. I was glad to be off that truck. I was not jubilant to the point of wanting to hold a parade or anything like that, but I was glad, glad, glad that the freezing, jouncing, bouncing, tormenting thirty-mile truck ride from the front lines was over. I smiled inwardly, remembering back up the road when our convoy had passed an army unit that was on its way to a mess tent, the soldiers carrying metal mess trays, and the whole goddamn convoy of us started barking and yip-yipping at them. This one guy, not a very big guy, raised his mess tray, his metal knife, fork, and spoon rattling, and he yelled at us, "Go ahead and bark like dogs; you're nothin' but a bunch'a sons of bitches, anyway!" Maybe he was right.

So there we were in the middle of the dirt road, Soupy Campbell, Bill Baxter, and me, clumsily moving through the bone-chilling cold toward the welcome sight of heat shimmering up around a smokestack sticking up through the top of a tent. I suspected this was the mess tent.

I had this really weird sensation in my face and ears, in my feet and toes, in my hands and fingers, a feeling like, well, as ridiculous as it may sound, it was a feeling like they were on fire, but it wasn't the kind of fire heat you would get from a flame. Anyway the three of us walked, gingerly picking our way, the short distance to where smoke was coming out the stovepipe, billowing upward in black puffs. And, oh! Get a whiff of that hot, fresh-made coffee smell—perked coffee. And, so help me God, the warm, yeasty smell of fresh bread. Oh, mother! I truly have come home to die!

It didn't take but one minute to scramble inside the tent. Supply chief Cpl. Lob Stratton and chief cook Albert Truelove were there.

"Welcome home," Lob Stratton said, pouring out three cups of hot coffee, pushing forward bowls filled with cream and sugar.

"Eat! Eat!" Albert Truelove said, a big smile on his face as he hustled our way thick slabs of freshly made hot bread topped with melted cheese. "I worried about you guys. And John Francis McLaughlin, too. He's back home, now. I prayed for all of you. I'm glad you're down safe."

I thought, So who needs a brass band, anyway? The coffee was just the way I like it, hot, sweet, and strong. I was wolfishly gobbling down slice after slice of the cheese bread, washing it down with gulps of coffee, when suddenly some of it went down the wrong way and I was red faced with hacking and coughing, trying to get my breath. But I've got to tell you I was feeling great. Little did I realize that within twenty-four hours both Lob Stratton and Albert Truelove would give me reason again for another fit of coughing.

As the company supply chief, Lob Stratton had the job of getting enough pyramidal tents, canvas cots, new clothing of all types, enough of everything a supply chief needs to keep his ass out of a sling and his company in the lap of luxury. That was a tall order for such a short supply chief in the middle of a really cold winter.

As the company cook who worked for a chief cook who was drunk most of the time, Albert Truelove had the job of setting up a cooking galley and a mess tent, of doing whatever was necessary to produce enough good food to feed more than one hundred eighty hungry mortar men three times daily, men who wanted more than just warmed-over deadly three rations.

To a certain degree, both Lob Stratton and Albert Truelove succeeded in their jobs. I think Lob Stratton succeeded by default; Albert Truelove was successful because he truly was a born scrounger.

Somehow, somewhere, and nobody questioned him too closely, supply chief Lob Stratton had picked up about two dozen pyramidal tents. The entire company would sleep under gray canvas at Camp Tripoli. No one questioned the color of the tents. Gray was a color usually reserved for the navy supply system, but as Lob constantly asked everyone loudly and clearly, "Now you tell me why the navy needs pyramidal tents."

It was Lob Stratton, the mighty pip-squeak, who straw-bossed the local labor force—Korean yobos—in not only erecting the tents but in "strong-backing" the tents as well.

When putting up pyramidal tents by placing them side by side in a row, strong-backing is needed to gain not only a neat military appearance, but also to provide added strength. Strong-backing was accomplished by digging heavy posts in at the four corners of each tent. Long poles were then lashed between the tents. Tents next to each other shared the same long poles. Similar poles were placed at the rear of each tent; shorter poles were at the front, permitting a doorway to be used. The canvas sides of each tent, with canvas strips already sewn in place, were tied to the long poles. When the center tent pole was raised, the canvas would stretch tautly, and the tent city would have a neat, uniform appearance.

Lob Stratton was a well-meaning but officious prick who nearly did not qualify for the Marine Corps when he first sought enlistment for four years. He was barely up to enlistment requirements. He was the smallest man in the outfit, just barely reaching the required sixty-four-inch height. Lob had not grown any since joining the marines. So when the supply manual recommended that the long poles of the tents being used for strong-back purposes be placed "about chest high," the book was assuming that a marine of average height would be erecting the tents. The end result of Lob placing his long poles about chest high was tents that were saggy-looking at the bottom and stretched mighty tight at the top. His tent-raising efforts did not result in row after row of neatly erected tents with a distinct military look to them. But nobody gave a good rat's ass; those tents, baggy bottoms and all, looked good to men who had been living in sandbagged holes in the ground. Still, nobody was taking pictures of the tent area to send home to their family. I mean, shit, even combat grunts had a certain amount of pride.

Lob remedied part of this situation for a few tents the following day. I don't think he intended to do so. It was just one of those things that happened when you were around the Lob.

I've got to tell you this about Lob Stratton. He could play poker. He was either the luckiest man in the Marine Corps when it came to playing poker, or he was the cheatingest. Mostly, when we played poker, we played by candlelight, candles being our prime source of illumination. Lob, our supply NCO, would requisition case after case of the white, inch-thick, five-inch-high wax candles.

Everyone had his own candle holder, usually a modified dry C-ration can. With the top of the can removed, a man could carefully cut one third of the side away. A small candle placed inside would then be protected from drafts and the inside mirrorlike silver surface of the can would reflect the candlelight two, perhaps three times its normal brilliance. It was the drafts of wind, strong enough to cause the candle flame to flicker and waver, throwing shadows about, that were of main concern to the cardplayers. Lob Stratton's card playing was at its very best when the candles guttered, causing long shadows to dart around the card table.

Pay call would come while we were in Camp Tripoli. We were never paid when we were on line, so most of us had one, two, even as much as three months' pay due us when we were in reserve. Lob Stratton, with his winning ways and his winning smiles as he cheerfully raked in pot after pot in a tent filled with flickering shadows, would have ended up a very rich man had he stayed in Korea longer than just a one-year tour.

A couple of men who had earlier fallen victim to Lob's winning ways decided we ought to have better lights at future poker games than just those squat, flickering candles. The word went out to the supply chief. "Either you get something better than those goddamn candles or you stay out of the card games," was the way the Big Dog put it to Lob Stratton. Witnesses to this very brief conversation later said that Lob Stratton first had a very depressed look about him after the Big Dog delivered his ultimatum, a look like that of a man who had just lost a gold mine, followed quickly by a look of anxiety, like that of a man wondering if he could find his gold mine again. As you might imagine, the Big Dog was always a heavy loser at the poker table.

Hard-pressed, the Lob took his problem to Albert True-love, a man who claimed he had Armenian Jew cousins in all the armed forces supply circles. Albert Truelove looked like a hard guy with his chiseled stone face, his square, heavyset body that was already starting to get fat, his thick, muscular arms and short, stubby-fingered hands; but in all reality, the Armenian Jew was a real pussycat, a pushover for a hard-luck story.

It was Albert Truelove who, after hearing Lob Stratton's hard-luck story, showed up late that afternoon with two wooden cases in the back of a jeep. Each of the wooden cases held two dozen Coleman lanterns—a veritable treasure trove of light. The jeep and the wooden cases had U.S. Army Quartermaster markings.

Lob Stratton and Albert Truelove quickly knocked apart the wooden cases. They placed the wood slats, which had U.S. Army markings stenciled on them, face downward on the ground floor of their supply tent. The wooden floor offered better footing than the cold, damp ground.

Albert Truelove was off again in the jeep. He soon returned with quite a few five-gallon cans in the back of the jeep. A navy seabee was sitting in the passenger seat. The two men unloaded the five-gallon cans, each marked "white gasoline," the only fuel that should be used in Coleman lanterns. It was almost impossible to get during the winter months of 1951.

With the jeep unloaded, the seabee got into the driver's seat and started the motor. "Anytime you get another jeep, Albert, you give me a holler, you hear?" the sailor yelled as he gunned the jeep out of our compound.

Lob Stratton gave Albert Truelove the eye, and then asked his question. "Albert, did you steal those Coleman lanterns and that army jeep?"

Albert Truelove, a good and true man, did not answer the question directly. Instead, he countered with a question of his own: "Lob, is it true that you really are a fast shuffler in a card game?"

Captain Massey was delighted with the Coleman lanterns. There were plenty to go around, with two allocated to each tent. In addition to giving off more than sufficient light, the lanterns also gave off heat. In the wintertime in Korea, anything that produced heat was welcome, no matter how it arrived. Well, almost anything.

The Lob would prove us wrong.

While the captain did not press for answers on how the

Coleman lanterns were obtained, he did insist that Lob Stratton "hold school" on the use, care, cleaning, and proper manner of lighting the lanterns.

All of which was the reason why a number of us sergeants were sitting on canvas cots in the supply tent, which held the only large table in camp. It was around this table that the big-money poker players sat night after night. And it was on this table that Lob Stratton had placed a single Coleman lantern.

Officious. That single word described Lob Stratton best after he had been assigned a job by the captain.

"Okay, you people! Knock off the grab-ass and the bullshittin' and pay attention here! The cap'n wants me to hold school on these Coleman lanterns. I've read up on them, and I'm gonna show you how they operate. And when I get done, I'm gonna ask questions, and you people better have answers for me," was the way Lob Stratton started his lecture, easily winning friends and influencing people with his mild manner and grace.

I've got to give the Lob credit. He really had read up on the Coleman lantern, to a certain point, anyway. He quickly pointed to and then named correctly all the parts of the lantern, giving at the same time the function of the part in making the lantern work properly. He demonstrated how to tie the asbestos wick in place, how to burn it with a match prior to turning on the white gas, and then how to light the fumes coming through the wick.

The Lob showed us how to fill up the Coleman lantern with fuel, how to screw the fuel cap back on tightly, and how to pump up the lantern to get the pressure necessary for the fuel to spray in a fine, easily ignitable mist. He also showed us how to keep the carbon off the protective glass.

The Lob did everything right except for one thing; he used regular gasoline in the lanterns instead of the white gasoline required for them. The Lob used regular gasoline simply because there was a fuel can nearby that contained regular gasoline. Then, in spite of having just said that only white gasoline must be used in the lanterns, the Lob filled the reservoir of the lantern he was using for school purposes

182

with regular gas. As a result, the Lob could not get the lantern to light.

Officious to the end, the Lob ordered Albert Truelove to bring in some of the white gasoline. All the while, the Lob was unscrewing the locking nut from the base of the Coleman lantern, smirking and making light of the matter, informing all of us who were seated on those canvas cots listening to his lecture and using the task at hand to enforce his words: "Well, you guys know how to keep a woman from getting pregnant, don't ya. Ya get right back on top and you unscrew her, that's what you do!"

Vapors of gasoline hissed out when the pressure that had built up inside the reservoir was released with the locking nut loosened. We all cringed, sitting as we were on those canvas cots, suddenly surrounded by the gasoline vapors.

The Lob compounded his initial mistake. Without rhyme or reason he upended the Coleman lantern, splashing the regular gasoline out on the wood-slatted floor.

"Oh, you fuckin' Lob! What an asshole you are! Tell me, when you asked your wife to marry you, how'd you ever convince her she needed two assholes?" the Big Dog hissed out at Lob Stratton. The Big Dog and all the rest of us sitting on the canvas cots were waving our hands about, fanning the air, trying to get rid of the gasoline fumes.

"Not to worry, Big Dog. I can get rid of those gas fumes easily," the Lob said.

Right then was when Albert Truelove walked into the supply tent. He was carrying a canteen cup filled with white gasoline. That also was the precise moment when the Lob stopped chewing on the kitchen match he had in his mouth, removed the match from his mouth, and struck its sulphured end on an abrasive.

And that was when the whole fucking supply tent exploded into an immediate ball of fire, the sound of it something like a drunken elephant farting: Baaarroooommmm!

The fire was gone as quickly as the noise it made.

It took only a moment. That contained flame, inside the supply tent, devoured all the hair around our eyebrows; it singed our whiskers and mustaches and all of the fake fur of our Mickey Mouse hats. It turned to immediate ash the canvas of the cots on which all of us had been sitting and the next thing we knew there we were with our knees hooked over the wooden side railing that had slipped through and supported the canvas, our asses now about two inches off the floor, and our necks against the wooden railing of the back side of the cot.

That flash fire demolished the canvas tentage of the supply tent as well as the tent next to it. Everything made of navy gray canvas just crumbled into dust.

When the Lob struck his match the regular gasoline vapors went up in a blue-gold whoosh, and the white gasoline Albert Truelove was carrying vaporized with the big boom sound.

When it was all over, the Lob was standing at the instructor's podium, his face black sooted, white eyes blinking, and him never losing his cool.

That fucking Lob Stratton!

"Now that," the Lob said, officiously, "is just one of the dangers of using a Coleman lantern improperly in a closed area."

So I ask you, would you play poker with someone who could keep their cool like that?

Or, maybe, like the Big Dog said, on this and many other occasions, "Lob Stratton really is an asshole!"

CHAPTER
15

Albert Truelove had his opportunity to show us he had all the traits of an exceptional conniver and an extraordinary thief right after we arrived at Camp Tripoli. He used all the leadership traits of a marine NCO, only he used those traits in an end-around kind of way to gain whatever it might be that someone in the outfit needed.

The traits of leadership had been pounded into Albert Truelove while he was at Parris Island. A litany of words—similar to the Boy Scout oath—the leadership traits had to be learned by all marines, along with examples of how those traits could, and should, be applied through dedication and service. As the Boy Scout oath dealt with the traits of being trustworthy, loyal, helpful, and a whole lot more, so did the marine leadership traits deal with the qualities of integrity, knowledge, courage, decisiveness, dependability, initiative, tact, justice, enthusiasm, bearing, endurance, loyalty, unselfishness, and judgment.

I guess when you got right down to it, there really wasn't a whole lot of difference between the Boy Scouts and the Marine Corps, except possibly the fact that the Boy Scouts were pretty much assured of having adult leadership.

Captain Massey was one marine officer heading up a combat outfit who exercised all the traits of leadership expected of a marine commander, especially when he had to administer disciplinary action against Albert Truelove. I'll say this for Captain Massey; when it came right down to the crunch, he saw his duty and he did it.

The same held true for Albert Truelove, but in a different sort of way. He saw what had to be done and he, too, went right ahead and did it. This time he was doing it as much for himself as for the rest of us.

Albert Truelove's main job in the Four Deuces was to fill the boots, by default, that Sgt. Ben Baker was supposed to wear; he was expected to be the chief cook of the outfit.

Sergeant Ben Baker—a man who did not live up to the expectations of his last name—was a tolerated drunk who couldn't boil water without fucking it up. Baker, in spite of his nonproductivity as a cook, continued to hold on to his three stripes primarily because of certain skills learned back home in the mountains of Tennessee. Baker knew how to combine raisins or prunes or canned peaches and apricots in proper combinations with sugar, yeast, and water; he brewed up batches of mean-but-mellow moonshine in five-gallon cans.

Baker was the kind of marine who believed that if a cook couldn't offer a grunt decent food, then it was incumbent upon the cook to at least offer that grunt a right-smart drink instead. Baker had the knack. In his more sober moments, Baker told us he wasn't much out of short pants when he first started helping his grandfather brew the tastiest moonshine in Tennessee. Baker brought his skill to Korea to the advantage of the thirst of the Four Deuce mortar men and to the disadvantage of their hunger. Following his arrival in the company, Four Deuce mortar men developed a lean, mean, slightly intoxicated look. Baker's three-day brew was more than just tolerable; his seven-day batch was strong enough to walk right over to where you were sitting and pour itself right into your canteen cup. The really good stuff that Baker aged for more than two weeks was reason enough to keep the Korean War going on for as long as possible. I guess the reasons why there was a war in Korea were about the same as the reasons for any other war; the fragments from exploding mortar rounds were all about the same size, too. People who shoot mortars in a war often have good reason why they need a stiff drink every now and then, no questions asked. So Ben Baker, because of his knack as a brew master, remained a sergeant; he spent his days "testing" his various types of brews, mixed as they were in five-gallon cans that lined the mess tent walls.

It was a matter of record that Albert Truelove, assuming the duties of chief cook, had very little to work with in the way of preparing really decent food. He knew where to find supplies; he had proved that in finagling for the white gasoline. He readily helped others, but he needed a little motivation in helping himself.

Thanksgiving was just a day away. I had stopped at the main mess tent to get a helmet full of hot water for shaving and there was Albert Truelove with a long face.

"How many different ways can I fix the deadly three, Cautious?" Albert Truelove was still referring to me by my FO name, but that was okay with me. Almost everyone had gotten used to calling me that.

Albert Truelove had asked the question, but I don't believe he was expecting an answer from me. With Thanksgiving Day coming up, all he had to work with were the same old canned foods, hardly the tools to build a feast. From the talk around the poker table, the men of the Four Deuces expected to be thankful on Thanksgiving Day. They quite candidly informed Albert Truelove that it was up to him.

Right now Albert Truelove was making meat-and-beans potpies. They looked savory enough and they smelled great. The half-inch-thick crust was an exceptional golden brown. Everyone was going to eat the crust, I knew that. But not too many men were going to dig in deeper than the crust. Even though the meat-and-beans filling would be hot and would even smell good, it still had that sort of grayish, lumpish, go-to-hell characteristic about it that nobody could stomach.

"You'll never sell it to them, Albert," I said, washing

187

under my armpits. How great that warm soapy water felt. Albert Truelove had gas-operated immersion heaters he could light and then stick down into metal GI cans filled with water. With a small stovepipe sticking upward, the immersion burner heated the water almost to the boiling point and kept it at that temperature. Albert Truelove was no fool when it came to the comforts of life in the field.

At one end of the mess tent he had built wooden stands that would accommodate, through formfitting holes, helmets filled with hot water. On shelves located below small mirrors, Albert Truelove had an array of shaving materials. Now I knew who was responsible for a similar setup at the base of Hill 854. The only difference was that it was much warmer in the mess tent with the stoves and ovens heating the area. Albert Truelove treated us right, there was no doubt about that.

A couple mortar men had already been through the chow line. They had eyed the meat pies without enthusiasm. The few who took meat pie portions ate the crust only, peeling it carefully away from the gray mass underneath. They ate the crust and then dumped everything else in the garbage cans with a loud banging of metal trays.

"It's the same old shit! Only today he tried to hide it under a pretty good crust. He shoulda made apple pies, only I guess he ain't got any apples. Well, he better goddamn sure have pumpkin pie for Thanksgiving."

Albert Truelove told me he just did not have anything to work with, foodwise.

Courage and dependability were just two of the traits of a good marine NCO. Courage comes in two packages, physical and moral. Albert Truelove, like all other marines, had been taught in boot camp that if he ever got into a tight place and felt fear, that he was to recognize the fear, gain control over the fear, and then make the fear work for him. Some of the veiled threats coming at him concerning something palatable served in his mess hall seemed to me to be very real threats from men fully capable of carrying them out.

"If we don't start seeing something in that mess line that makes it worth breaking into a card game for, why then maybe there might be a mistake made in FDC and maybe a round will poop up into the air and come right down on top of your mess tent, Albert," the gunnery sergeant heading up the FDC said as he emptied his mess kit into a GI can.

"Albert," said a staff sergeant who was on perimeter defense and who was the man in charge of positioning the light and heavy machine guns in defense of the camp, "me and my men are going to have machine gun practice right after the noon meal on Thanksgiving Day." There was no real threat you could put your finger on, but, whatever it was, it struck home with force on Albert Truelove.

That was the way of things when the Armenian Jew decided to put his fear to work to his own advantage. Albert Truelove knew he had to take some action, even if it might prove to be the wrong action. He knew that what he really needed was some decent rations. He knew he was a good enough cook to make a decent meal if he had the right ingredients.

Albert Truelove knew that if one word of all the traits that describe a marine NCO was to be selected as the keystone word, that word would have to be "dependable." When he had accepted his corporal stripes as a marine NCO, Albert Truelove was expected to get his job done, and to get it done right, never mind any obstacles that might be in the way.

The real prime mover for Albert Truelove was the trait of decisiveness. He had it hammered into him by his drill instructor at Parris Island: "Get all the facts. Consider the facts carefully. Don't waste time haggling with minor points. Then, and only then, make up your mind about what it is that needs to be done, and then, by God, go ahead and do it."

Albert Truelove knew it was time right now to put into action all the leadership traits he had been taught. He asked Captain Massey if he could leave the company area.

"Captain, what I want to do is see if I can find any of my Armenian Jew cousins in any of these rear-echelon army outfits. I've always scrounged for somebody else all the time; this time I want to scrounge and get something for the mess tent."

"Well, I certainly applaud your view, Corporal Truelove. It surely would be a break for this outfit if we could tap into the army supply system. We certainly do need quite a bit that we can't get through our own supply system.

"While we're on this subject, I liked the way you took the initiative this morning by getting the Coleman lanterns and the white gasoline.

"Too bad about the fire. According to Corporal Stratton, you'll take steps to gain two other tents since the fire was caused by you in some way or another. He explained it so quickly to me, and you know how he can confuse any issue."

That fucking Lob Stratton, thought Albert Truelove.

"Yes, sir, Captain. Other than the tents and decent rations, what do we need most of all? I need to know so I can sort of keep an eye out for it."

"Well—and this is really Corporal Stratton's problem— I'm very concerned over the fact that we don't have any of those new winter boots, those thermo boots the army's been issuing to its troops.

"A lot of our people are going to get frostbite without them . . . the gun crews, especially, what with them being out in all kinds of weather, day and night, and you know how wet it gets in those gun pits. But, Corporal, that really is my problem. Mine and Corporal Stratton's."

"Yessir, I understand, sir. But I'll keep my eyes open. I might find one of my Armenian Jew cousins in the right spot. You never can tell about these things, Captain."

"Perhaps. Well, you asked for the rest of the day off. I'll okay it. If you must stay out of camp overnight, please call back to the switchboard and notify the duty officer."

"Yessir, Captain. There's just one other thing, sir."

"Yes, Corporal."

"Well, sir, I hate to ask, but I was wondering if I could borrow a clean set of your starched dungarees. When I'm with my Armenian Jew cousins I'll be sort of, well, you know, sort of representing the marines and I'd like to give them a good impression. I've been cooking in these dungarees for the past couple of weeks, and they're kind of dirty."

The corners of Captain Massey's mouth sort of turned

down a bit at this unusual request. But fifteen minutes later Albert Truelove was off, walking away from Camp Tripoli in clean, starched dungarees. I hollered to him and he looked back over his shoulder, waving his hand.

I've got to admit that it was the first time I had ever seen Albert Truelove all cleaned up, all freshly shaven. He had even washed his yellow leggings. He was wearing a shiny black holster on his web belt, a .45 automatic tucked carefully inside. Truly, when given the opportunity, Albert Truelove showed a certain panache. I watched him walk away from camp with a sort of dashing elegance to his gait, something totally unexpected from a mess cook. He had a carefree, spirited, self-confident spring to his step and his manner. He looked very military in those clean and starched dungarees with a black globe and anchor neatly stenciled on the left breast pocket. As he strutted off, I could hear him humming the marine corps hymn, and I thought to myself, God help those army Armenian Jew cousins.

Albert Truelove was still waving his hand when he came back to Camp Tripoli very late that same day. He was driving a new U.S. Army jeep, towing a new jeep trailer behind it. Both the trailer and the seats behind and beside Albert Truelove were loaded down, covered over, and tied down with light green tarpaulin sheets.

Albert Truelove drove the jeep and trailer right up to the commanding officer's tent, honking the horn all the while.

"Captain! Captain Massey!" Albert Truelove hollered. "I hit a gold mine right down the road near Wonju, down where the army has their big supply center. One of my cousins is the skipper down there. He's a bird colonel! He gave me anything I wanted. He was a marine buck sergeant in World War Two, and he's a really great guy.

"When I told him I had to borrow a clean uniform from you, Skipper, why, sir, he thought that was decent of you. Look! He gave me a bottle of scotch, the real stuff, to bring back to you."

"That's just great, Corporal," Captain Massey said, holding the bottle up high. "I surely do thank you. But I can't accept it just for myself. We'll water it down and share it with the whole company." There was a great roar of approval from all of us at the generosity of Captain Massey, a great skipper.

"No need to do that, Captain," Albert yelled out. "I brought back the whole case." He flipped up the tarpaulin and showed us the wooden box, minus one bottle. "I've got enough for the entire company to have a drink after a big feast tomorrow." There was an even bigger roar of approval, led by, of all people, Sergeant Baker who, I guess, approved of really good booze as much as the rest of us did.

"What do you have in the trailer, Albert?" someone yelled out.

"Well, for starters, I've got six frozen turkeys, big ones, and a couple of canned hams. I'm gonna start cooking right away."

We really roared out then. Albert Truelove knew just what to say to capture our hearts and minds and stomachs.

The jeep and trailer were quickly unloaded; five sacks of big Idaho potatoes, two sacks of sweet potatoes, three sacks of white rice, three baskets of red apples, cases of corn, tomatoes, spinach, applesauce, and jellied cranberry sauce.

"Be careful lifting out them sacks of white flour from the backseat of the jeep," Albert Truelove cautioned. Beneath the flour, cushioned from the jolting jeep ride, were big glass jars of sweet pickles and pimiento-stuffed green olives. On the passenger seat was a large cardboard box filled with canned spices of all types.

In addition to food, Albert Truelove had brought back a case of heavy wool socks and a case of wool underwear, enough so that everyone in the company would get some.

"But no thermo boots, right, Corporal?"

"Wrong, sir! I can't get enough for the entire company, but I can get enough for all our mortar crews, and the FOs, too. I couldn't load them today. If it's okay with you, I'll go after them next week."

The jeep and trailer were unloaded. Albert Truelove looked at them, hesitantly, and then said: "Oh, uh, Captain. My Armenian Jew cousin, the army colonel, said we could keep the jeep and trailer, if we needed it, and if we would paint it marine corps green, and put our own serial number

192

on it. He even said he had a six-by-six truck we could have, if we needed it, and that I could pick it up on my next trip to see him."

This bit of generosity raised the eyebrows of everyone just a bit. But, since Albert Truelove said he had already been given the marine corps green paint and brushes necessary to the job, no one questioned the gift further.

We started eating well right away. In less than an hour Albert Truelove was emptying his field ovens of some of the best white-flour biscuits—with bits of grated cheddar cheese baked right in them—we had ever had. He quickly broke them open and filled the biscuits with hot chunks of pink ham; it was hog heaven time. We glutted ourselves, and Albert Truelove, wiping greasy hands across his neat, clean borrowed dungarees, looked very pleased with himself, basking as he was in our praise of his culinary skills. He opened cans of real butter and jars of thick golden pineapple jam for the biscuits. Threats were a thing of the past; only accolades showered down on Albert Truelove as he prepared the Thanksgiving Day meal.

Albert visited his army cousin twice more within the next few days. He brought back two light machine guns and one heavy machine gun, along with plenty of ammunition. Everyone who worked in the gun pits, and all the FOs, each got a pair of thermo boots. I felt self-conscious in mine; they were so big, black, and bulbous looking.

He brought back more wool socks, more heavy winter underwear, a couple of cases of olive drab army flannel shirts, two cases of assorted-size woolen gloves, and a good supply of all-weather rubberized trousers. He replenished his mess tent with case after case of canned goods of all types. We repainted the truck marine corps green and, in bright yellow paint, gave it a new serial number.

On his last trip Albert Truelove brought back two very big army enlisted MPs and a rather pompous-acting snit who identified himself to Captain Massey as being an Army Criminal Investigation Department (CID) officer.

"I'm Lieutenant Tracy, of Army CID. Are you the commanding officer here?"

Eyeing Albert Truelove sitting in the rear of the jeep

crowded between the two large enlisted MPs, Captain Massey acknowledged the snit's salute, and said he was the Four Deuce mortar skipper.

Albert looked the worse for wear sitting between those bandbox, perfectly groomed army MPs who could have stood any kind of an inspection and passed it with flying colors. They wore their uniforms proudly, but you could tell they were just rear-echelon pogues, not mud soldiers.

Albert was still wearing the uniform he had borrowed from Captain Massey some two weeks earlier. Not only had the dungarees been through the preparations for a tremendous Thanksgiving Day meal, but through quite a few meals afterward. They were dirty and smeared with grease and other mess tent residue. Quite conspicuously on the collar tabs of the borrowed dungaree jacket was a pair of silver railroad tracks, the rank of a captain. Apparently Albert Truelove had borrowed more than just a pair of clean dungarees from Captain Massey.

The snit was talking: "When we apprehended this man, he was driving an army truck filled with stolen property of an unusual nature, such as sandbags, barbed wire, shovels, picks, axes, rolls of tarpaulin, and such. We never would have stopped him at the supply dump gate except for the fact that it was strange to see a marine captain driving a truck, dressed so very much as you would expect an enlisted man to dress, dirty uniform and all, if you know what I mean," the snit said to Captain Massey, who, if you could read his red face and tightened lips correctly, was getting angrier and angrier.

"We all know officers do not drive trucks and do not look or dress like the ordinary soldier, wouldn't you agree, Captain?" the snit continued, blathering on in a very supercilious manner, a manner that did not fit our skipper at all.

Barely able to contain himself, Captain Massey snarled: "Get to the bottom line, Lieutenant. You apprehended this man, you identified him and brought him back here. What is it you want to have done? Have you already preferred charges? Do you intend to press charges?"

Suddenly feeling the air become electric, the snit looked about him to a sea of tight-lipped faces.

"Actually, Captain, on apprehending this man, I brought him immediately back to your outfit. Since the truck and its contents never left the depot, there was no actual theft. I haven't made any charges. Still, I wanted you to know of his conduct. He was, after all, impersonating a marine officer of captain rank."

"Very good, Lieutenant. I think you saw your duty, and you did it. I thank you for that. I will personally take charge of this matter. There will be no need for you to follow it up with a report in your command, since you have not yet done so. Since it is after the fact, your command might not appreciate it, and neither will I, if you understand what I mean, and I certainly hope you do," Captain Massey said, his voice striking out with a this-is-the-end-of-it tone.

"Well, uh, in that case, sir, I will get on back to my duties," the snit said. His jeep left a cloud of dust on departing the marine compound.

Captain Massey was still looking sternly at Albert Truelove. And then the captain's face broke out in this tremendous ear-to-ear grin.

"Did you really have all that stuff in the back of the truck, Corporal? Damn, but we could have used all of it when we go back up on line next week."

"Yes sir, I sure did. Captain, I've got to tell you, begging your pardon and all, sir, but them army people are all overcome with rank. Those depot soldiers will bust their asses filling a truck for any officer, especially a marine officer who looks like he's been in a war, and no offense meant to you, Captain. All a man has got to do is a lot of yelling and cussing and looking real pissed off, as if you need the stuff right away, and like you have the authority to get anything you need."

"And they got you because you were wearing a dirty uniform, is that it?"

"Well, not the enlisted men, sir. Not the ones working in the depot area. Just them people on the gate. And I didn't have any trouble with them, either, as long as I was wearing

195

a clean uniform. It's just that I've been cooking in these dungarees too long. That Lieutenant Tracy, he acted like he never heard of dirt."

"Corporal Truelove, why didn't you come and get another set of clean dungarees from me?"

"I really didn't want to impose on you, Captain."

Captain Massey remained quietly in thought for a moment. "Tell me, Corporal, are there other army supply units down the road that you have not yet visited?"

"Just one more, Captain. I was saving that one for just before we went back up on line."

"Corporal," said the captain, smiling his fine white-teeth kind of a smile, "why don't you go on up to my tent and get into a clean set of dungarees. Knowing the way the army works, they'll never suspect you coming back down the road again so soon.

"You go get cleaned up. And, uh, by the way, you'll also find a pair of major oak leaves on my table. My wife gave them to me some time back, to wear should I be promoted. I'm certain you'll know what to do with them," Captain Massey said, now wearing the shit-eating grin.

"And, uh, by the way, Corporal Truelove, when we go back on line next week, consider yourself under base restriction for two weeks. That ought to satisfy Lieutenant Tracy, just in case he asks for a follow-up incident report."

CHAPTER
16

"Reddup, frawnt!" The first sergeant who had replaced the Funny Gunny barked out his command to the Four Deuce Mortar Company as we raggedly aligned ourselves in formation on the parade ground at Camp Tripoli. It was the nature of the beast for us to quickly interpret the first sergeant's growl to mean "Ready, front!" This was the command for us to drop our extended and held-shoulder-high left arms. We had only moments before been given the command that caused us to align the company properly, each man taking short side steps until we were all abreast of each other, arms up and extended, stretched-out fingertips touching the shoulders of the man next in line, necks craned so that we faced that man. On the command of execution our heads and eyes snapped forward, our arms snapped down quickly, our backs braced stiffly in the position of attention.

"Persons to be decorated . . . front and center . . . MARCH!"

I sensed movement in the area of the rear ranks. Two men stiffly moved forward; marionettes militarily squaring corners until, in position, they faced Captain Massey.

One of the men was Lob Stratton; he was to be awarded the Purple Heart. I didn't know the other man but had been told he was a radioman who had taken over the duties as an FO, back in February, and had called in some good shots after the assigned FO had been severely wounded; he was to receive the Letter of Commendation.

I tried to hear the words being read from the citations before the medals were pinned on Lob and the other man. But between the snuffling and the coughing and the hacking of the men around me I couldn't hear a thing. A few minutes later the ceremony was finished and the company was marched off the field, headed back to the tent area. This was our last formation together; we were headed back up on line the following day, December 17.

There was a chill to the late-afternoon air and the wind seemed to be picking up. It was a blustery day, one with a cold blue look to it, the look we had come to expect before it snowed. I hoped the snow would hold off until after I got up on Hill 849 with Easy Company. That was my new assignment. We were to relieve the 7th Marines on line. On my map I estimated my new position to be about two miles to the left of where I had last been assigned duties as the FO with Item Company.

Later, that last night in Camp Tripoli, we robbed each other in a nickel-and-dime poker game played in the supply tent; all of us cardplayers were armed with a canteen cup filled with Ben Baker's best two-week-old raisin jack. In the dim light of guttering candles the Lob had smirked and simpered and told how he had gotten his Purple Heart. I almost didn't want to believe him, but everyone else was nodding their heads in agreement.

One of the other FOs, Tom King, a staff sergeant from Texas, said, "That was the way of it, for both the Lob and that radioman of ours. Well, at least one of them deserved his award." King took the last drink from a small silver flask he carried close to his heart.

"I'm not belittling anybody's heroism, but I'm here to tell you that Dugout Doug MacArthur, and at least one other general officer, has screwed up this business of awarding medals. They've taken the challenge out of earning medals in combat, they've cheapened the awarding of medals, and they've made it an easy thing for the undeserving to be heroic.

"It's well known that MacArthur always carried a bunch of medals with him wherever he went. A man had to watch out or Dugout Doug would run him down and stab him in the chest while pinning some kind of a medal on him, and then he'd need to put the guy in for a Purple Heart as well."

King said he knew for a fact that some of the nation's highest and rarest medals for heroism, the Distinguished Service Cross—which usually was awarded for extraordinary heroism, usually against an armed enemy—and the Silver Star—which usually was awarded for gallantry in action—were often awarded to ranking officers who, apparently, did not qualify for the award.

King said, "MacArthur has given out so many medals, those two in particular, that they seem to be neither so highly nor so rarely placed.

"Air Force Lieutenant General George Stratemeyer seems to be competing with Dugout Doug in handing them out. To my way of thinking, it makes the getting of them seem cheap and easy, and that ain't right, especially to the men who earn them, really earn them."

King said he had his facts right: "I read about it in *Time* last February. That magazine's never wrong."

According to the magazine article, King said, MacArthur had awarded a Silver Star to his surgeon general and his chief of intelligence. The reason, if any, for awarding these men the Silver Star was not provided in the article, "but try to imagine either man performing gallantly in a combat action." King made a put-down face. "It just doesn't go with the jobs those men have been assigned."

King said, "Later, during the Inchon landing, MacArthur was coming into the beach aboard a landing craft, following too close on the heels of the marine landing party, when—and, mind you, I'm not taking any credit away from MacArthur, he's a tough old bird, always looking for a fight—he was persuaded by Vice Admiral Arthur D. Struble, the Seventh Fleet commander, not to get any closer to the beach at that time.

"You got any idea who was later awarded the Distinguished Service Cross by MacArthur? The records will bear me out when I tell you that, heroically speaking, Struble did little more than stand on the bridge of his ship, and in a calm sea at that."

King continued, "Vice Admiral C. Turner Joy, the Far East naval commander, got his MacArthur-awarded Distinguished Service Cross, too. God only knows how he qualified for extraordinary heroism against an armed enemy."

I could see by his glazed eyes that King was really hitting his silver flask a lick.

"When MacArthur finally got ashore at Inchon, one of the first things he did was to pass out three Silver Stars to three marine officers. Apparently in a show of United Nations support, he stopped two South Korean naval officers, who just happened to be passing by, and gave each of them the Silver Star, too.

"Gallantry in action, that's what it was all about."

King bummed a cigarette, choked while lighting it, and then said, "MacArthur and Stratemeyer almost got into a daisy chain with their awards."

MacArthur, King said, gave Stratemeyer a Distinguished Service Cross for "continually subjecting himself to great danger" when Stratemeyer was said to have been "directing the evacuation of U.S. civilians from advanced airfields."

"Now you tell me the last time you saw three big Silver Stars directing air traffic for civilians on an advanced airfield.

"And here's the kicker: Stratemeyer turns around and awards MacArthur the Distinguished Flying Cross for either heroism, or extraordinary achievement, or maybe both, while participating in an aerial flight. Stratemeyer's write-up for the award said MacArthur's flying visits to Korea were made under conditions presenting the threat of hostile air interception.

"Whooee! Now ain't that a kick in the ass! All I can say is that you can now roll me over, in the clover, lay me down, and do it to me again."

King told us that a check of air force records showed that

Stratemeyer was no chintz when it came to awarding medals of distinction to his own men, either.

"Back in his headquarters in Japan, Stratemeyer awarded Silver Stars to seven of the officers on his staff. A brigadier general got his Silver Star for 'assuring the constant and uninterrupted flow of material,' and, golly gee! girls, ain't that something?

"Other officers got their Silver Star awards for being subject to enemy air and ground attack 'during their occasional flying trips' to Korea."

King was bleary-eyed by this time, and his silver flask was nearly empty. "I'm gonna hit the rack, folks. You people have won all my money and I've got a long day tomorrow. I'm going up with Baker Company. You take care, Cautious. Be careful you don't get around some of the army and air force generals and get your back knocked outta shape carrying around any medals they might award you.

"Better yet, why don't you let the Lob tell you all about how he got his Purple Heart?" King lurched out of the supply tent and headed for the last good night's sleep he would get for a month or so.

I knew that Lob Stratton got his nickname because of what he had hanging between his legs. For such a small guy, he had about the biggest lob in the Four Deuces. So it was only natural that we called him the "Lob." He, too, had started out his time in the Four Deuces as a wireman.

Lob was wounded as a wireman. On receipt of his Purple Heart, Lob asked for and got the job as the company supply chief. He didn't want to tempt fate—in the form of a bullet or shrapnel—again.

I knew that a lot of grunts poked fun at the Purple Heart, saying the only thing it really signified was a fast-moving piece of metal and a slow-moving grunt. The Lob proved there was a lot more to getting the Purple Heart than meets the eye.

According to regulations, medals and decorations were to be awarded to military men for acts of bravery, outstanding service, taking part in a war or campaign, or being wounded. The Purple Heart was the first medal for bravery

201

to be awarded to the common soldier. Established by George Washington during the Revolutionary War in 1782, the medal was initially called the Badge of Military Merit; it acknowledged "singular meritorious action."

The Purple Heart in its modern form is conferred on any person wounded in action while serving with the U.S. Armed Forces. It is awarded posthumously to the next of kin of those who were killed or who died of wounds received in combat action.

The present day Purple Heart medal is still heart-shaped; it is the best known and one of the most beautiful of the U.S. military decorations.

The key factor behind the Purple Heart medal is that the recipient must have been either wounded or killed in action against an enemy in a combat zone. There are a lot of marines who have the medal who would not have rated it if the letter of the law, wounded by enemy action, had been taken quite literally. Lob Stratton qualified for his Purple Heart, figuratively.

Granted, the Lob was hit by the jagged edge of an exploding projectile during a combat engagement in Korea and, granted, if measured from end to end the Lob probably had the longest scar in the outfit, a thin, ragged scar well over three feet long. Nothing serious was cut when the Lob was hit, but it could have been the worst thing to have happened to him in his young life.

The card game was now forgotten and Lob Stratton, a two-canteen man working on his third canteen cupful of Ben Baker's best, was telling me just how it was the day he got his Purple Heart.

"We had been movin' out all day long, from real early in the morning. We walked a lot, mostly jockeying back and forth, and we hadn't gone far. I don't believe we had covered more than maybe half a mile or so. I was the telephone man for Captain Massey. And I'm here to tell you that he either ran, walked, creeped, or crawled over every bit of that half mile. Mind you, we were behind the grunts. The grunts had a good lead on us, but we still had lots of gooks in the area, and we were catchin' a round or two every so often."

The Lob wet his whistle with a sip from his canteen. "We

got to an open area that had some worthwhile defensible positions, an area that would do okay for our guns. The captain wanted to check it all out, so back and forth he went, and I was humpin' right along with him, keepin' in contact with the company switchboard through this EE-8 I was carryin' and what felt like three, maybe four thousand pounds of telephone wire I was carryin' on my back and layin' down as fast as I could through them disposable reels, you know the ones I mean, they call them doughnut reels because of the way they're shaped."

Lob said it was late in the afternoon when Captain Massey telephoned for the troops to move into their new positions, to find a good spot that had plenty of firing room on all sides, to set up the mortars and dig in their defensive positions.

"The Old Man told the Funny Gunny—remember him? a real great guy—well, he told the Funny Gunny to pass the word that any food or rations that we had brought with us could be heated and eaten as soon as we got our fightin' holes squared away.

"That's when I got my Purple Heart. Right when we were heatin' up our rations. All I had was a can of meat and beans. I'm gonna tell you true, I was some kind of hungry, and a hungry man will eat just about anything."

The Lob took another few swallows from his canteen and continued, "You know how you heat up rations when you're on the move. You sort of dig up the ground a bit, chunk it up, and you pour some gasoline over the dug-up dirt, and then you light it off. And then you stick your can of rations into the gasoline flames. That's what I did, anyway. Only I was so tired I forgot to puncture my can first, you know, to let the steam out."

The Lob said five or six guys from the company, the captain and the Funny Gunny included, were all sitting around the edge of the fire waiting for their rations to heat up. "We was sort of squattin' like the gooks do when they rest, sittin' down on our hunkers, our knees spread wide open for balance, and our asses restin' on the heels of our boondockers. We were like a bunch of yobo workers sittin' around that fire."

In the meantime, the unpunctured can of meat and beans was sitting in the middle of the blue gasoline flames, and the can was getting hotter and hotter. "It seemed like it just sort of swelled all up, its sides bulgin' out and the top gettin' puffier," the Lob said. "Well, that can of deadly three meat and beans finally exploded. I mean to say it came shootin' out from the fire with its top all blown out, meat and beans gettin' impaled on the jagged end of the can."

The Lob sipped his drink, chuckling, lost in memory.

"BOOM!" said the Lob, waving his arms about in a boom fashion, "that can came right at me. It hit me just inside my right knee and it traveled around the inside of my legs because of the way I was sittin', cuttin' and gougin' its way around in a semicircle, and then it tore away from my left knee and headed straight back into the fire area, hittin' and scatterin' all the rations like crazy. It was like a mortar round going off . . . BOOM!"

The Lob said it took about a quarter of a second for everybody in the immediate area to get on their bellies, weapons in their hands, everybody ready to shoot it out with the gooks. "As soon as that can came boomin' out of the fire, and in almost the same moment goin' right back into it again, Captain Massey was yellin', 'FIRE IN THE HOLE! FIRE IN THE HOLE!' like he knew for certain we had just gotten an incoming round of mortar fire.

"In the meantime," Lob Stratton said, "I was still sort of hunkered down in that Korean squat, fingerin' around among the meat and beans, and the cut dungarees, and the jagged edge where I had been scratched all around on the inside of my thighs. I was bleedin', mind you, really bleedin', but it looked a whole lot worse than what it really turned out to be. Still and all, I was fingerin' around down in my crotch area hopin' against hope that I wouldn't come up with even the tiniest part of my family jewels. That jagged end of the meat-and-beans can cut me about a quarter-inch deep in a couple spots."

The Lob smirked: "Lucky for me I got such a small pecker or I would've been in trouble."

According to the Lob, Captain Massey put himself in a tight spot when he yelled out "FIRE IN THE HOLE!" That kind of a yell always signifies that you are sending out some of your own rounds or, worse luck, that you are on the receiving end of some incoming rounds.

"It was the first bad call the captain made all day. I've got to hand it to that guy, he was some kind of a hustler the way he kept going. For about ten, maybe twelve hours under constant fire, he made all the right decisions.

"So you see, even while the corpsman was scrapin' away all that meat and beans I got loaded in my crotch area so he could get a bandage on me, we all sort of got to act like it really was a gook mortar shell and not just a can of deadly three meat and beans that fucked up our meal. Nobody wanted to see Captain Massey humiliated," the Lob said. "The captain called it a gook mortar round, and since he was the boss, why then we all called it a gook mortar round."

I sort of shook my head over the story.

The Lob, with a big grin all over his face, said, "Can you beat that, Cautious? Two weeks in a Japanese hospital and the Purple Heart all because of a hot can of meat and beans.

"I call it singular meritorious action. I sure wished either MacArthur or Stratemeyer had been sitting around that fire. I wonder what I would've gotten from them."

CHAPTER
17

It took the first dead grunt to make believers out of the rest of Easy Company. We had been told about Luke and Luke-the-Gook's castle first thing that late December morning, some four hours before the first man became a casualty at about 0700. It was almost as if Luke the Gook had waited for the pink of dawn's early light to shoot out the lights of a red-eyed grunt. The Easy Company rifleman died with a large-caliber bullet entering just below his helmet and directly above his nose. A perfect killing shot, the round then exited through a large hole in the back of his head, scattering bone, brains, blood, and blond hair all over the sandbags of the trench line behind him. That's all it took, the brains of one man, and we all learned our lesson the hard way, as I suspect the marines we were relieving had learned before us.

When we relieved grunts of the 7th Marines at their covered fighting holes in the trench line of Hill 849, they tried to give us the word. They said that we really didn't want to fuck around with Luke the Gook when he was in his castle. The word was that our grunts could man the fighting holes on Hill 849 during daylight hours, but Luke the Gook controlled the trench line access routes to those holes. Sitting in covered and well-concealed sniping positions, positions so located in a large outcropping of granite that he could fire at will at us and yet still be in defilade, unable to be harmed by our return rifle fire, Luke the Gook was the man who decided when Easy Company grunts could use their trench line.

"He's got you bore-sighted with a Russian-made 61-millimeter antipersonnel and antitank rifle. You better move fast in the trench line on the eastern side of the hill, and you better keep your ass way down because he shoots through sandbags" was the word that had been passed on to us.

At about the time I was getting the red-ass treatment from Easy Company grunts because of my huge, bulbous-looking black rubber thermal boots, that was when the booming sound of a large-bore rifle shattered both the morning calm and the young grunt's head. Me, and Soupy Campbell, my radioman, and Billy Baxter, my telephone man, were the only three marines on Hill 849 who had the outsized winter boots, thanks to Albert Truelove. The three of us fumbled and stumbled with awkward steps through the trench line, passing grunt after grunt in their firing holes. We finally regrouped where the kid was being looked at by a grim-faced corpsman.

"Get your asses down!" the Easy Company first sergeant said, and just as he barked his command we heard the outsized boom again and a round hit the radio on Soupy Campbell's back, ricocheting off with the whining of a missed shot, and knocking Campbell on his butt in the trench line.

"Can you get him?" the first sergeant asked me, nodding his head in the direction of Hill 975, as he continued to supervise other grunts in removing the young kid's body to a more protected area.

I had absolutely no idea where to shoot; no one had seen any movement by Luke the Gook at this time. I plastered the hard rock area with a dozen or more rounds, and barely scratched the granite surface of the castle. I established three concentrations in and around the spot known as Luke-the-

Gook's castle. Later in the day, I would know exactly where Luke the Gook had his sniper holes, for all the good knowing did.

Luke-the-Gook's castle—the name was appropriate. In a great outcropping of granite halfway up the slope of Hill 975, a mountain area to our front owned and operated by the North Korean People's Army, an area of unyielding firmness and endurance, the gooks had enhanced natural characteristics of the terrain with man-made entrenchments. Their sniping holes were constructed of logs and sandbags impregnably positioned in and around the hard igneous rock. They had constructed killing spots on the living mountain. The name Luke-the-Gook's castle would come to signify to us a keep for killing, a tower of terror.

With the help of Easy Company grunts looking for the sniper positions and informing the FOs of them, it was determined that the North Koreans were using at least three different shooting locations in the castle area. Riflemen there commanded an easy-shooting, easy-killing view of more than half our trench line. Fortunately, our fighting holes were protected, covered over with planks and sandbags. Unfortunately, the slug from the 61mm sniper gun could pass through one sandbag and still kill. Getting to the fighting holes during the daylight hours was a real man-killing proposition. Easy Company grunts countered Luke the Gook by using the British Army system called "stand to." Under this system, the men would go to their firing holes half an hour before dawn, while it was still dark, and stay in their firing holes until half an hour after dusk, when there was no light for Luke the Gook to see or aim by. The disadvantage of stand to was that once a grunt was in his protected firing hole, he had to stay there all day, or else risk being sniped at while moving in the trench line.

In retaliation, word was passed by the Easy Company first sergeant: "Any time we get a round in on us, I want everyone on line to fire at least five rounds at Luke-the-Gook's castle. That should give them gooks a return of about a hundred to one on bullets fired." This was sound infantry procedure against the most common type of sniper, but not against Luke the Gook.

Snipers usually are well-concealed marksmen who shoot from a range of 250 to 300 yards. Generally, the sniper is used as a harassing element, shooting a single, sometimes a second aimed and directed shot at a selected target from a hidden position. The sniper, after firing, normally moves quickly to another preselected position and perhaps fires again. A large volume of quickly returned rifle fire usually discourages and sometimes, through a lucky shot, kills the sniper, according to the Easy Company first sergeant, a man who seemed to know about these things.

But with Luke the Gook it was a different story. He used three well-protected holes, and no amount of rifle, machine gun, mortar, or artillery rounds was going to hurt him. Like a turtle, Luke the Gook would pull back into his protective shell and wait out the return fire. All we were really doing with the return fire was giving relief to our frustrations while diminishing our ammunition supply, which had to be replenished daily.

Under the glare of a cold winter sun on that clear blue and ice-cold late December day, just a week or so before Christmas 1951, the first day of many we would spend on Hill 849, Easy Company grunts saw how Luke the Gook operated.

The three firing positions we had spotted were placed with skill near the outer edges of the granite rock location of the "castle." The enemy sniper positions apparently commanded an excellent view of a large portion of the trench line we used on Hill 849. Armed with a Russian-made antipersonnel rifle of tremendous proportions and firing a large-caliber slug, a rifle made further deadly with a specially mounted sniper-scope, two men worked as a team in dealing out death. One man would throw the front end of the huge rifle (its large barrel exceeded four feet) out in front of the sniper's hole; a second man, the shooter, would quickly position the rifle, line it up on a target, and then slowly squeeze the trigger. As quickly as the rifle had been flung out into a firing position, it was retrieved, but by way of pulling on a wire connected around the barrel, dragging the weapon back to the sniper pit. The whole operation took about five seconds.

209

Actually, Luke the Gook tried to shoot Purple Heart bullets. His rifle slug was big enough to maim or seriously injure any grunt it hit. His purpose was only to wound a grunt, and then be afforded an opportunity to shoot again, and again, into those who came to give aid to the wounded man. As men moved the wounded grunt through the trench line, more and more of them became exposed to the sniper's eye. An infantryman helping a wounded man was not a threat; so it figured that the more grunts Luke the Gook could wound, the fewer men we would have available as a force in our fighting holes. Luke the Gook played a vicious game on his castle grounds. He would play a still more vicious game.

The day before Christmas, a murky cold day, Easy Company got a present in the form of the Candy Bar Kidd, possibly the best marksman in the division. It had been decided to fight fire with fire, pitting our best sniper against what apparently were some of their best marksmen. Easy Company had already lost eight men to Luke the Gook's sharpshooting—two KIA and six very badly WIA. Morale on the eastern side of Hill 849, which had been plummeting, soared with the arrival of the Candy Bar Kidd.

He was just a kid, for all that implied. He had the face of a boy, but his eyes had seen something; they belonged to another time, another place. A quiet kid, he wasn't talking about what gave him that look to his eyes. He had the quiet manner of someone who, it seemed, wouldn't say "shit!" even if he had a mouthful, but somehow no one wanted to provoke him into saying even that. There was a swagger, a confidence, and a hardness to him. He was a minor celebrity, and marines like to pin names—easy-to-say and easy-to-remember names—on their celebrities. His real name was Charles Browning Kidd, shortened to C. B. Kidd. When he went out on a sniping assignment—always alone and generally for a couple of days in front of our main line of resistance—the Candy Bar Kidd took as rations two canteens of water and a pocketful of the flat gumdrop type of candy disks that came in C rations. It was a natural for us to change the C. B. initials of his name into Candy Bar.

The Candy Bar Kidd had earned his reputation as a

marksman in both interservice and international shooting matches, in civilian- and military-sponsored large- and small-bore competitions. He was an expert marksman with the military .45-caliber automatic. He shot in a peculiar manner by holding his weapon straight-armed out in front, the other arm, his left arm, cocked at an angle on his hip. He would stand sideways to his target, presenting only a profile of himself. Sure, a lot of marines used that position to fire a .45-caliber automatic. The Candy Bar Kidd, however, held his automatic horizontally out in front of him, not vertically like everyone else. Ask the Candy Bar Kidd why he shot that way and he would tell you: "I don't know. It just feels natural for me to do so." As far as the Marine Corps was concerned, he could hold his weapon with his feet as long as he consistently shot high expert, and that's what the Candy Bar Kidd shot, high expert, dropping just a few points, never more than three, in championship matches.

While the Candy Bar Kidd was great with a sidearm, he was clearly the best rifle shot in the Marine Corps, and he proved himself on rifle ranges throughout the world. It was unusual for the Candy Bar Kidd to drop even two points in a large-bore match. Generally, the Candy Bar Kidd fired a perfect score, centering his bull's-eye shots within the small center-core black, placing shot after shot within millimeters of each other at ranges exceeding five hundred yards. He was truly a shooting machine.

The Marine Corps permitted the Candy Bar Kidd to carry his rifle with him wherever he was stationed. He carried only the standard M1 rifle, slightly modified. The main modification dealt only with the sear of the rifle. The Candy Bar Kidd would file away on the sear until all he really had to do, when shooting, was think about pulling back on the trigger; then CRACK, another round was on its way, dead on target.

"If you're gonna fuck up on a shot—miss what you're shootin' at—chances are it's because you're anticipating the shot, you're aware of the five-to-seven-pound pull on the trigger. And while you're thinkin' about the pull, chances are you're gonna let the front sight drift, and if you do that, chances are you'll screw up a good shot," was the way he explained why he filed his rifle sear to the point of it having less than a pound of pressure release.

"You've got to concentrate on the shot you're taking. When you're shooting, nothing else should matter to you at all. Nothing should distract you in any way. The only thing of any importance occupying your mind should be the lining up of your sights, your rear sight and your front sight, on the target." That seemed to be the creed of the Candy Bar Kidd.

He was quiet, making about as much noise as a shadow would, moving about in the dark of night. I found out that you knew where the Candy Bar Kidd was located only when he wanted you to know. He seemed as expert a stalker as he was a shooter, moving effortlessly and noiselessly. He seemed spooky, if that's the right word to use, and I was glad he was on my side.

"Are you Cautious?" he said. The Candy Bar Kidd was standing right at my side in the FO bunker. He startled me. I had been standing at the parapet of the bunker, my binoculars to my eyes, studying Luke-the-Gook's castle area. Maybe I had been concentrating too hard looking out there, but it was the first time anyone ever came into a bunker where I was on watch when I was not aware of their arrival. When he asked his question in his quiet voice, he really startled me.

"Yeah. Who are you?" I asked. And he told me his name.

"I wanted to check in with you FOs over the next day or so, to sort of let you know where I would be out there. Do I need to speak with all of you, the artillery and the 81s, too, or will you tell them?"

I said I would pass the word on to those who needed to know it. With that out of the way, the Candy Bar Kidd pointed in the general direction of areas well in front of Luke-the-Gook's castle, yet still in front of our lines. The two of us agreed on times and general area locations.

When the Candy Bar Kidd and I talked in the FO bunker on Hill 849, I realized he was different in more than just his ways and manners; he was unique in his uniform as well. He was not wearing the washed-out, bleached-white, formerly green herringbone twill dungarees the rest of us wore. So help me, his battle uniform was made of a dozen or more

212

camouflage helmet covers, all taken apart at the seams and resewn together into a jacket with large pockets at the sides, and trousers with equally large pockets at the sides and rear. His soft cap was made of the same camouflage material. The only incongruity was a red bandana, which he wore around his neck.

"I can turn them inside out—I had them made that way—and have the darker green camouflage, or I can wear this washed-out light brown side," the Candy Bar Kidd said, adding that he needed to "blend in with the surroundings. You won't see me when I'm working."

We talked a bit more, the Candy Bar Kidd telling me that I might hear his shots, perhaps even see the flash of burning gunpowder during the night.

"You won't see much, or hear much either. I don't like to kill people. But if I have to kill them, then I like to do it quickly. If I can—and I usually make sure that I can—I do it with a single shot. I try for their head, if they aren't wearing a helmet, or for their heart. I prepare my own bullets. One will do the job."

After we had agreed on areas where he might be located during the next forty-eight hours, I gave my attention back to the right side of Hill 849.

"We've been giving Luke the Gook most of our attention since we came up on the hill. And that gave the main force of gooks over on Hill 975 an advantage. They hit us last night and kicked ass on the other side of this hill," I said. "They got close enough to throw some concussion grenades into a fighting hole. I think they wanted to take a prisoner back with them."

Easy Company fought back, I said. "We chased the gooks off after a firefight. As far as I know, we only had two grunts wounded. They had busted eardrums."

I expected the Candy Bar Kidd to make some comment, and when he did not, I took my binoculars down from my eyes and turned, looking toward where he had been standing. He was gone. He had departed as silently as he had arrived. I had no idea how long I had been talking to myself.

There were some rifle shots during the night, mostly

coming from scared kids in our fighting holes, some shooting at shadows, some shooting at noises in the night. And right after those single shots, or maybe a burst of shots from an automatic weapon, there would be a platoon sergeant all over somebody, pissed off with this breach in fire discipline: "Use a fuckin' grenade, asshole! Nobody can tell where a grenade is thrown from. It ain't got a fuckin' muzzle blast to give it away! How many times do I hafta tell you that, you fuckin' asshole?"

I suspected that a few of those shots heard in the night might have been from the Candy Bar Kidd. I hoped so, anyway. I hoped he could get rid of those sharpshooting gooks in the castle area.

True to his word, no one saw the Candy Bar Kidd out in front of our lines while he was working. But on his second night out we heard him.

Wounded men make different sounds—depending on the extent of their wounds—but nothing compares to the moaning-mewling sound a wounded man makes when he is out beyond your reach and he knows he can't bandage himself, restricted, maybe, because he has broken bones. The slightly wounded marine—and even some of the more seriously wounded—know they have a good chance to make it if a corpsman can get to them soon enough. They are the ones who make the crying sounds, sounds torn from their throats, sounds they later are ashamed of having made, sounds they make as they plead and beg to be rescued. The grunt who has the more serious wounds, the guy who is trying to hold his guts in place, or who is strangling on his own blood because he has no jaw, or who can't breathe because of the holes in his chest, or can't move to you because he hasn't any legs, the grunt who knows there is no way for him to recover from his wounds, he's the guy who begs, piteously, for release from his agony. A lot of times corpsmen give them morphine shots, plenty of morphine shots, and a lot of times someone else has to give them shots, too, just one or two.

A grunt holding down the fighting hole closest to Luke-the-Gook's castle first heard the moans an hour before dawn. The sounds were of someone in mortal agony; they were strange-sounding moans, not words, really, just moans of someone hurt, very badly hurt.

The 81mm mortar FO popped a couple flares over the castle area. Hissing high overhead, the flares swung pendulumlike, swinging a bluish magnesium light that cast great shadows eerily between our lines. We couldn't see anything. The moans continued. It was the sound of a man greatly filled with pain and distress of both his body and mind.

We were all praying—and nothing is more sincere than a prayer from a fighting hole—that it would not be the Candy Bar Kidd we were hearing. But we knew it was him.

Someone in ripped and torn camouflage dungarees was spread-eagled on his back in the flat, open area in front of the main Luke-the-Gook's castle. The arms and legs of whoever was there were widespread and staked to the ground. The communication wire used in this crucifixion dug deep into the flesh of the wrists and ankles, pulling the limbs straight.

Those of us who had binoculars could not remove them from our eyes. We stared at the grisly sight.

The face of whoever it was—and Easy Company grunts knew exactly who it was out there—was definitely that of a Caucasian with blond hair. Through the magnification of the binocular lens, I could see that the puffy face had no eyelids, no nose, no ears, and no lips. The camouflage jacket was ripped open; the rips down his chest and stomach opened to puffy, purple-gray, sluggish worms of intestines pushing through the long slashes. The crotch area of his trousers was hacked out; he was butchered, and whatever had distinguished him as **a m**an was no longer there. We could see no toes on his shoeless feet, no fingers or thumbs on his hands.

And yet this body moved. Like a grotesque marionette, it twitched convulsively.

Easily seen were the booby-trap wires leading from the arms, the legs, the neck of the tortured soul to the cast-iron serrated body of a fragmentation grenade. There was just enough slack in the wires to prevent the Candy Bar Kidd from pulling the grenade pins. In agony, there on the

215

ground, the Candy Bar Kidd thrashed and pulled as best he could, wanting to pull the grenade pins, wanting to end his torment. The gooks who did this were experts; they tortured not only the body of the Candy Bar Kidd, but his mind as well. And in torturing him, they tormented all of our minds; we could not shut out his sounds, we felt his agony and we knew we would long remember this day.

At the head of the mutilated body was an M1 rifle with a sniper's scope attached, the bayonet jammed into the ground. The red bandana of the Candy Bar Kidd was fastened to the butt plate, a challenging flag to our guts and integrity and maybe our stupid pride.

Marine grunts had it drilled into them, time and again, that the marines take care of their own: "Nobody gets left behind, not the dead, not the wounded." There was this unwritten pledge of loyalty among marines; nobody would ever be left behind, no matter what had to be done. You didn't need to like a man living; but you knew you could not break faith with him dead. In the marines, grunts would make a corpse of themselves trying to retrieve the body of another marine. If men would do this for a corpse, imagine what they would do for someone alive, someone they cared for and respected.

It was good knowing that; it was good knowing that someone would come get us if we were wounded or killed. Easy Company grunts would go out after the Candy Bar Kidd. This was our creed. It was what marines lived by in combat and, sometimes, why marines died in combat.

The gooks knew this too, and they were going to make us pay for having all that trust in each other.

An Easy Company grunt alerted the company that Christmas Day morning. He cried out: "Oh, shit, no! Them fucking gooks have got a body staked out in front of Luke-the-Gook's castle! Somebody get the captain and the first sergeant down here, on the double!"

Minutes later, another grunt, binoculars to his eyes, shouted out: "Oh, fuck! It's the Candy Bar Kidd! Goddamnit! It looks like the Candy Bar Kidd!"

That word passed electrifyingly from fighting hole to fighting hole, from bunker to bunker.

The company commander and first sergeant rumbled through the trench line, hunkered over, with shouts of "Get outta the way! Get outta the way!" In a crowded fighting hole they studied the grim scene.

"Is he dead, Top?" the captain asked the first sergeant.

"God knows he oughta be, but he ain't."

"He's bait, isn't he?"

"He sure as hell is, Skipper."

"We'll lose more men going after him, won't we?"

"Yes, sir, we sure will."

"Advise me, goddamnit! Don't just agree with me! Tell me what we should do."

"What we should do is call in some Four Deuce fire and just obliterate him and every goddamn thing else that's out there, Captain!"

"But we won't do that, will we, First Sergeant?"

"No, sir. That ain't our way. You know it. I know it. And every goddamn grunt on this hill knows it. Those goddamn gooks know it, too. That's why the Candy Bar Kidd is pegged out like that. It's the only reason why he's still alive!"

"How many men do you figure we'll lose, Top?"

"Just as many as it takes to go out there and get him—or what's left of him—and bring him back to our lines, Captain. And not one man more than that, however many it might be. I ain't no fortune-teller. But I can tell you this, there are some grunts here in these trenches that have only a little bit of future left to them."

"That's the way marines do it, right, First Sergeant?"

"If the Candy Bar Kidd is still living—and it don't make a big rat's ass whole lot of difference whether he's living or he ain't—we got to go out and get him. He's out there. He's one of us, and we sent him out there. We'd expect him to come get us if we were there, so we gotta go out there and get him and it don't really matter if he's dead or alive when we get to him. That's the way it's done, Skipper," the first sergeant said. He sighed a great big heaving sigh and his lips sort of tightened up and I could almost feel him thinking about his wife and two kids. "I'll take the first bunch out."

The first sergeant asked the platoon sergeant for five volunteers; the platoon sergeant said he could easily get four more men. I volunteered to go with them. I knew full well that I would be turned down and I was turned down. I knew it was my job to shoot the Four Deuces and I knew it was the job of an Easy Company grunt to go out and get the Candy Bar Kidd. All of a sudden I felt ashamed of myself. I felt flushed and I shivered, pretending the shiver was from the cold, knowing it was from the tickle of a yellow feather.

Sure, okay, I had played the role. I had volunteered. The captain had taken note of it. But deep inside me I felt ashamed that I had volunteered knowing full well that I would not be selected. I wondered if I would have the guts to volunteer, like those young grunts did, had there been a chance, a real chance, that I might have been selected to go with them on this very dangerous assignment.

My job was to put some smoke, lots of smoke, on the area. I quickly called for a fire mission, gave my concentration number, requested five rounds of WP, and in less than two minutes my smoke was impacting, billowing up, clouding everything with a pure white. I ordered one WP round to be fired every thirty seconds in the same area, right in front of Luke-the-Gook's castle.

In the trench line closest to the castle area the captain asked the first sergeant, implying with his words the question of whether or not the older man still packed the gear, the strength, necessary to going out and bringing back the Candy Bar Kidd.

"Can you do it, Top?"

"I can do it, Captain."

And with that the first sergeant, the platoon sergeant, and four grunts from Easy Company were up and over the trench, heading into the smoke.

The gooks—those crafty bastards—used our smoke to hide their movements. They came down in strength to the area where the Candy Bar Kidd was anchored to the ground. In our trench line we could hear the frantic, fearful, hand-to-hand fighting with men shooting, stabbing, gouging, killing each other, close enough to each other to see both fear and terror in the eyes of their enemy.

Five times that morning Easy Company grunts went out into purgatory in groups of six men each. The second patrol brought back the mortally wounded first sergeant, still alive but fading fast from both bullet wounds and bayonet slashes.

"Get him back, Captain! He's dead! Now, he's dead! Bring him back!"

Later, other men would confirm that the first sergeant had gotten to within five feet of the Candy Bar Kidd, close enough to shoot the Candy Bar Kidd five times with his .45-automatic pistol.

There were no heroics in sending out the five patrols of men. As each group went out, they passed others who had gone before them coming back in or being brought back in. There were no heroics beyond that of one man willing to give his own life for someone else.

"I got close enough to tie a rope around his ankle," the platoon sergeant said. He had gone out four times. He would lose his right hand, one of the hands that had tied the rope around the ankle of the Candy Bar Kidd. The pin had pulled out of the grenade tied to the ankle when he had knotted his rope. The platoon sergeant had grabbed for the grenade to throw it when it went off, leaving him with a bloody stump.

The last patrol went out and pulled on the rope. The patrol had taken empty burlap sandbags with them. Three of the sandbags were filled and bloody when they dragged them back.

Including the Candy Bar Kidd and the first sergeant, Easy Company lost four more men KIA and ten WIA on that terrible Christmas Day 1951.

The day after Christmas we were still getting sniper shots on the trench line on the east side of the mountain. All three of Luke-the-Gook's sniper positions were back in business. We still hunkered down when we moved in the trench line.

CHAPTER
18

One of the two Luke-the-Gook casualties that Easy Company suffered the day after Christmas died soon after being evacuated to the MASH hospital at Yong-Dong-Po. He was a new second lieutenant, new to Korea and new to Easy Company. No one even knew his name. But everyone knew that twenty-four hours earlier he had gone out to help bring back the Candy Bar Kidd. The other casualty was a grunt Pfc who had been taking a leak in one of the trench-line piss tubes when he was shot clean through his chest, a real messy hit that was going to get him home.

Luke the Gook had to go. Easy Company just didn't want to keep on taking casualties at his whim. Since conventional infantry weapons had little or no effect on the three known and mainly used sniper positions, some other method was needed to bore-sight in on him and blow him right out of his socks. Since Easy Company was assigned to defend Hill 849 for another two months—until their scheduled relief off line at some time during late February—ideas on how to do the job were discussed.

In conference with his platoon leaders immediately following the evacuation of the grunt Pfc and after the rescue team had been fired upon and, surprisingly enough, missed by Luke the Gook, the Easy Company commander said he was having an M-26 tank brought up Hill 849.

The word was passed. We started making bets on how long the tank was going to last on the hill, and then we made bets on how long we were going to last after the North Koreans were fired upon by the tank. The NKPA forward observers would make our lives a living hell of shrapnel from their mortar and artillery rounds soon after the tank fired. That was a foregone conclusion not hard to reach. We all opted for another layer of sandbags on our bunkers.

It wasn't as though tanks had not been used to help out the grunts in the past. It was the concept the Easy Company commander wanted to try out that was new.

"I want to use the tank as a sniper rifle," the Easy Company commander said. He explained the tank would bore-sight in on its target, and that its only targets would be the three Luke-the-Gook sniper positions. He said he wanted the tank gunner to open the breech of his 90mm gun, look through the barrel straight at each of the three Luke-the-Gook sniper positions, and then fire up to ten rounds of high-explosive shells at each position.

"That oughta shake their shit," the Easy Company commander said, adding, "We've got to be prepared to protect the tank once it gets up on the hill."

To do that, it would be necessary to construct one hell of a big bunker. He put a hard-working staff NCO in charge of the job, a platoon sergeant with a grudge, a man who had already lost three men to Luke the Gook.

"You figure it out. You tell me what we'll need. I'll get it. You use it. And then the tankers can do their job for us," the Easy Company commander said.

Late that afternoon supply trucks brought quite a few pieces of L-shaped quarter-inch angle iron, each twelve feet long with four-inch flanges. Laid side by side with their ninety-degree angle pointing upward to form the ceiling of a bunker, each piece of angle iron would cover a six-inch span. Most of the angle iron would be used on the bunker top, supporting five layers of sandbags; the remaining angle iron would be used for side reinforcement of the mammoth bunker needed to house the M-26.

The supply trucks also dropped off fifteen hundred sandbags, tied in bundles of fifty. Picks, long-handled shovels, sledgehammers, and mallets were delivered. A team of forty Korean yobo laborers would be marched to the area under protective guard at about 1900, just as soon as it was dark. Since the artificial moonlight would not be turned on until after midnight, the yobos would have five hours of darkness to move the materiel up the hill.

"I figure the tank is gonna need a bunker that's ten feet high, twenty feet long, and about eleven feet wide. I've already figured out where we'll put the bunker. Leave it to me, Skipper," the platoon sergeant said, confidently. He arranged for sufficient yobos to be at the bottom of Hill 849. Under his direction the yobos would carry up the ordered materiel and then build the tank bunker. To help in excavating the hole needed for the bunker, he had a quantity of C-3 explosive gently brought up the hill by a division engineer.

The plan was for the yobos to bring the materiel up the hill that night. Most of the yobo working party would each carry two bundles of sandbags up the hill; the remaining yobos would bring up the tools. It figured to be a long, tiresome, and dangerous job on such a cold winter night.

Work would commence with the excavation of the bunker under the artificial moonlight. Two nights had been allocated to this herculean task, with the yobos working constantly. The division engineer during the afternoon hours had set off C-3 charges; later the yobos attacked the blasted ground with picks and shovels, filling the sandbags and then stacking them nearby.

When dawn ended the first night's work, great strides had been made in excavating the bunker area. Through the day the division engineer again exploded carefully placed C-3 charges, shattering rock, loosening the iron-hard ground. The outline of the huge bunker had taken shape. Three sides were of the mountain itself; the fourth side opened to a sandbagged driveway that extended out from the bunker about thirty feet and then angled sharply to the right about half that distance.

"The idea is for the tank to come out of the bunker, drive to the end of the sandbags, execute a right-hand turn, shoot the shit outta Luke-the-Gook's gun pits, and then back up like crazy before we get rounds in on it. The tank will be safe in the bunker; it'll be sturdy enough," the platoon sergeant said.

I believed him. Even without a cover over the top of the mammoth hole, it looked secure, with slabs of the hard rock shining on three sides.

The job was finished just before dawn on December 28. It was rough and ragged-looking but, as promised, it was solid. Sandbags still needed to be placed for the driveway to the shooting spot on the east side of the hill.

"I'll get that done tonight, Skipper," the platoon sergeant said.

And he did.

Without incident.

Well, almost without incident.

"I'm gonna go tell the skipper we're damn near done with this job," the platoon sergeant said to the division engineer, who had come up on the hill to give advice on the use of C-3 explosive.

The Easy Company commander was not in his bunker when the platoon sergeant entered it. Instead, by the light of a small, squat white candle burning in a dry C-ration can holder, the platoon sergeant saw a Korean yobo. The yobo was leaning over a makeshift desk in the bunker, folding a map.

Later, after the Easy Company commander and a number of other grunts responded to the three loud blasts from the platoon sergeant's .45-automatic pistol, the gook was packed down the hill on a stretcher carried by other yobo workers, finally finished with their labors.

"He was a fucking spy, Captain! He was supposed to be working on that fucking bunker! I don't know how or even when he slipped away from the working party, it's so fucking dark and shadowy out there, you know how it is! I sure as shit didn't send him to your bunker, that's for sure!

"He was in your bunker! He was reading your goddamn maps! As far as I was concerned, that makes him a fucking spy! And you shoot spies in wartime, Captain! You shoot them where you find them!"

That's the way the report went into Division G-2. It was the talk of the hill for the next day or so.

In his report the Easy Company commander noted that his platoon sergeant had worked nonstop for three days successively. The captain noted that Easy Company had a continued loss of men for the past ten days—nine KIAs, seventeen WIAs. The captain conjectured that it was spies, like the one killed by his company platoon sergeant, who had aided in the deaths and the wounding of his men. When questioned a few days later, the Easy Company commander could verify only his first two statements.

The M-26 grumbled up the hill, engine laboring, inching its way up in a metallic dance to music provided by humming motors. The tank rolled over antipersonnel mines, ripping them up, setting them off. Buttoned up, the tank was not damaged in any way by the mosquito stings that would have taken arms, legs, fingers, toes, feet, and heads off grunts. Night ended when the M-26 backed into its freshly dug home. Soon it would be the first morning of a brand new year.

The sharp crack followed immediately by the cold whiplash of air seemed anticlimactic as the tank fired its first round on a day that promised snow, lots of snow. With sharp resounding cracks followed closely by impacting booms, 90mm HE shells of the M-26 smashed into the three Luke-the-Gook gun positions, blasting them into oblivion.

We were like kids at a ball game, the way we cheered every time a bore-sighted shot slammed into one of Luke-the-Gook's castles. Thirty sharp cracks later and it was all over. The captain was right; it took a sniper to get a sniper.

It was a great way to bring in a new year.

Over the next couple of days we had some long-range rifle shots zinged at us from Hill 987. Nothing accurate. Nobody even flinched as they walked the trench lines on the east side of the hill during the day.

The platoon sergeant was arrested by Division G-2 officers on January 5, 1952. He was charged with murder. He was taken off the hill to be sent home under guard to a general court-martial to be held in the States.

For a couple of days, anyway, Easy Company felt like it had been shot at and missed. When the platoon sergeant was arrested, everyone in the company felt like he had been shit at and hit.

CHAPTER
19

All of us suffered through the cold days of January, when it seemed there was no bottom to the thermometer. The temperature, day after day, dropped to the vicinity of 25 degrees below zero.

I was luckier than most of the grunts in Easy Company on those cold winter days. At least when I went on watch in the FO bunker I had the dirt walls of the mountain and the overhead sandbagged roof to cut the wind that knifed into watch standers who were exposed to the weather in trench-line fighting holes.

I would put on as many layers of clothing as I could: heavy winterized olive drab trousers, woolen socks, heavy shirts, thick gray sweatshirts, and my flak jacket; then I topped it all off with a fur-lined parka. I would pull down and fasten the ear and neck flaps of my Mickey Mouse winter hat and would push my hands and fingers inside thick woolen gloves. And then, thermo boots on my feet, I would trundle as best I could to the FO bunker.

Inside the FO bunker, protected against wind and weather and with my face wrapped with a woolen scarf, I would shiveringly look out through the observation slit at the frigid winter scene of war on the mountains of Korea.

I scanned the contested area between the North Korean positions and our front trench lines by moving my eyes from side to side over ever-increasing distances. I was looking over a virgin blue–tinted covering of snow that stretched tautly down the mountainside to the valley floor far below our hilltop position. I saw a snowy field that, like an old mirror broken here and there, still brightly reflected the rays of a feeble winter sun.

During daylight hours the sun could and would, if only momentarily, melt the snow. Almost immediately, the melted snow, as if in response to a chill wind blowing, would freeze, and on freezing would coat the area in front of our trench-line positions with what seemed to be a thin, translucent covering, a superficial veneerlike finish, a finish marred only by those blackened areas where grunt-thrown fragmentation grenades had exploded during the dark of the previous night.

I saw movement in the trench line just to the right of the FO bunker. I recognized Corporal Castaglia, who was in charge of the Easy Company .30-caliber Browning light machine gun section. He was a gunner on one of his own guns. I could identify easily with his chilled look, with his shivering. The two of us, and many other Easy Company grunts, were pulling the 0800 to noon watch in fighting positions dug into the front side of the trench line facing the North Koreans on Hill 987.

Castaglia and I, for a few moments, had talked about the cold that day when we had come on watch.

Cold, Castaglia said, was when you had to stick your hands under your armpits to keep them warm, when your whole body was shaking, shivering, telling you to pull your arms in tight, to tense your neck and chest muscles, and to throw your chin up and forward.

Castaglia told me he was proud to head up the light machine gun section that Easy Company had in its weapons platoon. He said everybody was awfully happy to have the extra firepower his guns provided when it came right on down to the nitty-gritty needs of a shooting war.

227

Nodding his head at his machine gun, Castaglia said, "Them rapid-fire buggers can go through about a hundred and fifty rounds per minute. And that, Cautious, really eats up an ammo box filled with linked rounds.

"These grunts like the machine gun in a firefight, but take a look around when we need ammunition and you'll see there just ain't a helluva lot of volunteers who want to hump those more-than-fifteen-pound metal ammo boxes."

Castaglia told me the light machine guns were ideal for use in a rifle company. The guns were relatively small and not too heavy; they could be hand carried anywhere a grunt could go.

I could look out the viewing slit of the FO bunker and see Castaglia in his dark green sleeping bag cover, leaning against the sandbagged wall of the gun pit. I was thankful for the sandbagged barrier stacked over my head, protecting me somewhat from the wind and the elements, and I was awfully sorry for Castaglia and all of his light machine gunners in their open firing positions.

The Easy Company skipper had okayed his men to stand watch in their sleeping bags, never mind the fact that everyone knew about marine grunts being bayoneted in their fart sacks earlier, when the war in Korea was so fucked up. The skipper okayed the sleeping bags to keep his men from freezing.

The word that was passed by the new company gunnery sergeant threatened, "You better be standin' when I come around. Not sittin', but standin' up. And, by God, you better be awake! And that front zipper better not be zipped all the way up! I want you people to be ready to shoot if you need to shoot!"

It was a quiet cold and it was sitting on top of about a foot of snow. There was a glare from the winter sun, which was trying to shine through all the hazy-gray clouds overhead, trying to reflect back off the unbroken sheen of thin bluish ice that extended from our gun pits all the way down to the valley floor in front of us. The only thing showing out front was jutted-up metal barbed-wire posts; the barbed wire slumped in irregular circular coils that slouched from one metal post to another, looking tired, not dangerous.

228

The sheen of ice was still unbroken when this North Korean suddenly materialized some twenty feet in front of Castaglia's light machine gun position. The enemy soldier was wearing a filthy gray-white padded winter uniform—a jacket with a round collar and large cloth buttons in front, which hung down to about mid thigh over bulky padded trousers. A cloth cap of the same dirty material fitted his round head, covering it completely.

Like a fuse lit in the middle, rapidly sizzling in opposite directions, the word "Gook!" fizzed quickly in the trench line, alerting everyone in a fighting hole to the possibility of an attack.

I was in a position to both see and hear Castaglia and the North Korean soldier, whose purple-black hands, with their sausagelike fingers, held a surrender leaflet overhead. The North Korean soldier was calling out something in a high-pitched voice. I could see his lips moving, but I couldn't understand him.

I think Castaglia would have shot the North Korean where he stood except for two things: One was that Castaglia still had his hands inside his winter jacket, up under his armpits; and the second was that Castaglia's assistant gunner earlier had the meaty part of his right hand frozen, briefly, to the cocking lever of the light machine gun. The assistant gunner said he wanted to be sure there was a round in the chamber while he was on watch. So he took off his glove—no one knows why—and attempted to cock the weapon. The only way the kid got loose was for Castaglia to stand up and unbutton his trousers, root around trying to snag onto his pecker, which was diminishing in size with the freezing cold, and then piss on the kid's hand and the machine gun. That short burst of steaming urine was enough to thaw everything sufficiently, and the assistant gunner pulled his hand loose, leaving behind a bit of skin. So anyone could easily understand why Castaglia wasn't about to put an ungloved finger on the trigger of his weapon, at least not for an enemy soldier who was standing up in front of him waving a surrender pamphlet.

After a transfixed moment of surprise mixed with a little bit of terror on seeing one of the enemy so close to his position, Castaglia brought one hand out from his jacket and waved the North Korean soldier into the trench line. Everyone could hear what Castaglia had to say to him, he was shouting that loud, maybe in excitement.

"Holy shit! Where the fuck did you come from? Howja get yer fuckin' ass out there in front of me like that? Is there any fuckin' more'o'ya out there?" Castaglia had his shooting hand out from under his armpit now. He placed a gloved hand around the grip of the weapon and a gloved finger on its trigger. With his other hand Castaglia beckoned the surrendering soldier to come forward. Castaglia motioned for the soldier to slide down into the trench line.

The North Korean wasn't hesitant about surrendering, but he was awfully slow-moving coming in toward the trench line, scuffling his feet rather than picking them up, cracking the thin coating of ice on the snow, punching his way forward. Watching the gook move, I felt that something was wrong, horribly wrong. And then I saw his feet, and I thought, Oh, shit! That shouldn't even happen to a fuckin' gook!

Rags, pieces of rope, and communications wire were wrapped around his ankles and the bottom of the rubber-soled half sneakers the North Korean wore, binding the sneakers to his feet. He had no socks on his feet, just the rubber sneakers, and they came up only as high as his ankle bone. The sneakers were split along the sides. Ugly black folds of swollen flesh with dirty red streaks pushed out from the splits. Just looking at the terrible condition the North Korean's feet were in was enough to make me feel sick inside. It was so readily apparent why he wanted to surrender; his feet were frozen into icy blocks and were three and four times their normal size.

I could not understand how he had the guts to walk on those feet, how he could suffer the anguish of standing upright, how he could brave it through in silence and not scream out in agonizing pain. But the North Korean soldier showed no emotion and I thought, just what kind of men are we fighting?

Castaglia had captured an enemy soldier and, in turn, had caught himself in a dilemma. He had an enemy prisoner standing in the trench line less than four feet away. He knew that any man who took an enemy prisoner to Division G-2 for interrogation would automatically be awarded a five-day basket leave to Japan, that such a leave would not come off the time a man had accumulated in his service record book.

Castaglia looked from the North Korean to the still-unbroken sheen of glassy ice covering the snow in front of his machine-gun position, unbroken save for the path recently kicked through it. Castaglia was nobody's fool. He knew the back of Hill 849 would be just as icy, just as slippery. Questionable footing was a very big consideration. A grunt could break his leg, or his back, or his neck slipping, falling, sliding down the path to the bottom of the hill. A man would have to go down the hill slow, really slow, and with a gook prisoner in front of him, his downward progress would be more severely curtailed. Castaglia was an old hand on the hill; he knew all about how the enemy looked for a target of opportunity.

"Huh uh, gook. Mama Castaglia didn't raise no fool for a son. You're in the trench line now, but I ain't takin' you prisoner. *Kada,* gook, like they would say in your language. Go on over tuh the next fighting hole and surrender yourself there," Castaglia said to the North Korean, who could not understand him. The machine gunner gestured with his arms, motioning the enemy soldier to the next fighting position.

And that's the way it went. No one wanted a prisoner this day. The North Korean was shuffled from fighting hole to fighting hole, going all through the Easy Company trench line and then being passed on to grunts in Dog Company, marines who were tied in on our right side.

Quite late in the day the soldier came stumbling back, still waving his surrender leaflet; he was exhausted beyond all measure. When he reached Castaglia a second time, he just stood still, shaking his head from side to side, reaching out pathetically with his surrender leaflet, trying to give it to Castaglia, pleading to surrender.

Castaglia motioned with his hands to the front of the main line of resistance, the trench line. He even helped the North Korean to climb over the trench itself. Castaglia waved the man out in front, farther, just a bit farther. And then he triggered off a burst of about twenty rounds from his light machine gun, catching the North Korean soldier in the middle of his body, doubling him at the waist, slamming him backward, a puppet with all its strings cut, knocking the enemy soldier back and down, tumbling him downhill, the soldier's gut-shot body rolling over and over in a gigantic snowball that broke the beautiful ice sheen, splintering it, placing an ugly mar on it. The rolling body set off two boot mines in passing and finally, almost at the bottom of the hill, it became snagged in barbed wire and was held fast, crucified.

We all heard Castaglia. "You just can't trust a fuckin' gook. Here the fucker comes in sayin' he wants tuh surrender, and then all he does is walk up and down our lines, checkin' out every goddamn fightin' hole. And then the fucker tries tuh run off back tuh his own lines. I hadda shoot him! Anybody woulda shot him! He was a fuckin' spy, and there ain't no two ways about that!"

Castaglia told his story to anyone who would listen, repeating it daily until we were relieved off the hill during late February. Castaglia told his story so often he came to believe it to be the truth. No one disputed him. We couldn't have cared less.

From that day on every time Castaglia had watch in the machine-gun position, he immediately would cock the gun twice, charging the weapon by putting a round in the chamber. He was always prepared to fire.

And every day Castaglia would look down the hill in front of him and yell out to the rags and bones and flesh that wouldn't rot or decay and go away because of the terrible cold weather, look at the body long dead with countless bullet holes in it. Castaglia would yell out, "You should'na have tried tuh be a fuckin' spy!"

CHAPTER
20

Someone called it the "twilight war" and the name stuck in describing the activity going on all along the battle lines held by the United Nations command above the 38th Parallel from late January through the end of February. It was as good a catchall phrase as any to describe the way we fought the war from entrenched and heavily fortified positions.

We had some night patrols going out, maybe as many as one each week, but to tell the truth most of us believed the night still belonged to the enemy; most of us were still afraid of the dark.

Forward observers attached to Easy Company were seldom asked to accompany either night or day patrols, although sometimes we volunteered to go. Mostly we were told to be available in the FO bunker, to monitor the radio there, and be ready to throw out some mortar fire if and when it was needed.

I tried as best I could to figure out just where the patrols would be located out in front of our lines. I've got to admit I really never knew for certain exactly where the patrols were located. In a shooting situation, as far as I was concerned, it would have been a by guess and by God situation. Luckily, I never had to fire to help out an Easy Company patrol. I was glad about that. The few times I had to fire when an Easy Company patrol was out, I made certain I was dropping mortar rounds way out, well beyond the range of the patrolling units. Even so, I remembered being just a bit reluctant to call in my shots on those few occasions. Big Dog Ondrak had taught me more than one lesson in being a good FO; I wanted to be damned sure I knew who was out in front of Easy Company, and exactly where they were located, before I fired my rounds.

All along the main line of resistance it seemed like the infantry grunt was dug deeply in his trench-line fighting hole. Based on reports received by radio—when we could tap into the right channels—we knew the twilight war was being fought high overhead, with pilots on both sides flying their sophisticated flying machines at incredible speeds and shooting lethal weapons at each other.

Newspapers, when we could get one to read, and outdated magazines said the hottest fighting going on day after day in Korea was the air battles. United Nations airplanes— usually U.S. Thunderjets, Shooting Stars, and Mustangs— went after ground targets and, far too often, found their targets surrounded by antiaircraft guns. By mid-February the North Korean shoot-down tally that started with the tallyho war cry of UN-U.S. pilots was that Red gunners had shot down 111 United Nations fighter-bombers. The still-smoking verified fact was that 56 jet-propelled aircraft and 55 propeller-driven aircraft had been knocked out of the sky and out of control to a final rough landing, which generally destroyed the sophisticated aircraft on impact in million-dollar fires.

Marine grunts seldom saw aerial action, since the air war was fought far away to the north, well beyond our range of mountains.

What the marine grunt saw was those little spotter airplanes that buzzed about on what seemed to be faltering motors as they dipped, ducked, and daily drew rifle fire as they skittered here and there, spotting new digging activity being done by the North Koreans. The spotter pilots charted plenty of the new bunkers and trench lines that honey-combed every Red-held mountaintop and ridge line facing United Nations troops.

From the way most grunts talked, I thought they were pissed off by the dillydallying at the peace-talk tables. None of what was being discussed—or what was being used as a means to stop the discussions—seemed to be of much merit. I was way out of touch with the world and war events on a daily basis. I got my news on a catch-as-catch-can piecemeal framework of facts.

I was concerned that back in September and October when we had the North Koreans and their Chinese partners on the ropes, back when we could have knocked them out of this war, we didn't do it. Instead we went to the peace table, and that's where we started to take a beating. When grunts talked about the war, we pretty much conceded the fact that the Reds went to the peace table only because we had been kicking their asses and they were definitely facing the prospect of a defeat.

One of the grunts who had gone to college said it seemed to him that we were in a no-win situation, because a United Nations spokesman who had tried to put together a peace program was supposed to have said that "only by constant pressure could peace be resolved."

According to the most recent figures released by Division G-2, the communist forces facing south were double the number of troops we had facing north. Actual figures released said we had 450,000 on the United Nations side, against 900,000 on the side of our enemy. I was telling just about anybody who would listen to me that after I had met the enemy in Korea I had stopped believing that bullshit about one marine grunt being worth any ten North Koreans. Personally, I wasn't too happy with the current odds, which favored the enemy with a margin of two to one.

All of the Korean War situation seemed to be kind of heady stuff to me, even though I was fighting in it, because I had so very little knowledge concerning it. Maybe being ignorant was the price me and the other grunts paid for being actively involved in this war. All I knew for certain was that for the past two months I was attached to Easy

Company and we had come off the lines late in February after being relieved by grunts of the 5th Marines.

I was very happy to trudge down the hill in my now-almost-worn-out Mickey Mouse boots. The boot had been developed by the navy using the vapor-barrier principle to keep feet from freezing. The vapor barrier resulted from layers of rubber placed one on top of the other with an air pocket between them. The boot wasn't much for walking, but it sure kept your feet from freezing. The word had been passed that you could pour cold water in the boot, stick your feet right in the water, lace up the boot, and then go outside in below-zero freezing temperatures. We were told that in a few minutes the water in the boot would be as warm as our normal body temperature. Arguments developed saying that a grunt might get immersion foot, but that he wouldn't lose toes to frostbite.

Arguments like that just naturally arouse the curiosity of the average grunt. Most grunts have to see something, have to feel it, experience it in some way in order for them to believe it. It was pretty well known that most grunts had the type of mentality that wouldn't even let them believe that shit stinks unless they could smell it. So my boots, early on, had been on the feet of just about every grunt in Easy Company, including the company commander. I'd guess about three barrels of water had been heated to body temperature inside the boots, a canteen cupful at a time.

Easy Company grunts, marines who were long on courage but short on brains, sought any diversion from the hum-drum life of winter war in the trench line. Bets were made as to who had the hottest body temperature. Funny money in the form of military scrip dollars was bet on who could get the cold water poured inside the boot down to the lowest temperature in just five minutes.

Doc, our corpsman, used a thermometer from his medical kit to determine the winner, dunking the thermometer into the water inside the boot to get a reading. He got lots of laughs when he pulled on the tongue of the boot just before sticking in his thermometer and then commanding, "Now say ahhhhh"!

A grunt who had pneumonia and a fever of 104 degrees

236

was the uncontested winner. Oddly enough, when the Doc shook the thermometer down and popped it back into the mouth of the sick grunt to recheck his temperature—right after the grunt had warmed the water inside the boot—he was quite surprised to find the temperature of the grunt had dropped by one degree. Doc thought he might have stumbled onto something important. Medical experimentation was delayed when the grunt and his pneumonia were evacuated to a MASH (Mobile Army Surgical Hospital) before more tests could be run. Further testing was delayed when no one else came down with pneumonia right away. Eventually the novelty wore thin. By the end of January most grunts on line had been issued their own thermal boots.

With snow deep on the ground, it was a tough proposition to do more than just shoot at each other with artillery and mortars. Patrolling was infrequent. We just stayed in our own trench lines. Occasionally we lobbed a mortar round or an artillery shell at each other to sort of keep in touch, to keep the war going. We were barely earning our forty-five-dollar-per-month combat pay. Because we weren't being harassed, we maintained a status quo situation: We fired when the gooks fired and neither of us showed many real targets of opportunity to the other guy.

The brief cold days and long frigid nights of January and February icily attached themselves end to end, passing with glacierlike slowness into a deep freeze of back-to-back solidly frozen Siberian weeks. Living in 25- to 30-degree below-zero temperatures was hardship enough; never mind having to die in it because some gook was shooting at you.

We looked for and finally got our reserve time at Camp Tripoli. Even in a reserve status, just trying to get warm and then stay warm was a hardship. Our only relief was in being in a place where there were no incoming rounds; but then, that's what being in reserve was all about. As much as possible we stayed in the tents provided to us and avoided going outside into the bitter, biting, cutting, blue, stone-cold weather. Once daily we would go down to the mess tent and eat some food, make up a sandwich or two, fill up a canteen with hot coffee, and then return to put a piss can under our cots. That done we would just stay wrapped up in our sleeping bags, crapped out in the rack for a day or two at a time. Some of us had radios that blared out; we would lay in a half-asleep stupor listening to the news and music over the Armed Forces Radio. I was surprised to be told the winter we were experiencing was supposed to be the mildest in the past twenty-five years. Maybe so, I thought, wondering just a bit about my brief case of frostbitten toes a couple months back.

A lot of the men in the company—some with fewer stripes than me, some with a stripe or two more, and once or twice an officer—asked my opinion concerning FO duties, what it was like up on line, and the best way to call in shots. I would answer them as truthfully as I could using my own experiences to help formulate answers. But far too many times, concerning all the many other subjects about which I was asked and felt I had too little knowledge, I felt awkward in trying to pose an answer. But, posed answer or not, most of the new men seemed to think I knew the answers to their questions on how to fight a war with the North Koreans. I suddenly became aware that due to having been up on line twice for a period of about four months total, I was now considered to be a veteran. I looked around and saw there were an awful lot of new faces.

The cook who relieved Ben Baker just didn't have the knack for mixing up home brew, so we lay in our bunks, hungering for a drink, and for the very first time realized that Baker had really contributed something to our outfit. To make matters worse, Albert Truelove had been given an emergency leave; his father had died. It was uncertain when he would return or even if he would have to come back to Korea. To a man, we hungered for his cooking and missed all the many different ways he looked out for us.

The Big Dog and Lob Stratton had both rotated home during late February; some of us made small talk about how the Big Dog took a pile of bucks from the Lob in a final poker game played under the brilliant light of four Coleman lanterns. A lot of the new men just couldn't understand how talking about that one particular poker game could bring

238

such satisfaction, especially if we hadn't been the big winner.

I was happy for Soupy Campbell, my radioman, and for Billy Baxter, my wireman, when I found out they both were scheduled to rotate home about mid-March. I should have realized they were short-timers. Soupy had brought that fact to my attention at the very end of our time on Hill 849. With just two more days to go, I volunteered for a reconnaissance patrol out in front of the lines. Because I had volunteered, Soupy would have to go as my radioman.

I can still see him standing over me in the trench line, his booted legs spread wide apart, his arms bowed at his side, his hands knotted into fists, his face furious. I had felt the sharp sting of his punch on my right cheek, a roundhouse punch that had knocked me right on my ass.

"You fucker! You're gonna get me killed! You didn't hafta volunteer for that fuckin' patrol! You didn't hafta put me on the spot! Why can't cha carry the fuckin' radio yourself, you sonovabitch?"

I was confused, lying there on my back, my head ringing. Soupy was a big guy, someone who packed a mean punch. All the time we had been together he had always helped me, calling in shots, going wherever it was we had to go, doing whatever it was we had to do to get the job done. We had gone out on recon patrols lots of times, and Soupy had always been ready to go, never holding back.

Billy Baxter helped me sit up and then stand up.

"He didn't mean it, Cautious. It's just that him and me are so goddamned short. We don't want to push our luck. We just wanta go home in one piece."

Two minutes later while I was still trying to get my head on straight, Soupy was back in the trench line again, his radio riding high on his back, reaching out a hand to help me stand upright. "Goddamnit, Cautious! Don't you get me killed here in this fuckin' shitass of a country that's as useless as tits on a boar hog! Let's get this fuckin' show on the road!"

Now, thinking back on it, with both Soupy and Billy gone, I would have to break in a new team when I went back up on

239

line at the end of reserve time. I wasn't too excited about that.

The only really great news was that Captain Massey had been selected for promotion to major; the bad news was that he would be transferred to a staff job in regiment very soon. No one knew yet who our new skipper would be.

I was bunking in a pyramidal tent with four FOs. I knew them, sort of, but had not made any real friends with them, up to now. Mostly I stayed quiet, just listening to them talk. I hardly ever added anything to the conversation except, maybe, a comment or two about something announced over the Armed Forces Radio Network. I wasn't trying to be standoffish. I just wasn't too anxious to make any new friends. It hurt too much to lose a friend, even if he only rotated home or got reassigned out of the outfit. I sort of stayed noncommittal, and that bothered me. I had never before found it hard to be a friend or to make a friend, to have someone to pal around with, to talk with, to share things with.

Time dragged by. When the word was passed, first over the radio and then later at a company formation, that the division would be shifted to the west coast, I couldn't have cared less. From the talk I heard, most of the men in the Four Deuces felt the same way. It didn't take someone long to assess our attitudes. It was time for school, and so we went to an all-hands lecture to learn all about our prospects over the next couple of months.

Major General J. T. Selden—who had relieved Maj. Gen. Gerald C. Thomas on January 10—was now the marine division commander. We were told that when General Selden was in conferences with Army Lt. Gen. James Van Fleet, the two men discussed the probability of still other marine amphibious landings. I remembered the USS *Marine Lynx* and Sochiri and was glad that nothing resulted from their discussions.

But Van Fleet informed Selden it was necessary for the marines to move from their present positions, to shift 180 miles across Korea to the far western end of the line, and then guard the vulnerable corridor leading to Seoul and overlooking the Panmunjon truce site. The marines were to hold down a strategic thirty-five-mile front, which was longer than that held down by any other division in Korea. The British Commonwealth Division would be on our right flank. We both would face Chinese troops.

A look at maps of the area showed that, tactically, we were getting another chance to hold the wrong end of a shitty stick. Three rivers would screw up our war zone; most of the main line of resistance was in front of the Imjin River and our division reserve and other support areas were behind it. Two other rivers, the Sachon and the Han, either cut through or bordered part of the front lines.

According to scuttlebutt, Van Fleet told Selden he could afford to give up real estate on the east coast, but he had to hold ground on the west coast. The marines, Van Fleet said, could be trusted to hold the line there. Van Fleet said that with army headquarters as well as those of Korean President Syghman Rhee located on the west coast, and with the peace conference going on at Panmunjon, just north of the new lines the marines would control, he had a corridor located where he could not yield any ground at all.

"Your marines must not only occupy that ground area, you must keep it safe for me," Van Fleet told Selden.

Van Fleet had recognized the tenacity of the marine grunt in holding onto ground he fought over and won. Time and again in skirmish after skirmish, in both light and heavy action, the enemy facing marines could not take fought-over land back from them. If they were going to get any marine-occupied ground, it was going to have to be given back to them, and the giving up of ground that had soaked up a lot of marine blood would be a bitter thing.

But General Selden was convinced the coast-to-coast move was necessary to the further prosecution of the war. Besides, he knew his two stars were talking to the three stars that belonged to Van Fleet.

The division was going to move lock, stock, and barrel. We gave up our hills to relieving army units. We bitched about it: Some of us didn't like the idea of moving; some of us didn't like the idea of the army coming in and taking over our positions; and some of us, me included, didn't give a big rat's ass one way or the other.

241

We climbed into the back ends of open six-by-six trucks, prepared for a cold two-day trip. Everyone had sleeping bags and coarse wool blankets to help ward off the cold. Without warning, the convoy started, trucks jolting, moving with muttering motors and smelly exhaust fumes. We soon became comfortably dazed with the swaying, the lurching, the soft squeaking and dull, throbbing rumble of the truck. No one said a word about leaving Camp Tripoli, about leaving the east coast, about leaving the Punchbowl hills. No one even looked back, except those facing that direction, and they were already half-hypnotized by the truck's motion. We were off to fight the Chinese.

Our trail across Korea was marked by all the garbage a man can throw overboard, shit-canned over the side of the trucks. Half-eaten C rations and empty cans were dumped. We had boxes of waxed paper—wrapped sandwiches made at the mess hall for the trip. The waxed paper went first, then the half-eaten sandwiches, and pickles, and hunks of cake. When we saw little kids scramble after the cans as we went through a village, we hammered on the top of the truck cab and told the driver to stop. The truck driver yelled back, "Fuck no, asshole! Goddamn, we're still above the parallel. We're in North Korea!" But in the truck I was in, we forced the issue, and the driver stopped.

"You got five fuckin' minutes to take a piss break," the driver said, unbuttoning his trousers.

In minutes we gave away just about everything edible on the truck. For the first time in my life I understood the phrase used often by my grandfather when he spoke of "a contradiction in terms." Right at that moment none of us grunts really cared anything at all about an adult gook, and it didn't matter all that much whether or not he was from either North or South Korea. But, almost to a man, we cared about the young Korean kids, their big potbellies pushing out thin winter coats; anyone could see they were starving, that they were suffering from malnutrition. No grunt wanted to see those kids get hurt, or be cold, or be hungry. Right at that moment it never entered our minds that those kids might grow up to be North Korean soldiers looking to whip our asses. Even if it had entered our minds, we couldn't have cared less.

We stopped for piss calls every hour, and stopped for chow at noon. Cooks and bakers had started out two hours earlier than the convoy and, after arriving at a predesignated location, set up a galley. I ate my food at the extreme edge of the stopped convoy, or near a ditch. I guess some of the new guys thought I was kind of snotty or something, going out and away from the crowd, not joining in the skylarking that always goes on when grunts get together. But I couldn't shake the bunch-up at the bottom of Hill 854 out of my mind.

We finally pulled into a large, flat area that had raggedy-assed tents erected around the perimeter. Someone said we were near Ascom City; others said we were closer to Yong-Dong-Po. I saw two lines of grunts in front of two of the tents. At the closest tent the grunts had mess gear in their hands; that line seemed to move pretty fast, with grunts bringing their chow outside to eat.

The line to the second tent seemed to move very slowly.

"They got six gook women in there. They ain't much, I'll tell you that, but . . . what the hell, it only costs five bucks a throw. Some guys are gettin' off one and going right on to the next in line, walkin' with their britches draggin' on the ground."

"You gonna get some?"

"Are you shittin' me? Half the goddamn company's already screwed them. You'd hafta tie a goddamn two-by-four across your ass so you wouldn't fall in. Besides, they probably all got the clap."

"Well, I'm gonna get some, clap or no clap. It's been a long time with nothing but hand jobs between times."

"I didn't say I wasn't gonna get some. All I said was that I needed to find a goddamn two-by-four."

I made a quick decision. I was hungry so I went to chow first. Damn! Warmed over meat and beans!

Later, I used a rubber. By the time I got to the josan and paid my five bucks I figured about fifty guys had already screwed her.

So much for the good things in life.

BOOK III

Small Hills and Big Chinese

CHAPTER
21

It wasn't as if I had a chip on my shoulder or anything like that. I didn't. It was just that I always got pissed off anytime someone sneered at me: "Four Deuces! Shit! When did you ever see the front lines?" and I'd bark right at them, loudly, "Only when I looked back!" As far as I was concerned, that was the way of it late in March after I joined Able Company, going up on line again, following the move to the west coast. Scuttlebutt said we were to relieve a unit of the Republic of Korea (ROK). Nobody thought much of the ROKs before we relieved them; we all thought they were a bag of shit after we moved into their position. **One**—and I'm not shitting you telling you this—just one fucking ROK soldier was waiting for us when we humped our way in from the staging area where the truck convoy had dropped us off.

Able Company was moving forward in single file formation on the foot-wide path that topped the rice paddy dikes when our scout saw this ROK soldier standing on the path. I figured he was the guide who would lead us to our new position. Instead, the ROK soldier gabbled at the skipper of Able Company, gesturing wildly and pointing at a small mass of hills still a hundred yards or so away. As it turned out, this gook was a representative of the ROK company we were to relieve. He was the only fucking representative. Through our interpreter, the ROK soldier said his company had already left the main line of resistance (MLR) position about three hours earlier. And then the fucker just walked off, heading back toward the rear, with never a backward look. What it amounted to was that Able Company was walking into a cold position, one that we might have to fight for in order to occupy. We didn't go in scared, but we went in the rest of the way very carefully, like we were walking on eggs.

Combat orders handed out by battalion had tasked Able Company with the relieving of two ROK companies and then with the holding down of that part of the line on the MLR that the ROKs had occupied, a line just about a mile long from end to end. That one company relieving two companies on the MLR was really going to stretch Able Company thin. The MLR was a line located at the forward edge of the main battle position. It was not a rigid line; it was, instead, flexible. Its purpose was to coordinate the fire of all our unit and unit supporting weapons, our rifles and machine guns, mainly. Later, we would be asked to stretch ourselves even thinner, after we found out all about the salient, which jutted out about a half mile from the MLR, and the need to establish an outpost position on that salient.

Going up with Able Company would be my third time up on line with a letter company. Last October when I had so recklessly, careless of all consequences, volunteered to become a Four Deuce FO for Captain Massey I had absolutely no idea of what I was letting myself in for, dutywise. I remembered the Funny Gunny had tried to clue me in on a few things, but I wasn't listening. At that time my mind was cluttered up with the importance of having just been promoted, of getting my three buck sergeant stripes. Both Captain Massey and the Funny Gunny were gone now, as well as most all of the other people I had known, really known, in the Four Deuces. I'll tell you true, I felt like a stranger in the Four Deuces. I had already been in the outfit for nearly half a year, but had spent most of that time up on the hill as an FO to one of the letter companies.

Spending time up on the hill makes a big difference in the way you feel about things. Actually, I thought I fitted in a whole lot better with letter company grunts I didn't know than I did in my own outfit with people I just barely knew but who I had to work with when shooting a fire mission. When I was on the line and the gooks were shooting at us like crazy, when the shit was really hitting the fan and I was downright scared, right then I had this feeling of contempt aimed at anybody who wasn't up on the line with me, getting the shit shot out of them. The way I felt about it was that anyone who was not up on the line was a pussy, and that was that.

An Old Salt, one of the old Easy Company platoon leaders who had been up on Hill 849 with me earlier in the year, had tried to provide me with an explanation of these feelings. "You're exhibiting all the symptoms of what is called 'the arrogance of survival.' I know about it because it was part of the course I used to teach officers when I was an instructor at the Basic School at Quantico, Virginia. Usually grunts, even officer grunts, who are young enough and naive enough get their bellyful of it about halfway through their hitch over here.

"Right now you're feelin' cocky about having lived so long in a combat situation. You feel a hell of a lot superior to them pussies who are, theoretically, 'on line,' yet who are stationed in the rear with the gear."

The Old Salt explained about the invisible yet still-tangible bond that existed between grunts who lived in the trenches, on the front-line positions that could come under enemy fire at any time, day or night. That bond, according to the Old Salt, a man who had fought in two major Pacific campaigns during World War II, "was due to the shared experience of constantly being afraid, and then of havin' to overcome that fear, somehow, someway, maybe by braggin' about how tough they have it up here on line."

He said, "The 'on-line' fighting grunt wants everyone to know that he has pulled his time as a combat grunt, and the combat grunt wants people to know he has earned his combat ribbons. He figures that maybe some other guys wearing the same ribbons haven't paid their dues. And so he holds those people, the rear-echelon pogues, in contempt. The 'on-line' grunt wants other people to know that he has suffered. So he shares his suffering by talking about his role in the fighting and, maybe, by lying about it a little bit."

One thing I knew for certain was that I didn't feel any contempt at all for the commander of the outfit I was going to be stationed with for a while. I felt good knowing that Able Company had a Mustang first lieutenant as its skipper, a man who had made his way up from the ranks. I always felt good knowing that the officer in command of the company where I was assigned had earlier been an enlisted man. Luckily, the Marine Corps felt the same way; more than half its present officer personnel strength had been former enlisted men.

At any rate, the Able Company skipper was sure of himself, and he passed that feeling on to the grunts in his company. His name was Able, 1st Lt. Lester Able. Since we were going on line, and since it was policy not to call an officer by his rank while we were on line, we sometimes called the skipper by his nickname; we called him Les. There was more than just one reason for us to call him by that name. He had this one church hymn that he kept on humming to himself. Naturally, his grunts, and that included me and my FO team, had to change the words of the hymn to suit our fancy. Les would start humming, and right away we'd all start singing, interrupting his song, bellowing it out as loud as we could: "Lord, he is Able! His first name is Les! Remold him, remake him, 'cuz he is a mess!" And then we would chuckle and chortle, and snort and fart around, whooping it up.

And Les, our skipper? He'd just smile and keep right on humming his favorite hymn.

Let me tell you something. Grunts take to a man like that. Give the grunts a leader like that and they'd do just about anything he would ask them to do. Grunts always followed a leader like Les Able. Well, almost always, anyway.

So Les walked us right into our new position. He was right

250

up front, telling his grunts to "Follow me!" And he walked, very cautiously, right into the MLR area.

The place was unoccupied. It was a low-lying hill mass of small, sort of mounded-over peaks, the highest of which was scaled, on our maps, at just fifty-two feet. We didn't know whether or not to identify our position as being Hill 52, or Rock Mound 52. The ground composition of the MLR was mostly hard rock. It was easy enough to see there would be no continuous trench line along this part of the line. Right away we knew we were going to have to build bunkers and other firing positions, placing them carefully, delineating not only the normally established fields of fire for our weapons, but our final protective line (FPL) of fire as well. We hadn't needed an FPL in the high mountains of the east coast. We would need it now.

The FPL uses the interlocking fire of all available flat trajectory weapons, especially light and heavy machine guns, along and across a predetermined line in front of the MLR where the gooks had to be stopped. Sustained fire from selected and emplaced weapons was fixed as to direction and elevation. Preplanned and prefired, the FPL type of fire was expected to be delivered under any condition of visibility.

Les Able was everywhere. He had his grunts reinforce the tactical obstacles in front of his position. The tactical obstacles, in the form of both double-apron and concertina barbed wire, were layered back from the rice paddy edge to right in front of the MLR, neatly covering what would have been easily negotiated slopes to Hill 52.

A movable gateway made of barbed wire on a wooden frame was placed so as to give access to the pathway edging the rice paddy in the center of the Able Company line. The path led forward about seventeen hundred yards to a triple-crowned hill mass of higher ground. Some of us would suffer foolishly at this outpost. We would suffer hurt, stupid hurt, the kind of hurt that comes with an explosion and hot metal.

We heard Les Able say it time and time again that first day: "That hill out there doesn't look good to me. The gooks could use it as a staging area, or just sit on it and look right down our throats." We all knew we were in for some patrolling in the next day or so.

But right now, initially, the protection of the MLR was paramount. The area out in front facing the gook line was checked for antipersonnel mines. None were located. We wondered aloud what the hell kind of a deal those ROKs who had occupied this location had going for them. The whole MLR was unprotected.

It didn't take the grunts in Able Company long. The first strand of regular double-apron barbed wire—with razor-edged protrusions all along its length—was placed six inches off the deck, just inches in from the rice paddies and well beyond hand grenade range. Empty ration cans with small stones placed inside were hung on the wire, making an effective alarm system for dark nights. Trip flares, booby traps, and blocks of TNT laced around with nails were placed carefully. Les Able knew how to protect his front and his flanks, even in a position that at first seemed indefensible.

Humming his favorite hymn, Les was all over the MLR, and under his instructions we dug deeper and extended farther all existing trench lines. The gooks knew exactly where we were, so it wasn't as if we were trying to hide something from them. What we wanted to do was to dig into the ground far enough to protect ourselves from aimed small-arms fire and exploding artillery and mortar rounds. I was surprised that we worked without hindrance. We used two days to improve our position on the MLR without a shot being fired.

Jutting up like a sore thumb at the far end of the rice paddies fronting our position was a three-spired hill mass, Hill 104.5, named after its highest point. Just seventeen hundred yards away, Hill 104.5 would give the Chinese an advantage over us; they would be looking down our throats. Moreover, they could use Hill 104.5 as a staging area for a concerted attack on our MLR. Les asked for and was given orders to occupy the hill during daylight hours only.

"I'm sending out a reinforced squad every day, Cautious. And every other day that's gonna include you and one of your communicators acting as a radioman. You take turns with the 81-millimeter mortar FO going out every other day. The artillery FO and his radioman will go out every day," Les Able said during a meeting of his platoon leaders.

I said I would go out with the first patrol the following morning. We were to form up early and head out, in the darkness, at 0430, passing through the gateway. We weren't busting any orders from battalion; the first light of day would be about an hour later. Les Able figured to be at the bottom of Hill 104.5 at that time. He wanted to get there without being observed.

I had already established some concentrations in the rice paddy area. I put two concentrations on Hill 104.5, one halfway up the continuous S-shaped path that led to the top of the hill and one in the trench line that circled the military crest of the hill. I hoped I wouldn't need to use them on our way out to the hill.

I looked back at our front lines from about fifty feet out in front of the wood-and-barbed-wire gateway. By the time we all got together—a light machine gunner and his two ammunition carriers, a corpsman, the artillery FO and his radioman, me and my radioman, an infantry buck sergeant and his twelve men, plus Les Able—and had passed through our lines, more than half an hour had elapsed.

For a while there, it was fumble, stumble, and regroup, with some of the grunts on line in their fighting holes continually challenging us and asking us to give the god-damn password of all things. It took a new buck sergeant in the reconnaissance patrol to square things away.

"You fuckin' assholes! You're supposed to challenge people tryin' to come in through the goddamn lines. Them are the bad guys! Us fuckers going out through your lines are the good guys! Now you people knock off all this silly fuckin' grab-ass!"

That sergeant had a pair of lungs. His voice just kept echoing back from way out in the rice paddy area. Everyone got quiet quickly. Grunts listen to a voice of authority. And then the sergeant said, "Besides, I already forgot the god-damn password!" and everyone, including the patrol going out, started snickering and tittering.

Les Able said, "Let's go!" and we moved out with him,

humming his hymn and a couple of us singing out the words. So much for our silence and quiet integrity. We made the march to the base of Hill 104.5 quickly.

There had been two substantially built but small farmhouses, or at least that's what I thought they had been, demolished and in ruins some seventy-five feet up from the base of Hill 104.5. Two fire-blackened walls of cemented rocks thrusting up jaggedly were all that remained of both the houses.

On the first of the so very many S turns that led uphill—with the two war-torn farmhouses on our immediate left and under very careful scrutiny—we paused long enough for a scout to go ahead of us on the pathway, clearing the way of boot mines, looking for trip wires. The path was clean. Nothing prevented our use of it. While waiting for a report from the scout, Les Able had us all take a sitting or kneeling firing position, pointing our weapons outboard. He wanted us to be prepared just in case we suddenly found gooks all around us.

We halted a second time and took another defensive posture when the scout went over the lip of the trench at the military crest of the hill. The scout moved to his left as a second man joined him in the trench line, this man moving to the right. As we watched, the two men checked not only the trench line for booby traps, but all the bunkers dug into the hill as well.

Nothing! I couldn't believe it. The scouts had found nothing of consequence in the trench line or the bunkers. There were no Chinese, and no signs of any Chinese. The trench lines and the bunkers were picked clean; it was as if Hill 104.5 had been made as a defensive position but never used as one. There was no brass in or near the firing position, no spent rounds of ammunition. There were no empty C-ration cans, no empty ammunition cans, no worn-out and thrown-away pieces of military equipment. Nothing!

"Welcome aboard, Skipper," one of his scouts yelled, motioning with his helmeted head for the rest of us to come on into the trench and get off the exposed trail.

I followed the artillery FO and his team to the far side of

the hill, to where an observation bunker was located. I couldn't get over the good condition of the deeply dug trench lines and the bunkers. It was sure different than the MLR. It was almost like being back on the east coast again. There was still a slight chill in the air. The sheer physical and mental exertion on the long, time-consuming trek filled with imaginary hazards, the uncertainty of what we would find up on the hill, and the sheer joy of finding nothing had caused me to sweat. My undershirt and utility jacket, under my flak jacket, were soaking wet. I was soon chilled in the false dawn light of Friday, March 21, 1952, the first day of spring.

"It's spring, I'm tellin' you. No shit! Spring starts today," a loud voice was telling his buddy. Two men had occupied a fighting hole near the OP bunker. I didn't have to try very hard to overhear or identify the loud voice. It was the sergeant who had forgotten the password. I was surprised to find out he was a recent replacement. In time I knew he would learn to speak just loud enough for the person he was in conversation with to hear him, and not any louder. Small things like that are learned up on line.

I was just up the trench line a couple yards away from the firing position the two grunts occupied. Me and the artillery FO were placing some concentrations out in front of the outpost. We were taking turns shooting, so there would be no confusion as to where we put our concentrations. Right now the artillery FO was working and my mind was free to listen to whatever was going on.

The new grunt in the nearby fighting hole kept going on and on about how it was spring and how "me and my girlfriend, we'd make plans to cut a day at college every year at this time."

Spring, he said, usually arrives during the third week of March. "So we'd make a long weekend out of it. Go for a ride in the country, maybe, or take a hike up in the woods. We always wanted to find something that let us know that winter was over. You know what I mean, don't you?"

It was this talk about spring that I was eavesdropping on that made me suddenly realize that the whole time I was in Korea, I had never heard a bird sing. And I wondered why.

Maybe it was because I wasn't listening. Or maybe it was because there were no birds.

"Okay, Cautious. You put in a concentration now," the artillery FO said. I had already taken an azimuth to the rock outcropping I wanted to use as a concentration, and had located it on my map. I had made mathematical corrections, taking into account the discrepancies built into the map earlier when they had been drawn up by Japanese cartographers. My first round was exactly on target. "Mark it," I said to my FDC.

While the artillery FO worked on his long shots and short shots to fix his next concentration, I again let myself listen in on the conversation going on between the two grunts.

"Usually spring is the season of the year between winter and summer that includes the months of March, April, and May in the United States. Korea is located in about the same temperate zone, so I guess spring comes around at about the same time over here," the new sergeant was saying. Somehow I knew he gave this information as a sort of preamble to something coming that was going to be a bit heavier. He was showing off his smarts. For no tangible reason I got a little bit pissed off at him.

I was trying to tune out the voice of the new sergeant as he started to lecture his fighting-hole buddy about why "there would be no change of seasons if the earth's axis were perpendicular to the plane of the earth's orbit around the sun," when I heard the other man excitedly cry out, "Look! Look over there, to the left, by that big rock. It's a fuckin' pheasant! No shit! It's a fuckin' pheasant."

I craned my head around and looked through the parapet opening of the FO bunker. Jesus! The kid was right. I saw a small brownish gray feathered bird, one just a bit bigger than a pigeon. The bird pecked at the ground, then lifted its head, jerkily, its eyes bright, its head making quick, sharp movements, a few degrees at a time, warily.

PIK-Kuhh-h-h! The sound was sharp and loud and deadly against the spring day. The head of the pheasant disappeared in a cloud of feathers seemingly thrown out in abandon.

"I got the fucker! I blew his head right off!" I heard the new sergeant yell, boisterously.

Then everything started happening fast. I heard the new sergeant holler out, "I'll get that fucker and we'll cook him up!" and at the same time that he was saying it he had already thrown a leg up and over the trench and was bounding out and away, already three or four running steps into the forty-some-feet distance to the dead pheasant. The new sergeant, in his mad dash, was well into the mined area when a boot mine went off with a hellacious roar, throwing small chunks of dirt and pieces of his left foot all over the landscape. His foot exploded almost in a manner similar to that of the head of the pheasant he had just shot. The new sergeant was thrown up into the air. He made a half turn and fell heavily, his back striking the ground.

I was out of the FO bunker and over the trench line and halfway down to where the new sergeant was lying on the ground before I realized what I was doing, before I realized that I was violating all the rules the Funny Gunny had warned me about. I was reacting without thought, without plan, without looking where I was putting down my own feet on this dangerous ground.

Fuck it! I thought, and in two more steps I was by the side of the new sergeant. I hunkered down and drew air deeply into my lungs. My whole body was shaking. It had to be from something other than just that short run. I saw something very, very dangerous. At about the same time, I heard people behind me in the trench line. Someone was yelling for a corpsman. I wasn't at all sure if we had a corpsman with us. I yelled back, "Don't nobody else come out here! This fuckin' place is full of mines!"

The new sergeant was lying with the broad part of his back, an area just below his shoulders, on a trip wire to a Bouncing Betty, a land mine of the very worst type. It is a six-inch tube, two and a half inches in diameter, containing the propelling charge and a fused shell. This stands on an inch-thick base plate more than three inches in diameter. The eight-and-a-half-inch-tall primer and fuse assembly are also on the base plate, next to the tube. The Bouncing Betty

257

fuse is a combination pull-and-pressure type. This deadly mine requires a pull of just three to six pounds on the pull ring or a pressure of about twenty pounds on the pressure cap to set it off.

I remembered having been told all about the Bouncing Betty when I was in training. I know I had been taught how to lay and arm the mine, as well as how to disarm it.

But right now, shit-scared, sitting on my haunches beside the new sergeant, looking at the way he had fallen on the trip wire, at the way the wire angled up and out tautly on either side of his body with no slack in it at all, I couldn't remember dip-shit. My mind was a blank. All I knew was that the new sergeant had just a bloody stump with a white bone sticking out of where the top of his boot had been, and that he was soaking the ground with heavy spurts of thick red blood. I straightened up a bit and pulled my web belt loose from about my waist. I tied the belt as tightly as I could around his thigh.

The poor guy was not moving at all, but he was looking at me, his eyes staring glasslike. I guessed he was either in shock or was going into shock.

"Don't move a fuckin' muscle, you hear? Just sort of let me know if you can hear me." His mouth moved, his lips opening and closing as he stared at me, but he did not make any sound.

"Listen, you're lying on a fuckin' trip wire to a Bouncin' Betty. I don't know why the fucker hasn't gone off, but it hasn't. You're hurt. I gotta get you outta here, right away." The new sergeant gave a slight nod of his head and his helmet tipped loose and went bounding down the hill. I thought my heart was going to beat its way out of my chest.

"Just don't move, man. I'm scared. I don't know if I can lift you or not." I was trying to talk calmly, assessing the situation for both the new sergeant and myself. My voice came out about as loud as his had sounded earlier, only mine sounded scared.

"Are you Catholic, or something? Do you want to pray? I'm gonna give you about five seconds to pray, and then I'm gonna just plain lift you off that fuckin' wire and get you outta here."

The beginning of the Lord's Prayer started way back in my mind and came out loudly from my mouth: "Our Father, who art in heaven. . . ." I snaked my left forearm under the new sergeant's knees and simultaneously forced my right arm under his chest. I didn't think I could do it because I'm not that strong, but I heaved upward, my neck muscles stretched tightly, my back straining, my thighs and my calf muscles bunching and wanting to build into charley horses. I heaved up and stood upright and I pulled the new sergeant's body right into my face and neck and chest area, knowing that if that goddamned Bouncing Betty went off, the new sergeant would take the bulk of the explosive charge right in his back while I was somewhat protected. I felt he owed me that much.

And then I was turning and stumbling back toward the trench line. I handed the new sergeant down to whoever was there to catch him. It was Les Able. He looked right into my eyes and I was glad that I had done what I just did. Someone handed me a lighted cigarette as they hauled the new sergeant to the back trench line. I could hardly bring it to my mouth, my hands were shaking so much. I dragged deeply on it and then gagged and coughed, and finally turned around and puked my guts out.

I don't know when it was that Les Able came back to where I was standing. "You're a good man, Cautious. Here's your belt. Better put it back on before your britches fall down." Les Able chuckled at his own joke, and then more seriously he said, "I'm going to put you in for a medal for what you just did. I'm going to write you up for a Bronze Star."

"Do you really mean that, sir?"

"Yes, I do. I really mean that."

My mind was working overtime. I had come over to Korea looking for promotion. I had already gotten one rank. Why not try for another?

"Thanks, Skipper. I appreciate what you want to do. But if you really want to do something for me, why don't you put me in for a meritorious promotion to staff sergeant?" And then I tried to explain everything to Les Able, as if I really had to do so. "Actually, Skipper, that's the rank that a Four

Deuce FO ought to carry up on the hill. I'd just as soon have the rank as have the medal, if you don't mind. I've got a family. I could use the extra money from a promotion."

Les Able looked at me in a curious way. He shook his head affirmatively. "Okay, Cautious, if that's the way you want it." He started humming his favorite hymn as he went through the trench line to check up on his men.

CHAPTER
22

Les Able had a wealth of wartime experiences to draw upon, having been in World War II, and because he was smart enough to adapt those experiences to the circumstances of war in Korea, Able Company grunts were the luckier for it. They were luckier still when Les, most of the time anyway, acted like what he had been, a former staff NCO, instead of what he now was, a newly commissioned officer.

Most grunts, even young grunts, stopped thinking of war, this war or any other one, as an adventure after their first couple of firefights. But there were some—like Les Able— who couldn't or wouldn't let go of the adventure. Maybe that was the reason why Les was such an exceptional officer, especially in the eyes of all his young NCOs.

"If our company's tactics are strictly defensive, then the gooks will be free to pick the tactics they want to use against us. The initiative will be theirs. And if the initiative belongs to the gooks, then this illusion of security," and here Les would swing his arm about, pointing to Mound 52 defenses, "brought about by the barbed wire we have out in front of us, the booby traps, the TNT charges, would be disproved."

Les Able was talking to me. For some reason he had warmed up to me after I had rescued that wounded new sergeant. Les often came into the Mound 52 FO bunker when I was on duty. I didn't know if he was using me as a sounding board for one of his talks or not. Tactics for small or large units was not my bag. I was just a buck sergeant trying to do his level best to put a Four Deuce round where it belonged.

"Don't you see, Cautious? A defensive unit is a prime target for an attack!"

I agreed with him, not because I understood the tactics he was speaking about, but because he had demonstrated that he was a leader of men.

In talks with his NCOs, Les Able spelled it out for us. He was the only ground commander I ever had who took the time to tell his grunts why they had to do certain things. Improving our knowledge proved an effective way to keep down bitching. There had been some pissing and moaning about having to take a patrol out to Hill 104.5 every day, starting early in the morning and ending far too late every night. Les explained tactics to his NCOs, the NCOs informed the grunts, and soon the bitching and moaning ceased, well, cut down a good deal, anyway. And, okay, sure, we did have a bad second day, a very bad second day.

I was in the FO bunker early and had one of my guns standing by, ready to fire instantly, if the patrol going out walked into any shit. It was a cakewalk again. The patrol moved quickly from the MLR to the staging area at the base of Hill 104.5. Scouts checked out the path uphill. The platoon moved quickly from their defensive posture up and then into the trench line. No sweat.

The explosion thundered and threw up a tremendous black cloud. The middle hill seemed to shudder. It was not an incoming round. I knew their sounds. This was a mine that had exploded, a big mine. Another new Able Company buck sergeant had carelessly walked through the back trench line without checking it out first. I learned all the details later that evening after the patrol had returned to Mound 52.

"Les just got through tellin' us to watch where we walked. I'm not shittin' you, that's what he said. Les said it was a favorite gook trick to let you walk on safe ground one day, and then come in and mine it the next."

The mine was estimated at about twenty pounds of TNT set with a pressure cap. When it exploded it seemed as though about ten thousand metal balls about the size of a BB zinged through the confined space of the trench line.

"One grunt, the guy in front of the buck sergeant, actually stepped over the fuckin' mine. Lucky all of them guys were wearin' their flak jackets and helmets. The guy in front was peppered from asshole to appetite up and down the back of his legs, the back of his arms, and in his neck, too. He's got a thousand small holes in him." One of the grunts on the patrol was talking. I was listening in on his conversation.

"The guy behind was luckier. He was a couple of steps back. But he still got caught with a whole lot of them fuckin' little BBs. He's gonna have a hard time pissin', and walkin', too, 'cuz the blast about ruined his knees, and his pecker, too."

"The sergeant?"

"I think he'll live. One of his feet—I guess it was the one he stepped on the mine with—was gone. We only found pieces of his boondocker. It was just gone, that's all, just gone.

"And he lost an eye, too. It was lying on his cheek, you know, with somethin' like white string, or ligaments, that's it, ligaments holding it on him. Anyway, it fell off when we moved him.

"And his other foot was all mangled. His boondocker was still on, but the sole was about blown off and he wasn't carryin' nothin' but hamburger inside. He'll lose that foot, too.

"Sheeeit! Feet take a beating in this war. That new buck sergeant yesterday lost a foot, and this buck sergeant today loses both of his. Goddamn!"

The grunt took a long swallow of coffee.

"Les has got to be pissed off. Real bad. Here we make just two patrols out to that fuckin' hill, and we ain't yet seen a fuckin' Chinaman. We ain't losin' any ground, but them fuckin' gooks are already ahead by three feet."

It was just one of those dumb things a guy says when he's

263

under stress and he's trying to work up a laugh. But nobody laughed.

The patrolling continued. Les had made his statement concerning the need for us to patrol out to Hill 104.5. We were grunts. This was what we were getting combat pay to do. Still, we didn't see any Chinese on Hill 104.5.

Off to our left, less than half a mile away and sitting just northeast of Panmunjon, an area that was lighted up all night with searchlights shining straight up, was an angry-looking hill mass. Because it was a reddish orange color during the day when the sun shone down on it, we called it the "Red Hill." This looked like a bad piece of ground, even from a distance. The part we could see was a long, sloping hill suddenly torn off and jagged, like a loaf of bread torn in half. The Chinese controlled the long, easy slope as well as the top of the Red Hill.

My old grunt outfit, Baker Company, had that hill mass looking down their throats. Baker Company, I was told, had to make their way up that jagged edge, every day, just to kick ass and take names. We could hear them on the tactical radio network when puffs of red smoke thundered upward and small pop-pop-pop sounds came muted to our hill. Baker Company was taking a lot of casualties. I was glad the luck of the draw had me with Able Company.

On our hill, after those first two casualties, the Chinese troops facing us just plain ignored us. The only time we saw any enemy troops was when one of us FOs would spot them, and we had to use binoculars to find them. Nobody wanted to rattle any sabers; we would throw out a couple of rounds and get in a couple rounds and that was that. The unfortunate part about not finding any of them was that we were starting to become complacent in our patrolling. Going out to Hill 104.5, daily, seemed to be no big thing.

It was my turn to go on patrol on Easter Sunday. After an easy early-morning walk out to Hill 104.5, a walk just as peaceful as we hoped the day would be, I was in the FO bunker, my binoculars up to my eyes. Morning had broken and the rest of the day was coming on fast. I was looking hard and thought I saw something move, way out in front. If it was a worthwhile target I would really be stretching my shots. I asked the artillery FO to take a look. He was a Swede. His name was, and I'm not shitting you now, it was Tenn Thousand.

"I think it's a Korean burial party, Cautious. I'm not exactly sure, but I think so. One gook is out in front with a rope, holding on to what looks like an ox. The ox is hooked up to, well, it looks like a cart with a big wooden box on it. There's a couple more people, a big one and a couple little ones, kids, maybe, at the ass end of that caravan out there. Are you gonna shoot?"

"Maybe. That's what I'm gettin' paid to do. How come you said you figured it to be a burial party?"

"Well, back in Seoul I saw a burial party. I took some pictures of it, in fact. It was a lot of people following a cart that had a casket on it."

"Do you remember if there was an ox pulling the cart?"

"No, come to think of it. All I remember seeing was people, just people. Maybe family members or somebody like that. They were either pushing or pulling the cart."

I looked out again at the target. Somehow I just couldn't convince myself that I was looking at a burial service. Maybe I didn't want to be convinced.

"That burial cart you saw. Were there any flowers or anything on it?"

"Well, I think so. Yep. I think they had flowers or something like flowers, anyway, all over the cart."

I took another look through my binoculars. Tenn Thousand had described accurately the target I had located; four gooks, an ox, and a cart. But I knew exactly what it was that I was looking at, or at least what I wanted it to be. I radioed my FDC. My first round was close, but not on target. It was close enough, though, to make a good correction from it. I gave the correction and ordered four guns to each fire two rounds of HE. The eight rounds were right on target. There were no secondary explosions. I studied the impact area for a long time. Nothing moved where I had fired.

"This is Cautious at Eight Able. Secure the fire mission. The gunners did a great job, right on target. Nothin' is movin' out there now. We shot the shit out of an ammunition supply wagon. The gooks were tryin' to fool us into thinkin' it was a burial party. Whatever it was, I turned it into a burial party, at any rate." I waited for my FDC to respond.

"Uh-huh. Yeah, well I'm pretty sure I killed the ox pulling that cart. My estimated guess on other casualties will include two gooks of average height, and two gooks of below average height. All KIA." I listened to the radio.

"Yeah. That's what I said . . . two gooks of below average height." I listened again to my FDC, and then said, "I don't know. They could'a been midgets, for all the fuck I know." I listened to the FDC talker for a moment.

"Yeah," I replied, "they might'a been kids, gook kids. Whoever and whatever the hell they were, they were out there where they should'na been." I listened again, and then I said, "Yeah, and a Happy fuckin' Easter to you, too. Why don't cha get your ass up on the hill sometime?"

For the rest of the day I felt at odds-end with myself. I was sort of psyched up and all let down at the same time. Les Able came by to talk with me.

"Heard you did some good shooting earlier."

"Not too bad, Skipper. I made a correction off my first round, then I closed the sheaf to get all eight of my rounds on target. Whatever was out there is dead."

"What was out there, Cautious?"

"I believed it was about four gooks escorting an ammunition wagon, Skipper."

"I understand some of the people out there were mighty small, sizewise, Cautious."

"Yep, Skipper. I already talked it over with my FDC. Well, I figure I made them all about the same size with my Four Deuce rounds. The way I figure it is if they are out there, and if I can see them, then I've got a right to shoot them." I looked out through the parapet of the FO bunker. I was talking, mouthing out words, but not really talking to Les Able.

"That's a killing zone out there, Skipper. You know that better'n me. Fuck it! I don't make the goddamn rules in this

266

war; I just play by them. Those two buck sergeants of yours, the ones who ain't gonna be marchin' in any parades any time soon, maybe I was thinkin' about them."

Les Able didn't need any morality statements from me. He didn't respond in any way to my last statement. Instead, he changed the subject and started talking about other events of the war. He said there was a serious break in the peace talks.

There always was a lot of saber rattling any time the ongoing peace talks were interrupted. It was pretty well assured that the United Nations was going to get fucked over again at the peace tables. The communist negotiators at Panmunjong had balked when told that only about a fifth of the Chinese and North Korean POWs who had been recently transferred to the island of Koje-do would accept repatriation. The communist high command was in a big snit about that fact. The peace talks should not have had an influence on the tactical war situation, but they did. Indeed, the peace talks had an iron-fisted grasp on the balls of our great green war machine and greatly influenced the way combat was being waged.

"From a tactical point of view, Cautious, last month during early March, this war became one of position and not one of maneuver. All we're doing is holding real estate. We're not trying to take any. It's why we don't stay out here on Hill 104.5," Les Able said.

He stayed quiet a moment or two, and so did I.

"I think we're going to have to pay for the past couple of easy weeks, Cautious."

I knew without being told that Les Able was going to come back out on the hill again the following day. I believe he thought the gooks would respond to my shooting. Les Able was the kind of a man who always did his own dirty work. I respected him enough to say I would come out on patrol again with him.

We made it without incident to the bottom of Hill 104.5 early Easter Monday. One of our scouts had just gone over the lip of the trench line and we all rose up to follow him when the feces hit the fan. Chinese were everywhere firing their burp guns. At least two were in the trench line above us. A half dozen more were on the small hill to our right.

Thank God they were firing high, way too high, and no one on the path was hit. We still had about twenty yards to go to get into the trench lines. The Chinese had all the time in the world to adjust their fire and ream all of us new assholes. Something had to be done to keep the attention of the enemy gunners off the fact they were firing too high. I was already on the radio calling in some shots on the concentration I had on the small middle hill, but it was going to take a long, long minute or two before they landed. I was kicking myself in the ass for not having my guns up and ready on that hill concentration, and at the same time I was keeping a tight sphincter muscle, hoping against hope that I wouldn't get shot, or that I wouldn't take a crap in my pants.

I think Les Able had lived all his marine corps life waiting to find himself in the position he was now in. He was at the head of his men, leading his men. Time and again he had said to his grunts: "A leader leads by example. If you want your men to do a dirty job, you've got to be ready to get yourself dirty."

Les gave it a good shot, I'll say that for him. He rose up, stood ramrod straight, and looked back at us still hugging the ground. He waved his right hand holding his .45 automatic forward, and he shouted: "Follow me, men! For God! Glory! And the Marine Corps!" He took four short steps up the hill before the gooks zoned in on him and about cut him in half. I guess he was hit six or seven times. But that fucker fell forward.

Even in dying Les Able was doing his job. In standing up the way he did, in taking the hits that he took in his face, neck, shoulders, and chest, he kept the gooks shooting high. They never did drop their aimed fire. They kept shooting high and I think it was because they hoped we all would jump up, giving them perfect targets.

Les Able was a great officer. He was also the only man who had moved forward. Moments later, artillery and mortar fire cleared the gooks off the small middle hill. A grunt scout in the trench line killed one of the enemy with rifle fire. The other Chinaman, on the right side of the trench line, stood up just as a mortar round went off. The rest of the patrol was home free in the safety of the Hill 104.5 trench line within two minutes.

We put the body of Les Able in one of the bunkers at the rear of the hill. Such a fucking waste.

CHAPTER
23

"Incoming!" a grunt shouted loudly. I had a choice. I could crawl into the bunker where we had just placed the body of Les Able, or I could make a run for it to the FO bunker. I opted for the FO bunker. I wanted to be in a position where I might be able to spot smoke rings, where I would be able to bring about some counterbattery fire.

The first of ten rounds hit Hill 104.5 about two seconds after I ducked into the FO bunker, pummeling the hill, causing brief vacuums of the cool spring air to be sucked in and blown out again, quickly, to the sound and noise of bursting bombs. I identified the incoming rounds as being 81mm mortar shells; when you hear enough go off, it's an easy identification.

Those Chinese were shrewd. They used everything in warfare to their own advantage. Their mortar tube equivalent to our 81mm was just one millimeter larger; they had an 82mm mortar. That one millimeter in the diameter of the tube—about the thickness of a cunt's hair—let the Chinese fire any captured rounds of ours with a great deal of accuracy, and effectively prevented their round from sliding down into our tubes. Who called them dumb gooks?

There was a slight difference in the way the Chinese made their rounds that caused a considerable difference in the way and manner in which their rounds exploded on impact. Our mortar shells were scored in such a way on the inside so as to break into many, many sharp pieces of shrapnel following detonation. The enemy's shells broke into pieces of shrapnel that were two, even three times larger than ours. The different sounds were easily identifiable. So when the first salvo of gook fire hit Hill 104.5, there was no doubt that it was our ammunition coming back at us.

I overheard Tenn Thousand, the artillery FO, calling in his fire. He was going to work his guns out in front of us; he was going after the guns that were pummeling Hill 104.5. My job, initially, would be to dust off the smaller hills to our right, ridding them of Chinese infantry who had been waiting in ambush for us as we came up the hill. I told my FDC what kind of fire I wanted.

"I want four rounds right on top of the hill. Then I want you to open the sheaf by about ten yards, and then I want you to walk it down the hill, shooting in a square. And then open the sheaf again by ten yards. And then again by still another ten yards. And then I want you to walk it back up the hill again."

When I got an "On the way!" from the FDC talker, I knew my rounds would be close. I went to the opening of the FO bunker and yelled loudly, "Fire in the hole! Fire in the hole on the middle hill!" I kept on yelling until the first of the grunts to hear me called out the signal, alerting others nearby that I had Four Deuce rounds coming in and they were going to be close.

I walked my shots up and down and all around the middle hill and then I pummeled the base and sides of Hill 104.5. These rounds joined those being fired at us by the gooks. Radio contact with the MLR position told the story.

"Able Forward, this is Able Rear, over." The radio operator seemed cool and detached.

"This is Forward! Go! Go!" The grunt radioman was nervous and excited. His voice gave him away.

"This is Able Rear. We see and hear much activity in your position. Advise, over!"

"This is Forward. We're catchin' shit! We walked into a reception committee, and they're throwing us one helluva party! Able Forward leader is ineffective! We're receiving much incoming. Our One Zero Fiver and Four Deuce Fox Oscar paren Sugar are responding! Over."

"This is Able Rear. I understand! Interrogatory the ineffectiveness of your Able Forward leader? Over."

"This is Able Forward. It's permanent! Out!"

CHAPTER
24

Living through combat, according to what the Funny Gunny had told me, was simply a matter of habitually doing those things that kept you from getting killed. Right now, in the FO bunker on Hill 104.5, I stayed busy calling in shots on selected targets on the middle hill, which was just a few hundred feet away, dropping my rounds time and again on tenacious Chinese who were located in well-constructed fighting holes. The Chinese, in turn, potshotted at every moving grunt on our hill.

My luck in calling shots was holding true. I was hitting my targets. The Chinese—at least initially—had us surrounded. The mortar and artillery fire that Tenn Thousand and I had called in had broken the chain of fire the Chinese ambush had earlier locked on us. The artillery and mortar rounds had impacted on the Chinese, disrupting their uncontested shooting moments after Les Able had been gunned down. Taking advantage of the lull, the rest of us then scrambled up the hill and into the relative safety of the trench line. Right now the reinforced squad I was with had Chinese on our right side and all around us down at the bottom of the hill.

In the brief moments after calling my shots on the middle hill—waiting for a splash and then looking out to see where the rounds were landing and then telling my FDC how to adjust the impacting rounds, moving them to hit in still another place—I had what seemed to be all the time in the world to think about the realities and the terror of war.

There was no doubt about it, I had finally gotten into the shooting war and it was scaring the crap out of me. It started scaring the crap out of me the moment I saw Les Able get hit. I had been under fire before, lots of times, mortar fire and artillery and an occasional rifle shot, maybe even a consecutive half-dozen shots or more, but nothing like this, not just me and a dozen or so other grunts being the specific target, not being all the way to hell and gone out in front of the main line of resistance, not being surrounded by an enemy who had us cold.

Finally, at long last, the shooting war in Korea had caught up with me. A few minutes ago when the squad was more than halfway up the hill, when Chinese small-arms fire from rifles and burp guns suddenly stuttered, that was when, for me, the Korean War took on a new meaning. That was when the shooting war in Korea had terrified me so badly I could not respond to Les Able when he had yelled out "Follow me!" the battle cry of marines at war. I don't think he really meant it as an order, but as a battle cry. I did not have the courage, the guts, to look into the face of war. Try as I might I could not will my legs, my arms, my body to stand up as Les Able had done, facing the terror of all the small-arms fire being thrown in at us. So I did nothing.

I felt shame the moment I heard the rounds impacting, hitting Les Able, the moment I heard him grunt when life went out of his body. At that moment I realized exactly why it was that all infantrymen were called "grunts."

I was ashamed that I had not leaped to my feet, ashamed that the other grunts in the squad had not leaped to their feet. As a squad we would have, could have, presented not just one but many targets to the Chinese, moving targets, placed over a large area, threatening targets that might have, during that frightening moment when the combat began, disrupted both the concentration of the enemy and their concentrated efforts to shoot at just one target.

I felt ashamed then and feel no less ashamed now, knowing that no one else in the reinforced squad had responded, either. Like the rest of the grunts, I just hugged the ground. I guess I was too scared, or maybe I valued a whole skin a whole lot more than honor. I had found out earlier that a grunt loses his cherry in a war the first time he comes under fire and then, like now, the grunt discovers that being under direct enemy fire is just as tough to live through every time it happens.

Right now, calling in Four Deuce rounds on the middle hill and waiting for them to land, waiting to hear the rounds explode so I could quickly pop up my head—if only out of habit—to look for black smoke and then call in any correction needed, I huddled in the FO bunker and thought about war. I realized that if a grunt did not think too much, did not let the war grip him completely, then the terror could be endured. A grunt had only to control his fear, had only to let his training take over at fearful times in order to deal effectively with the realities of war. So I tried to do just that and realized I had reacted to the situation the way I had been trained; I kept my ass down and I called in my rounds. But I was still scared.

After an eternity that lasted just a few minutes, the Chinese suddenly stopped their small-arms fire. I don't know if it was the incoming mortar and artillery fire that Tenn Thousand and I had called in on them to knock them off the middle hill or whether they just simply figured us grunts were no longer an easy target of opportunity. Anyway, they just stopped firing. And so did Tenn Thousand and I, even though we both knew we could fire just about as much as we wanted; our gun pits were not about to run out of rounds.

Resupply of ball ammunition for the rifles of the grunts was altogether another proposition. The staff sergeant leading the reinforced squad—now that Les Able was dead—knew that his grunts had only as much ammunition for their individual weapons as they had carried up on the hill with them. In the position we were in, resupply of rifle rounds was going to be a big issue with us before too long. The staff sergeant checked his men and the positions they had manned in the trench line the moment the firing had stopped. That was the way it should be; the grunt rule for fighting was simple: Each unit leader was responsible for the all-around security of his men.

As I watched that staff sergeant at work, it was easy for me to understand why grunts trusted their staff NCOs. He had already taught his men—and they were responding to his teachings—that it was not just the duty of the officer or NCO to see that the squad was protected at all times, it was inherently the first and primary duty of the grunts to see to their own positions and safety.

The staff sergeant's grunts knew that when the unit stopped its forward movement of a battle, when they could not advance farther, they needed protection quickly against the enemy small-arms, mortar, and artillery fire. The staff sergeant had taught his grunts that the protection should be simple, available almost at once, and capable of further improvement as long as they remained in that position. The staff sergeant moved his grunts into the trench line, into individual foxhole or two-man foxhole positions. He assigned each man a specific field of fire in front of his position, one that overlapped the field of fire of the grunt in the position next to him.

The grunt staff sergeant looked to his men first, and then he talked strategy with Tenn Thousand and me.

"Most of my grunts coming out here today brought just a unit of fire with them, a bandolier of ammo plus a clip of eight rounds in their rifles. That's about eighty rounds per man. Most of them have already gone through two clips, about sixteen rounds. The machine gunner has two boxes of ammo—about six hundred rounds, all told. You heard him, he's got a heavy trigger finger. Now he's got a kick in the ass. He busted far too many caps in that free-for-all we just finished; he's got about four hundred rounds left. Everyone's got at least two fragmentation grenades; some grunts have three. Most of us have nearly two canteens of water. Everyone has food enough to last the next twenty-four hours. And that's about the size of it. I'm open to any suggestions you got," the staff sergeant said, looking at Tenn Thousand but including me in the conversation as well.

We agreed the situation dictated that we conserve our small-arms ammunition. The staff sergeant would pass the word to his grunts that they should fire their weapons at definite targets only and not waste their ammunition. Tenn Thousand and I had plenty of artillery and mortar rounds back at the gun sites. We figured to use those rounds to keep the Chinese at bay. The three of us figured our squad of men would bust off the hill that night at a prearranged time. Tenn Thousand and I agreed to cover the retrograde movement of the grunt squad from Hill 104.5 with both HE and WP, blanketing the area of the three hills with steel and smoke. We agreed on midnight as the time to start the move off the hill. In communications with the MLR, we asked that artificial moonlight not be turned on until 0100, affording plenty of time for everyone to get down off the hill in darkness, with still enough time to make the move along the rice paddy dikes back to where we belonged.

Tenn Thousand said, "When the grunts make their move, Cautious, you and I will stay up on the hill. When the grunts get to the bottom of the hill and start for the MLR, that's when you call in the last of your shots. Then you make your move. I'll give you about thirty seconds and then I'm gonna haul ass out of here right behind you."

The staff sergeant agreed to the plan. He would be responsible for the movement of his troops. His squad would carry the body of Les Able and anyone else who couldn't make it down off the hill under his own steam.

"It'll be a headache," the staff sergeant said.

At that moment I had no idea of the headache I would carry off Hill 104.5.

CHAPTER
25

I was confused by the way the gooks were shooting. Up to now they always seemed to have had a definite purpose in firing their artillery and mortars. I based this conclusion solely on my past experiences as an FO. Right now, there didn't seem to be any reason behind the intense shellacking the gooks were giving us. A dozen rounds would pummel Hill 104.5 and then, minutes later it seemed, another ten to fifteen rounds would impact on us, and then maybe twenty to thirty minutes would pass without a shell landing on us.

There seemed to be no justification, no reasoning, to the number of rounds the Chinese fired. It seemed they were just firing for the pure hell of it because—at least from what I was able to see—Able Company grunts sure weren't giving them any targets to shoot at, ducked as the grunts were way down in fighting holes and not making any kind of movement at all. Everyone knew that if you gave the gooks a target of opportunity, they'd drop in a round or two right on top of you. Everyone knew that. They'd see a target of opportunity and, Boom! Boom! they would be right in on that target, and then they would secure their guns and wait for the next grunt to show himself.

That was how the Chinese FOs operated. That was how we had come to expect them to operate. Now they were throwing shit in the game by dropping rounds by the dozens on Hill 104.5. By noontime every grunt on the hill had been hit at least once, sometimes twice, by these small hunks of hot metal. We were lucky; all our flesh wounds were minor.

Artillery and mortar fire boomed in, pummeling Hill 104.5 with so very many rounds of thundering explosions. All a grunt could do was grit his teeth and pucker up his butt hole and hope that the next time he got hit it wouldn't be any worse than the last time. The best defense a grunt had against this type of shelling was to get up under a covered fighting hole—one that afforded a good view to the immediate front for overall knowledge and one that had a good overlapping field of fire—and just sit out the roar and the thunder. All of the positions selected had good observation and fields of fire. They were covered over with layers of sandbags. The staff sergeant had known about the grunts' fear of the unknown. He knew his men could endure HE rounds as long as they could see what was happening. He also knew that if you cut off the visibility to a scant ten, twelve feet out in front of the grunts' positions, you would have some mighty shaky grunts.

I think the Chinese knew this, too, because about midafternoon they lobbed in and hit the front of Hill 104.5 with nearly a dozen rounds of white phosphorus. Thick, heavy, ropy white clouds of billowing, choking chemical smoke spread up, over, and all about the hill. The thick, perfectly white mist produced a pall-like sort of scary effect that clung tenaciously to the ground. There was no breeze to dissipate it. The most frightening part of the impacting WP was that it blinded us so effectively. In moments, visibility was down to about fifteen feet. A lot of grunts were not aware of the dual role of the WP shell. When its phosphorescent component was coupled with other nonmetallic elements and prepared properly for use in an exploding mortar round, the WP gained a spontaneous inflammability that, upon contact with air, produced a billowing, thick, intensely white smoke screen. The WP round had both shrapnel casualty-producing and incendiary capabilities.

To do my job right I had to see. My first mistake of the afternoon was to leave the FO bunker in order to get a better view; I went into the trench line. My second mistake was to stick my head up above the trench in order to take a look around.

"Sheeeitt!" I yelled when a WP shell exploded directly in front of my position. My head snapped back; it was as if I had been kicked in my mouth where my lips joined at the right side. My hand reached up, thumb and forefinger and middle finger working, pulling out, snatching out the small bit of white phosphorus that had burned the end of my scraggly mustache, a piece of WP that had struck and was trying to burn its way through my lip to my gum. I snapped my fingers forward, flinging away the bit of white phosphorus, burning the tips of my fingers. The impact, or my reaction to it, or both, had caused me to reel back and bang into the rear of the trench line. I either fell or the impact knocked me to the bottom of the trench line.

Tenn Thousand shouted out: "Goddamn it, Cautious! Are you hit? How bad are you hit? Answer me, goddamn it!"

I yelled back quickly, surprise ringing in my voice: "Them fuckers! Them goddamn fuckers! They burnt off the end of my mustache!"

There was no blood. The skin was not broken, just burned. Almost immediately a large blister formed. It was as if I had been briefly poked very hard with the blunt end of a branding iron. Almost immediately I was aware of a numb and very uncomfortable skin-stretched sensation. This was quickly followed, in the area where the WP had struck, with a stinging, burning-like-crazy sensation. My tongue kept darting out, licking the tight half-inch oval-shaped bubble that had formed at the side of my lip. I scared myself when I thought that an inch or two higher and I could have lost an eye. That's when I started shaking.

I licked the tight bubble again with my tongue. There was no hurt, not at the moment anyway, just a swollen numbness. Out of the corner of my eye I could almost see where my lip swelled up and out. But there was no hurt. If I felt any pain at all it was from the tiny blisters that had quickly formed on the tips of my fingers from where I held the small hunk of WP after I ripped it from my lip.

But no fucking blood.

Damn! Hit by a hunk of shrapnel, a piece of WP, but there would be no Purple Heart because I didn't have any broken skin.

Maybe I'd get lucky.

Maybe before the end of the day my bubble would break.

CHAPTER
26

"Can you see them, Cautious?"

Tenn Thousand and I had come down, hunkered over and scrabbling through the trench line, to a point halfway down the hill, a point in our lines that was closest to the Chinese. Their WP smoke was behind us up on the hill. I felt like the two of us were actors on a bare stage with a white backdrop curtain behind us.

I was almost certain the Chinese had us spotted. I felt like I was bore-sighted and visible and under the scrutiny of their watchful eyes. But I needed to be at this spot on the hill. I had a suspicion of where the Chinese had dug in their mortars and I believed I could locate the mortars from this vantage point. That suspicion was formed solely from listening for the coughing sound of the fired mortars and then trying to place exactly where the sound came from as they shelled us. To be certain of just where their mortars were located, I had to see the smoke from their mortar tubes. In order to see the smoke I had to go out some ten feet beyond the trench line, out to where I would have the proper angle, the right view. I informed Tenn Thousand of the situation, at least as I understood it.

"I think we're gonna hafta use some sandbags and build something like an individual prone shelter out in front of the lines, maybe along that shelf over there," I said, pointing. "Then I'll crawl out and see if I can spot where the gook mortars are when they shoot."

The concept was not new. I had used this type of protecting shelter before, but never under such dire circumstances. Essentially, Tenn Thousand and I would construct a prone shelter out of sandbags stacked two high, just tall enough to protect from grazing fire the head and body of the person using the shelter. Building such a shelter would be a whole lot easier than trying to dig a shallow trench. In the past I had always constructed such shelters at night, with darkness hiding work efforts. It was a lot safer that way. But right now, Tenn Thousand and I could not wait for darkness.

Carefully, we pushed sandbags out in front of the trench line. We would initially form a line of sandbags straight out for about ten feet and then, using the first line as a shield, extend a second and parallel line, the distance between the sandbags just wide enough for me to crawl out with some protection. When the two lines were extended out far enough, closing sandbags would be placed at the far end. Because it was so shallow a shelter, it was not recommended for a rifleman; a grunt would have to really expose his body using it as a shooting position.

But all I wanted was to get to a location from which I could see the suspected area where I thought the gooks had located their mortars. I wanted a position from which I could bob my head up and down—up for a quick look and then down for concealment and protection. Tenn Thousand and I worked patiently on the shallow shelter, keeping our bodies close to the ground as we labored. Finally the prone shelter was finished.

"Good luck, Cautious," Tenn Thousand said as I slid over the lip of the trench line and started to inch my way forward. I was protected on both sides and in front by stacked sandbags, which rose up from the ground about a foot. Even as I crawled the few feet toward the end of the newly made position, I could hear the phlegmatic sound of three Chinese mortars coughing out rounds. I heard, quite distinctly, the pooping sounds of mortar being fired, one after the other. Now that I had this observation location, I had just the edge I would need to see beyond a fold in the ground of a smaller hill that was in front of Hill 104.5. I could see the bright, quick flash of burning gunpowder spouting from the end of mortar tubes. I had pinpointed the enemy positions.

The Chinese were shooting three rounds, one immediately following the other, with a short pause—just a few moments of hesitation—between their shots as they readjusted their mortars for the next sequence of three shots.

Having spotted the location of the Chinese mortars, I called shooting information back to my radioman, who had positioned himself in the trench line, and then I ducked my head down into the dirt, below the level of the double-stacked sandbags. I could hear my radioman talking with the Four Deuce FDC. For the first time I realized that I didn't know the name of my radioman, not even his nickname.

The first section of the Chinese mortar rounds impacted far below my position. I could feel their shot pattern—three rounds in a line, marching up from the bottom of the hill—each round about fifty feet in front of the previous one. They were walking their mortars up the hill. I raised my head and definitely established their pattern of shooting. The closest round of the three was about a hundred yards below me on the hill. The rounds were directly on line with my position.

Oh, shit! I thought. I felt the moment of absolute helplessness felt by a grunt under artillery or mortar gunfire when, after seeing the rounds flash from the enemy tubes, he knows that within seconds the propellant cause of that metallic arc will fail, and death, in a solid, streamlined form, will crash thunderingly down upon a designated point, shaking and blasting apart his small dirt world.

The brute force of the detonation carried still more hurt for the grunts who were lucky enough not to be bitten by pieces of the hot, flying fragments; it was the blinding, instantaneous headache caused by concussion. The great pulsing roar made by the impact of a shell self-destructing close by would be instantaneously superimposed in the permanent headache area of the brain, and no amount of headache pills would ever cause the pain to go away.

"On the way, Cautious!" my radioman shouted, telling me of my rounds being fired.

At the same time I heard again three muted pooping sounds coming from the enemy mortar position. Still another series of enemy-fired rounds had been fired at Hill 104.5 and were on the way. Because of the close proximity of the enemy mortars to Hill 104.5 and the far distance to the rear to where the Four Deuces had set up their guns, the Chinese shells would take less than one-third the time to impact on target than my rounds. At just about the time I could hear their rounds being fired, the three they had fired earlier were due to impact on target. Those goddamn Chinese made a science out of shooting mortars. They extracted the maximum terror from every round fired.

Three rounds had already hit Hill 104.5. Down the hill I heard the carrumping sound of three more impacting rounds exploding just as my radioman yelled out, "You got a splash, Cautious!"

Good! Now it was get-even time. Ten seconds now and then a couple more and I would raise my head for a quick look and try to spot the black smoke of my exploding rounds. Numbers in sequence ran through my mind.

Seven . . . eight . . . nine, I counted mentally. I tensed my body for a quick upward thrust of my neck. I needed to push my chest up so I could see over the sandbags directly in front of my helmeted head. I splayed my hands and fingers out on the ground on line with my shoulders. I felt the aching tenseness in my elbows, and the tightening of my neck and shoulder muscles. As I brought my knees forward, ever so slightly bent, I could feel my butt jut higher and I prayed I would not get hit in the ass. If I was going to get hit, then I wanted a visible and exciting scar, something warriorlike, something I could proudly display. I felt my thigh muscles bunch and the calves of my legs tighten. I was aware of my toes curling inside my boondockers as I waited for the critical moment when I would suddenly thrust upward, exposing my head, my face, my eyes for that fraction of a second needed to look for my mortar smoke.

Fourteen . . . fifteen . . . sixteen, I counted. I started my upward movement and the ground punched up at me and all the air around me was gone, and then it came back with a slapping, snapping sound that I could feel but not hear. I was suddenly all-over hurt, and behind my eyes and between my ears there was a great ringing sensation. I felt my eyes bulge out and then as quickly narrow again in a stabbing pain that was all of a sudden here and then gone again, leaving behind only its aching memory.

I knew only that red and yellow fire and screaming bits of metal had torn into the top sandbag that was just inches away from my helmeted head. Dirt from the blasted sandbag covered me like a shroud.

I knew it as a terrible mistake, a miscalculation, and then, just before I knew nothing at all, in that last microsecond, that final knowledge of events happening, I felt all that was inside me try to push to the outside, try to force a way out through my popping eyes, my deafened ears, my bleeding nose, and my dirt-filled mouth. Blood forced its way out through my rectum; I felt as though I had expended a great quantity of gas in a single wet and monumental fart; my penis was smeared, the result of an abrupt and bloody discharge.

In that moment of losing consciousness, that instant flash when my mind worked madly overtime registering all that had happened and all that was then happening, I was aware of all the details I would need for a later, more leisurely review. I was aware of and knew the tease and doubt of shelling, the terrible feeling that I had inflicted so casually on enemy targets over the past months, the tease and doubt the enemy gunners were now inflicting on me. I knew that I had been incapacitated through concussion alone.

I knew that I had not been cut, had not been pierced or gouged by shrapnel.

I should have been overjoyed, yet I knew no joy. I knew

only a disappointment beyond belief, a vast disappointment brought about by the knowledge that the corpsmen would have nothing to stitch or bandage.

I had missed out again on getting a Purple Heart.

And then I was comforted by the man-made darkness that came at noon.

CHAPTER
27

Light of day, as at dusk, flickered and shifted through every shade of red. I was in a bunker and I was on my back, my hands folded over my belly. My breath came shallowly, just barely enough to cause my chest to rise and fall with the effort of it. I sipped at the air through a dirty mouth, through nostrils caked with what had been a thick, sticky substance, something that had caked and dried. The taste in my mouth was putrid; the smell in my nose was fetid. I raised up and hacked and spit and gagged and coughed and then stopped suddenly as I felt the stiff body of Les Able, rigid with rigor mortis, rigid with the progressive stiffening of his muscles, the stiffening that would naturally occur within several hours after his death as a result of the coagulation of his muscle protein.

Ahhh, fuck it, Les, I thought, as I pulled quickly away from contact with him. His mouth was still open, and his eyes were only partially closed, and in my mind's eye I could still hear his last words. I had admired Les Able in life, was proud of any type of association with him, but even though I did not fear him in death, I did not want to be in the same confined bunker space with his body. I shuddered all over and then kicked my feet down toward the end of the bunker, scooting myself out into the trench line.

All was silent in the darkening of day. I raised my hands and with a finger dug into my ears, feeling a thin shell of substance crack and flake away. I brushed my ears quickly and listened carefully. Nothing. I could hear nothing except my own hoarse breathing sounds. I coughed and hacked more and then, on my hands and knees, crawled along the base of the trench line as it curved around the crest of the hill. I nearly bumped helmets with Tenn Thousand as he came crawling along toward me.

"Jesus fucking Christ, Cautious! You're fucking dead!" Tenn Thousand said, wide-eyed, looking at me from just inches away. He quickly explained how the last mortar round in the third series of shots the gooks had thrown at the hill had taken out the sandbags that had closed the end of the prone shelter I was using to call shots.

"Your radioman and me just pulled on your legs, hauling you back into the trench. Nothin' but blood. Honest to God! You were nothin' but blood all over your face. You weren't breathin' or nothin'. We thought you were dead. So we stuck you up in the bunker with Les Able. Jesus! You scared the crap right out of me." And then, almost as an afterthought, "Your rounds knocked out those gook mortars." He quickly cut me in on the scoop that the squad had changed the time when it would depart the hill.

"We figure to make our move just as soon as it gets dark," Tenn Thousand said. Looking at his wristwatch, he said, "And that should be in about another hour. You've been outta things for about five hours, Cautious."

While Tenn Thousand and I informed our guns what we wanted to shoot and the exact time we wanted the shooting to start, the Able Company staff sergeant had the rest of his men prepare to go down the hill. They would carry Les Able down with them.

It was time. The grunts went over the trench line. A grunt with an automatic weapon, a BAR, went first, eager, anxious to get off the hill, yet very much on the alert.

Up in the FO bunker, Tenn Thousand and I started calling in our shots.

And then it was my turn to head out the back door. I was still wobbly but could make it under my own steam. There was no one on the path down the hill in front of me. I was gasping for breath and making a hell of a lot of noise. I couldn't see or hear the grunts, so I figured that, handicapped with carrying the body of Les Able or not, they were well ahead of me. There was the hint of a moon, way off, just coming up in the sky, casting the faintest amount of light.

Suddenly, from one of the standing walls of the farmhouse at the bottom of Hill 104.5 came the stuttering sound of a burp gun. Behind its flashes I could just barely make out a man standing. I raised the muzzle of my grease gun and, without stopping my downward movement on the path, still taking long steps downward, I pointed the weapon and squeezed the trigger, emptying the banana clip of thirty rounds.

I must have shot up the whole countryside. I sure didn't hit whoever was there shooting at me. Still moving downward, I pulled out the used magazine and turned it around, inserting the second magazine I had taped end to end to it. I squeezed the trigger again in a long series of stuttering shots. No luck. I had missed with sixty rounds, for the burp gun continued firing.

Tenn Thousand seemed right on my heels. I knew he was armed with a carbine. Out of the corner of my eye I saw him point his weapon straight out, almost as though it were a handgun. He squeezed off one shot—one lousy shot—and the enemy soldier fell over.

"Go!" Tenn Thousand yelled.

Way up ahead, the first grunts of the reinforced squad had some difficulty making the outpost position aware of exactly who was trying to barge through the barbed wire protecting the company front. Flares went off and streamed downward, trailing long, intestinelike strands of gray smoke as curses flew back and forth. We passed through the wire. A heavy machine gun stuttered overhead, aimed well down the rice paddy pathway, insurance against anyone who may have followed us.

That night, Able Company was informed by battalion that it was not deemed advisable to occupy Hill 104.5 during daylight hours in the future. Able Company was advised to hold their own for the time being. The company completed its remaining time on line until late in May, looking out at the three hills, looking out at the hunk of real estate that would become important again later in the summer, to be identified then by the name of Outpost Reno.

There was no monkeying around about it; all we did was hang tight, holding the ground we were sitting on. A grunt with a sense of humor, quite talented as a cartoonist, drew a picture of a monkey, dressed in dungarees and boondockers, helmet, rifle, and all, and identified as an Able Company grunt, sitting on a couple of sandbags, holding tightly to a hardened and swollen peter that jutted out from between his legs. Exposing teeth in a broad grin, the monkey appeared to be saying: No monkeying around about it; I'm holding my own in Able Company.

Les would have liked that.

CHAPTER
28

Late in May, elements of the 5th Marines relieved Able Company at Rock Mound 52. On rejoining the Four Deuces for an anticipated and looked-for month of reserve time in a large open area filled with dust and pyramidal tents, I found that someone in the first sergeant's office had already made plans for my thirty days off the line.

"Tomorrow you get on down to division headquarters and check in with the G-4 section. You've been selected to go to NCO Leadership School, Sergeant Crawford."

This was my first introduction to the new first sergeant, although I had talked with him a time or two on the EE-8 telephone while I was up on the hill. He was a tall man weighing more than two hundred pounds. He carried his weight well, with bearing and dignity. There was nothing crass about him. He spoke well and without profanity and he made me understand, in a moment, that vulgar language is the lazy tool of men who had a limited vocabulary.

The first sergeant informed me that, in a crash course of about six weeks' duration, a course of intensified schooling that would end with a combat patrol in front of the lines, I would learn all there was to know about being a noncommissioned officer, or at least all that was necessary for a young NCO to know at the present time. The first sergeant ran down the syllabus of subjects that would be taught at the school: first aid, hygiene and sanitation, squad tactics, the use of both map and compass, scouting and patrolling, basic communications, and the use and care of small arms, the M1 rifle, the automatic rifle, both light and heavy machine guns, and grenades and demolitions. I didn't figure I would have any problems with the course of instruction.

"You will graduate around the middle of July, providing of course that you don't get killed or taken prisoner while you're out on patrol. That's a new twist the Marine Corps has added to its final exam for young NCOs." He gave me a quick smile. "But I believe you're going to do all right. You'll need this course in your service record book if you want to make staff sergeant."

My ears picked up on his last two words. He had my undivided attention.

"And when you get back to the Four Deuces with a diploma, I'm going to see to it that you get a week's basket leave in Japan, gratis, without it coming off your accumulated leave. It's called rest and recuperation leave. Not many people get to go on R and R. Just one man each month from each of the line companies. You've got to earn it; the skipper here thinks you've earned it."

I didn't know what to say to that. So I kept my mouth shut and said nothing. The first sergeant continued: "Coming and going and being in Japan and all will take about ten days' time. So, you see, I've got your reserve time all planned out for you, plus the first week or two when the company will be back up on line. What do you think about all that, Sergeant Crawford?" My smile answered for me.

I learned later that I had Les Able to thank for the plans that had been made for me. Les Able had informed the Four Deuce first sergeant that Able Company had named me for consideration for the award of a Bronze Star medal. The consideration was for rescuing that buck sergeant who had gone out in front of the lines up on Hill 104.5 to get the pheasant he had shot. Les Able had also informed my unit that, instead of a combat award, I had asked for a meritorious promotion.

Additionally, I learned that Tenn Thousand had contacted my company and informed the first sergeant that I would be placed in nomination for the Letter of Commendation for materially aiding in neutralizing enemy mortar positions during the time when the last patrol from Able Company was surrounded, briefly, on Hill 104.5.

Since the first sergeant had informed me that the successful attending and passing of the 1st Marine Division NCO Leadership School—a school that was held in a combat zone and included a class in an active combat situation—was the quickest way for me to get my ticket punched for selection to staff NCO rank, I looked forward to attending the school. I drew clean clothing and other supplies from the company supply sergeant and cleaned up. The company jeep would drive me to the NCO Leadership School. I was surprised to find the driver heading back toward the front lines. The schoolhouse, I was informed, was within a mile of the line. I marveled at the lengths to which the 1st Marine Division went to gain realistic training for the troops. School instructors were grunts who had learned their lessons on line.

I recognized both the New Jersey twang and the words—which I had heard muttered over and over earlier during January—while I was checking in with the clerk of the NCO school.

"A grunt just can't trust a fuckin' gook. That's all there is tuh that. Back in January on the east coast a fuckin' gook showed up in front of me on a day cold enough tuh freeze a well digger's ass, and he's wantin' tuh surrender, wavin' wunna them surrender passes in the air, and then after he scopes out our lines the fucker tries tuh escape by runnin' down the hill. I hadda shoot him! That fuckin' gook was a spy! And he fucked it up tryin' tuh run away like that! That fuckin' gook should'na have tried tuh have been a fuckin' spy!"

Former Corporal Castaglia of Easy Company, who had recently been promoted to buck sergeant, was still trying to

294

justify opening up on a gook with his light machine gun. Anyone who would keep harping at it this long maybe had something he had to justify. Only nobody checking in at the NCO school was interested. Maybe we all had something on our minds, something to justify.

The small class of fourteen students was provided quarters in a long, dirty-brown squad tent. I had the cot next to Castaglia's since I followed him, alphabetically, on the class roster. Rain or shine, classes would be held outdoors. There were no blackboards. No one had to take notes. Since the classes dealt with living and dying—us living and, hopefully, the gooks dying—the instructors had our absolute attention.

Classes began immediately, within an hour after the last man had been assigned his bunk. The classes were informal; everyone was asked to contribute some knowledge to each subject discussed. Instruction took on the manner of a continuous bull session; the instructors introduced the subject matter and then guided the discussion and kept it from straying too far afield.

As we had found out in actual practice, in actually fighting a war, there was no right way or wrong way to approach an answer to any question or problem posed. Constantly the class was told: "If your solution to a problem has already worked for you, then continue to use the solution, or modify it to your existing needs." There were, however, tried and proven ways that could resolve certain field problems. The instructors told us these methods and encouraged us to learn and apply them at the proper time. Classes continued throughout each day, including the weekends. At night we were assigned perimeter guard duty around the school area, which was close enough to the lines so that this duty was not punishment, or anything like that, but was an absolute need. Naturally, we were armed to the teeth. Days and nights passed quickly. It was soon graduation time. But first we would have a final examination.

"You people get yourselves ready for a night reconnaissance patrol. Pull this off successfully and you'll graduate," the class was told. There was a great hurray sounded to this remark. The skylarking stopped when the instructor continued: "If you don't pull it off successfully, we will give Purple Hearts to them as get hit, and sound taps for them that get hit real hard."

Reconnaissance patrols are sent out to gain information about the enemy or the terrain. The class was reminded that such a patrol engaged in combat only when it was necessary to accomplish its assigned mission or in order to protect itself. Imagine the luck of the draw when I found out that the patrol would go out to Hill 104.5. I was assigned duties as the Four Deuce FO for the patrol. If I could live through the night of July 14, I figured I would pass the course. If there was one thing I could do pretty well, it was shoot the Four Deuce mortar. Besides, I still had the maps I had recently used up on Hill 104.5, and my maps had all my former concentrations marked on them. All I had to do was contact the Four Deuces FDC of the 5th Marines. It would be easy enough to reestablish my old concentrations.

I felt like I would be cheating on the test. It was like I was taking a test and had all the answers.

At least I thought I had all the answers.

CHAPTER
29

I did not know Murphy or why they named a law after him but he sure must've been one helluva fuck-up to gain that kind of notoriety. Simply put, Murphy's Law stated: If it can go wrong, it will go wrong. Murphy's Law sort of applied to me and the rest of the NCO school class when we went out to Hill 104.5 for our final examination.

Instructors at the NCO school had communicated with regimental headquarters of the 5th Marines. Plans were coordinated for the NCO school graduating class to pull a reconnaissance patrol on Hill 104.5; I was to establish Four Deuce concentrations for use with that patrol. I had no trouble putting in the concentrations I needed. I purposefully shied away from putting concentrations near the two war-torn, bombed-out farmhouses located to the left of the S-shaped path at the bottom of the hill. I had already decided, without discussing it with anyone else, that if an opportunity presented itself, I would examine the area closely for my own personal reasons.

The NCO school instructors had formed the patrol by assigning duties and functions that used the expertise of class members to advantage. A newly promoted staff sergeant—who just that day had been selected for his rank—was designated the patrol leader. Castaglia would head up the light machine gun section. I had already been selected as the Four Deuce FO.

Since I was the only man in the class who had actually been on Hill 104.5, the patrol leader and I talked things over, with the rest of the grunts of the patrol listening. I told them what I knew about the rice paddy path that had to be used to get out to Hill 104.5. I told the class about the mines that men of Able Company had set off on the hills, and cautioned them in that direction. I told them about the trench lines and the bunkers on Hill 104.5 and where the best fields of fire might be located. I told the class about the ruined farmhouse and about the Chinaman who had blazed away at me with a burp gun.

I didn't tell anyone about my plans to visit that farmhouse if the opportunity presented itself. I had my reasons for wanting to go there. I knew the Chinese would not risk men to recover their dead if the dead man was in a position exposed to our fire. Morbid as it may sound, I wanted to examine that dead Chinaman if his body was still near the farmhouse. I couldn't believe I had missed with all sixty of my grease-gun rounds and that Tenn Thousand had done the man in with one shot from his carbine, a carbine held out in front of him like a goddamn sword as he was running downhill.

There was no grab-assing or anything like that when the patrol formed up at the wood-and-barbed-wire gateway at the bottom of Rock Mound 52. The patrol leader quickly went over the drill with us one last time.

"Our primary mission as a recon patrol is to gain current and valid information about Hill 104.5 and the area held by the Chinese to the immediate front," the staff sergeant said.

He continued, "You men are expected to look, see, and report anything that'd be of value to the Fifth Marines, since this is their area of operations."

In keeping with the spirit of a reconnaissance patrol, the staff sergeant said, emphatically, "Engaging the enemy in combat is a secondary role to this patrol. We should become engaged in a combat situation only if it's absolutely necessary in order to protect ourselves."

Covering all bases, the staff sergeant said, "If we get into a shooting situation, I want everyone to get off the hill as quickly as possible. We'll re-form the patrol at the base of the hill for a quick nose count."

That was when he asked me to designate a location that might offer protection and would be easy to find.

I designated the two bombed-out farmhouses, an easy-to-recognize landmark. I reminded the patrol members about the Chinaman who had been shooting at me with a burp gun when I had come flying down off the hill a couple weeks ago, and how Tenn Thousand, with one lousy shot, had knocked him down.

"If that gook could get into there without getting his ass blown away with booby traps, then we ought to be able to do the same thing," I said.

"Chancy?" the staff sergeant asked.

"Sure," I said, "it would be chancy. But then this whole business about taking a final examination with real bullets and all is just as chancy."

We were quiet, quick, and efficient as we passed through the wire and headed out to Hill 104.5.

I guess the class should have gotten good grades on getting out to the base of Hill 104.5 quietly. I pointed to the bombed-out farmhouses. The patrol carefully climbed the hill. We eased into the trench line and found positions where we could observe the enemy hill across the way in front of us. Patrol members quickly determined that Hill 104.5 was bare of the enemy, although we found evidence they had been using it.

The patrol had been on the hill for about five minutes when we heard Chinese, lots of Chinese, coming up a path on the far side of the hill, a path that must have been cleared earlier. I don't know exactly how many of the enemy there were, but in the darkness it sounded like there was a whole shitpot full of them, maybe a horde or more. It didn't take long to figure that maybe our reconnaissance patrol might, out of sheer necessity, be turned into a combat patrol real quick.

According to plans arranged earlier in the day, I was to have the 5th Marines Four Deuces fire illumination flares if and when the patrol made contact. The 5th Marines gunners already had both illumination and HE rounds primed and ready to put in their tubes. All it would take to get them in the air was my command.

In planning the patrol, the staff sergeant had figured the Chinese would continue to do exactly what they always did when there were flares in the air. The Chinese would stop moving; they would stand perfectly still. If that held true, our patrol would have some operating time, even if that time was counted only in seconds. The flares would be the signal for everyone out on patrol to bug out, to get down off the hill mighty fast.

That's exactly what happened. Well, almost.

When the flares went off, the Chinese, as predicted, stopped moving up on the trail. They went rigid on hearing the Pop! Pop! Pop! sound of flares igniting overhead. In the first shaky, wavering, smoky light of the flares, it didn't take anyone but a scant second to see that the enemy was coming up the trail to Hill 104.5 in force, maybe as many as a company of them. Someone sure had picked the wrong night for our graduation exercise. It was time for us to "cut-a-chogie," to haul our asses out of the area.

The word was passed quickly for the patrol to get off the hill and meet in the vicinity of the bombed-out farmhouses for the staff sergeant to get a quick nose count. Following the nose count, I was expected to call in some HE rounds, pummeling the top of the hill. Using the thunder and roar of the exploding Four Deuces shells as a diversion, the class would then shag-ass back to the MLR.

With that plan in mind, the patrol headed down the path toward the farmhouses. I was one of the first grunts to get to the bombed-out buildings. Since it was my idea to go there, the staff sergeant figured I ought to go in first to sort of find out if there were any mines or booby traps in the area.

I did and I satisfied my curiosity, much to my gratification. The body of the Chinese soldier was still there, kind of flattened out by now. As I had figured, no rescue party had been sent out to get his body. For the briefest moment I wondered about the marine standard for retrieving their dead and wounded.

By the light of the oscillating magnesium flares, I looked more closely at the caved-in body lying face down. He had two big holes punched outward in the center of the back of his cotton jacket. Tenn Thousand would have to share this kill with me. The burp gun the soldier had been firing was on the ground just beyond the body, a bit rusty from being out in the weather. I picked it up and, by its carrying strap, slung the weapon across my back. I was carrying a PRC-10 radio on my other shoulder in order to communicate with the 5th Marines Four Deuces, so it was getting a bit crowded back there.

Waiting for the rest of the NCO class patrol to get to the bombed-out farmhouses, I called for still more incendiary flares. Those 5th Marine mortar men were good. I no sooner asked for the illumination than it was in the air, with their FDC giving me a ten-second splash. Alone momentarily, I could hear, could actually distinguish the approaching shells in their trajectory, despite the other noises of the night. I heard the shells rumble a low thunder high overhead, and then I heard the heavy Chung! sound as the shell casings and the flares separated. The metal containers continued their thrumming individual ballistics arcs all the way down, punctuated with a peculiar whistling-moaning sound as they tumbled end over end. High overhead, each of the magnesium flares popped into a blinding white light, each swaying at the bottom of parachute lines, lurching, creating a grotesque shadow dance below.

Quickly now, other men of the NCO class came stumbling down the hill. A fast nose count.

"Goddamnit!" said the staff sergeant. "We're one man short. Who the fuck didn't make it off the hill?" His question was interrupted with the stuttering sound of a light machine gun.

Right away we all knew who either hadn't gotten the word

or—and there was a good probability of this—who was ignoring the word. Even at this distance, we could hear Castaglia roaring out in a gravelly voice as harsh as his barking light machine gun: "You fuckin' gooks shouldn'a ought tuh've been tryin' tuh sneak up here tuh spy on us!"

"Can you get some HE out in front of the hill?" the staff sergeant asked.

"I sure can," I said, all the while talking to the FDC by way of my radio.

"You got it," I said to the staff sergeant. "Three rounds of HE, each, from a section of four guns. On the way! If we head back up the hill, my rounds will be splashin' by the time we get there. I'll follow them with more illumination."

Back up the hill went the patrol. We got into the rear trench line as a dozen Four Deuce HE rounds pounded the front of Hill 104.5.

The thunder of exploding HE shells was still in our ears when the sky was lighted again with magnesium flares.

There were no living Chinese on the hill. Castaglia had piled up more than thirty of them in front of his machine gun position, the closest being about fifteen feet away.

All of a sudden Castaglia was aware that he had us for an audience.

"Did'ja see them? Did'ja see them fuckers? That ain't no way to attack a fortified position, is it, Sarge?" Castaglia asked the staff sergeant.

That numb nut Castaglia didn't even know he had been the only grunt on the hill facing the Chinese. He just kept on doing what he did best, chastising the enemy verbally, shooting the shit out of them physically. Castaglia was living proof, and the piled-up Chinese were dead and dying proof, that if you get too close to an asshole you were just bound to get shit on.

The last flare hadn't even burned out properly when the NCO class once again hurried back down the trail, moving for all it was worth back to the MLR.

The NCO school instructors got the word on what had happened. Everyone in the class except for Castaglia passed the final examination and got a diploma.

Castaglia failed mainly because he had turned the reconnaissance patrol into a combat patrol when there really had been no need to do so.

Castaglia didn't worry about it too much. He was the only man in the NCO class to be put up for, and then later be awarded, the Silver Star for gallantry in action.

CHAPTER
30

"You did real good in NCO school, Sergeant Crawford," the first sergeant said, fondling the burp gun I had just given to him. "You're scheduled for R and R, just like I promised you. You'll get a five-day basket leave from the corps, gratis, to go to Japan. You've earned it. My clerk is taking care of all the details now. You'll leave from Kimpo Airfield about 1400 tomorrow afternoon."

The selection criteria for R and R were determined by personal awards or decorations. I was selected because I had been nominated for both a meritorious promotion to staff sergeant and the Bronze Star by Les Able and, more recently, the Letter of Commendation by Tenn Thousand.

"And those two near misses. Don't forget about them," the first sergeant reminded me. "You came close, twice now, to getting a Purple Heart. Personally, I think you should have gotten one for the blister on your upper lip. It was WP that burned you, wasn't it? It left a scar, didn't it? And nobody can discount the fact that it ruined your mustache." The first sergeant chuckled about that and so did I, even though it wasn't a laughing matter at the time it happened.

The company jeep driver would take me to the paymaster at 1st Marine Regiment the following morning. I would give him my freshly typed-out SMR, a special money request, which authorized me to draw all the money I had on the books, pay accumulated but not received.

I figured I had about a hundred dollars coming to me in back pay. At the official exchange rate of 360 to one, my hundred dollars would amount to 36,000 yen, a real treasure trove in the economy-poor Land of the Rising Sun. Six years after World War II, the debilitated Japanese economy continued to struggle hard to recover. I would have enough negotiable yen to satisfy any yen I might have, enough to live royally for a week.

Following pay call, I was taken to Kimpo Airfield, located just a few miles northwest of Seoul. I waited there for a Fairchild R4Q Flying Boxcar flight to Itami, Japan, the main air base for the 1st Marine Air Wing. Everyone on the R-and-R flight was slated to stay overnight at Itami—with its Cinderella liberty—and then be authorized to go anywhere in Japan during the following week.

I was way out of my element and completely overwhelmed by it all. I had absolutely no idea where I would go or what I would do on R and R. As things turned out, I didn't need to worry. The first man I saw in the temporary barracks at Kimpo Airfield was Sergeant Castaglia. He greeted me like a long-lost friend and, I guess, maybe he was right, war friendships being what they were at the time. Castaglia, I later learned, had been assigned duty in Japan two years earlier. I was fortunate to have him latch on to me. At least I thought I was fortunate.

The R-and-R flight departed Kimpo Airfield on time, carrying about three dozen grunts. By 1700 we were being given an orientation briefing by a master sergeant. The briefing was short and to the point.

"Change your Mickey Mouse money to Japanese yen right here on the base or take your chances on getting shortchanged in town. You people can then wait around for about an hour and have a lackluster meal here on the base, or you can head right out on Cinderella liberty, where you

305

can part with a buck or two in town and eat Kobe beef washed down with a cool Asahi.

"Get back inside the main gate by midnight—and don't fuck it up or you'll be spending all your time and money here, locally, in beautiful downtown Itami, all in accordance with base liberty policies.

"Them that don't fuck up will have their leave papers endorsed early tomorrow morning. I'll sign you out and, in accordance with the wishes of the base commander—a bird colonel who was shot down while flying an F9F Panther jet over Korea and who was rescued by some grunt marines— I'll give you tomorrow as a free day, a travel day, so to speak. And, lucky you, I'll also give you still one more extra day at the end of your basket leave here in Japan, another travel day. That'll give you seven full days to get yourselves screwed, blue'ed, and tattooed."

Fifteen minutes later, Castaglia and I were seated, cross-legged and a bit uncomfortable, on the floor of a Japanese steak house, our shoes on steps outside and our stocking feet up under a large circular table. We had ordered thick Kobe beefsteaks, fried rice, and a garden salad. Milk, cold homogenized milk, had won out initially over Asahi or Nippon beer; it had been far too long between drinks of ice-cold milk for both of us.

A Japanese mama-san wearing a deep blue cotton kimono, a loose outer garment that reached down to a few inches off the floor and had short, wide sleeves and a bright red sash, came to our table after Castaglia and I had each demolished a second steak.

Bowing first, she sat down at the table and, with an elegant grace, poured cold Asahi beer in fresh, clean glasses. Castaglia, still seated, welcomed her to the table with a slight bow from his waist. In stilted English, mama-san asked if there were anything she might do for us.

Castaglia gave her a crooked grin. "We're gonna need just a cuppla things, Mama-san. Like, maybe, two number one josans who speak, maybe, a *sukoshi* bit of English. *Wakaru maska,* d'ya understand? We need josans for, maybe, one week, for *shichi* days. We both are ichiban boy-sans. We are numbah one. We will treat the josans right. But, maybe, we might wear them out, Mama-san, you know what I mean?"

Pointing at me, Castaglia said, "We are both numbah one skivvy honchos."

I believe I got a bit embarrassed at the blunt way Castaglia got right down to the nitty-gritty in defining our basic and base needs.

Mama-san didn't flinch one bit. She gave us a toothy smile and clapped her hands together smartly.

Two young josans responded to her bidding by quietly opening, entering, and then closing a sliding door, gaining entry to the small dining room. Both wore bright pastel-colored cotton kimonos that had wide sashes and a flat pillowlike arrangement in back. On their feet the josans wore heavy white cotton socks made with a special big toe feature, the better to wear their footwear of wooden clog-type shoes or woven sandals.

Each josan had coal black and very straight hair fixed in an elaborate hairdo held in place by long wooden pins, the symbol of their place in Japanese society. They were young —sixteen, maybe seventeen years old—and both were quite pretty in the Oriental way. Their attractiveness came from fine, almost exquisite features. They smelled very, very delectable. They had delicate hands, and fingers that fluttered like posing butterflies.

For my taste, the josans wore far too much makeup, especially around their eyes, which, instead of being slanted, were narrow and elongated, wider at mid eye than at either end. I had been told by other grunts and had expected to see women with flat faces and pug noses. I was surprised at the attractiveness of the josans.

One of the two josans seemed to be very thin, the other was pleasingly plump. There was no selection made by either Castaglia or me. The thin josan sat down next to me and the full-bodied josan sat next to Castaglia. My grim look turned round-eyed as the thin josan quite casually slipped her hands inside my crotch and caressed me. I looked up, sort of surprised I guess, and saw mama-san grinning at me.

"You like?" mama-san said, nodding her head.

"I like," I said, a crooked grin all over my face. The josan stroked me again. She gave no sign of embarrassment. She looked me straight in the eyes.

I gulped, "You speak, how much, Mama-san?" I sort of croaked it out. I wasn't in a dickering mood. Any reasonable figure would satisfy me. I quickly agreed that 500 yen, about a dollar and thirty cents American, was a reasonable price for the company of the thin josan for the evening.

I called the josan Skoshi, an abridgement of the Japanese word *sukoshi,* which meant little, or small, thinking I was some kind of a linguistic expert to have come up with just the right name right out of the blue. She responded far too well to the name and I was a bit miffed thinking that, in all probability, someone had earlier used the name on her.

In a nearby bathhouse Skoshi gave me my first introduction to the ritual of the Japanese bath. She told me to remove my uniform and as I did she folded my clothing in a practiced manner, placing everything in a neat pile in a small basket. With an expertise that could only have been born of practice, she dodged and avoided my hands.

"You wait," she said. And then she removed her kimono. She had a beautiful figure. Her petite, very erect frame carried small, pert breasts. She was thin, yes, but she had plenty of padding at just the right places. Her legs were shapely. Elfinlike, she had no fat around her waistline. She had no body hair, none on her legs, between her thighs, or on her arms. Her body was so very smooth to touch.

Skoshi led me by the hand through a wooden doorway and into a tiled washroom. She motioned for me to have a seat on a three-legged wooden stool.

"You wait just one minute," she said. "First I give you a bath, plenty wash, then you soak in hot tub, then I give you numbah one rubdown. I gonna treat you right, you wait and see."

Behind me now, Skoshi used a small water-stained wooden bucket, wrapped around with twine, which had a handle jutting out from it, the better to scoop hot water from the tub. The hot water was cooled somewhat with cold water from a nearby faucet; then Skoshi poured the now-warm water gently over my head. Another and then another small bucket of warm water was used to wet my body, preparing it for washing.

In the warmth of the washroom with its warm water smell, I relaxed, prepared to enjoy the bath. Lord knows, I surely could do with a bath.

The washing was good. I felt my body start to tingle. I could feel the past eight months of Korea flaking off me, coming out of my pores, and being washed away, bubbling, through a drainpipe fixed in the wooden floor of the bathhouse. I was content as I breathed the thick, moist air of the bathhouse as it mixed with her musk. I let my body relax as Skoshi washed me again and yet again from head to toe.

Following a final rinse of warm water, ridding me of soap, Skoshi told me to stand up and walk to the large, chest-high, round wooden tub, which was fashioned, giant-sized, in a manner similar to the water bucket. She lifted the wooden cover and placed it carefully along the back wall of the bath chamber. The tub was filled with water, very hot water. The middle of the tub was hidden by thick clouds of steam.

Pointing to steps placed on the inside of the tub, Skoshi preceded me down and into the tub, showing by gestures where I should place my feet. She seemed not to mind the hot water, which turned my ankles red. I stopped and minced from foot to foot and gradually became accustomed to the heated water.

Standing waist deep in the bathwater, watching me, Skoshi held a hand in front of her face and tittered. She pointed to a bench built along the inside of the tub. I was to seat myself again. Skoshi adjusted my head, permitting it to lie back on a towel folded at the edge of the tub. I couldn't do a thing for myself; she anticipated everything. I was quite consciously aware of her naked and lusciously thin brown body now and again close to mine, sometimes rubbing tantalizingly against mine, but I was so comfortably relaxed in the warmth of the bath that I was quite willing for Skoshi to perform everything according to an established ritual.

Skoshi broke into my contentment, saying, "You come, now!" Using the wooden stairs, she walked up and out of the tub. She motioned for me to sit again on the three-legged stool. I sat. Skoshi walked behind me again. I heard her filling the bucket with water.

My eyes widened and I gasped, deeply, my whole body tightening up as ice cold water cascaded over my head, splashing down, down, down. I turned quickly and again saw Skoshi had both hands clasped over her mouth, giggling, her slanted eyes smilingly wide. She looked ravishing.

Before I could grab her, she stopped me, saying, "You come now. Skoshi fix!" She motioned for me to lie face down on a massage table. I gasped in utter delight as I felt the heel of her palms hammer at my shoulders, felt the side of her hands drum along my back in short karatelike blows, felt the strength of her fingers as she kneaded my flesh, my muscles, as she smoothed away, caressed away all the aches and pains of Korea and combat with her gentle touch. She delightfully stroked, poked, and prodded my body—at the back of my head and behind my ears, my neck, my arms, my hands and fingers, my back, my buttocks, my thighs, the calves of my legs, the Achilles tendon area, my feet in and around the arch and each individual toe; all received their own special massage.

I was as relaxed as I had ever been. It had been a long, long day for me. The anticipation of the flight into Japan, the landing and the briefing, the meal and the quart bottle or two of Asahi beer, the warm bath, and the relaxing massage had just about done me in.

Skoshi made me put on a kimono and then dressed herself in the kimono she had worn to the bathhouse. She motioned for me to follow her and we walked a confusing course through wooden hallways to her room. She motioned me to lie down on the unrolled quilted bedroll on the floor. I did so.

Skoshi said, "I'll be right back." I nodded, heavy lidded, and then promptly went sound asleep. I never knew when Skoshi came back into the room to take her place on the bedroll beside me.

Castaglia barged into Skoshi's room with all the finesse expected of a slightly drunken grunt. He was drawn out and red eyed in a messed-up uniform and smelled of beer and strong drink.

"Ya gotta 'bout fifteen minutes tuh get yer ass in gear so we can check in at the main gate on time, Kawshuss!" Castaglia said, bringing me out of a deep sleep.

With a leer and a smirk, Castaglia eyed Skoshi and me.

"Did'ja get any?" he asked.

It was the type of question expected to be asked at a time and place like this. I don't think Castaglia expected any more of an answer than a shrug or maybe a grunt or two from me.

Still, I answered his question much in the manner I had learned while working the Quantico switchboard. I knew then, as I knew now, there just wasn't a marine around who was going to pay out cash money and who was going to come back off liberty and say that he hadn't gotten laid.

When it comes to lying about getting laid, I remembered that young marines have no peers.

I looked Castaglia dead in the eye and I lied.

Skoshi held her hand up in front of her face and tittered.

CHAPTER
31

The long summer drought, a normal occurrence in Korea, started during May and ended with the beginning of the yearly monsoon rains on the morning of July 28, 1952. I remember that day even though it wasn't a red-letter day for me, one that I wanted to live all over again. It was the day I went back up on the hill and I guess I was feeling antsy, a bit apprehensive, knowing that I was getting to be a short-timer, a man with less than two months to go on his hitch in Korea.

Just twenty-four hours earlier I had returned to Korea from Japan. Truck transportation was provided from Kimpo Airfield for those of us who needed it to get back to the 1st Marine Regiment. On arrival there I made a telephone call to the Four Deuces and talked the first sergeant into sending a jeep to pick me up. The ride back to the Four Deuces was subdued mainly because I made an ass out of myself. I didn't know the jeep driver; he was a new replacement who came in with the 22nd Replacement Draft in June. Like I said I had a case of the ass and just felt prickish and I didn't want to share talk about my R and R with him. I gave him short answers and shrugs until he finally gave up trying to hold a conversation and just concentrated on trying to hit every damn pothole in the road back to the Four Deuces.

Over coffee in the mess tent the first sergeant said I was to go up on line with George Company the following day. That was okay by me. I had been listening to the Armed Forces Radio the past week while I was in Japan. I knew there was little or no action going on other than the swapping of mortar and artillery fire and maybe some patrols to keep posted on what the Chinese were doing. It was just more of the same old shit that had been going on for the past couple of months. Going up on line would be a piece of cake, no big thing, an easy job.

And, as the first sergeant and I talked, I thought to myself that I needed whatever rest I could get. Up on line I knew I could get a rest that would be interrupted only by the exigencies of a shooting war. I could handle it.

I should have been all rested and recuperated. I had, after all, spent the past ten days in Japan on R and R in order to get that way. But then I met Skoshi that first night while on Cinderella liberty. I never left Itami. I spent half my R and R leave with Skoshi. I guess I enjoyed it too much because I felt a little bit guilty about it, too. I had mixed emotions and I didn't want to talk about it with just anyone.

Now that my illicit sex fling with Skoshi was over, I've got to admit I was just a little bit apprehensive about the next couple of days. Even though I showed none of the symptoms, I worried about whether or not Skoshi had the clap and, more importantly, I was even more worried that maybe she had given me the clap. One of the last things arranged by the master sergeant at the Itami Air Base for the grunts coming back off R and R was another reminder for them to view a movie dealing with the horrors of syphilis and gonorrhea. Mother marine took care of her own, right down to denying her brood good memories of Japanese sex.

Perhaps I really had nothing to worry about. Navy corpsmen in Japan had already shot me through and through with enough penicillin to kill off any disease I might have been carrying around. I had been informed—and as promptly forgot about the warning—that Japanese farmers used night soil, human excrement, collected in huge "honey pots," large barrels placed on sturdy two-wheeled wagons, as fertilizer for their gardens. Bacteria on the unwashed vegetables from these gardens could cause severe stomach problems to the uninitiated. During the brief time I was with Skoshi, I ate quite a bit of the locally grown fresh fruit and brightly colored vegetables that she chopped up raw into attractive salads. And then I doubled over with severe diarrhea.

In agony I asked Skoshi to find Castaglia. I don't know why I was surprised when she told me he had taken off for Nagoya with the other josan: "They be gone two days now." Between running to the *benjo* with the turkey squirts and shitting my brains out, I managed to get back into my uniform. I told Skoshi I had to go to sick bay at the base. She called a cab. I gave Skoshi a present, a five-thousand-yen note. The cabdriver drove me to the base at Itami and out of Skoshi's life forever. I spent the rest of my R and R in the sick bay at Itami drinking paregoric and getting penicillin shots.

All of which was why I returned to the Four Deuces tired, physically weak, and drained dry. For one thing, Skoshi had damned near screwed me to death. Follow that with a couple of days of debilitating diarrhea and a grunt was guaranteed to lose weight and become just plain worn out. I should have been rested, but I was not. I was quite the opposite. I felt weary and used up. I had lost nearly ten pounds in weight.

I spent the night of July 27 in the Four Deuce headquarters area, restless and unable to sleep. I remember it as a hot, humid night, one without relief, a sticky night made stickier with just trying to stop sweating, with just trying to breathe. It was an altogether uncomfortable night, relieved only when, after a brief and unsatisfying attempt at sleep, I got up to get some coffee to ease my still-aching guts.

The first sergeant was awake and in the galley. He, too, was feeling miserable with the sticky night.

In conversation over coffee, the first sergeant, an old-timer to the Far East, a man who had spent years in China, Japan, and Okinawa, told me that, following the June and

314

July weeks of day-and-night hot, dry weather, "if you have a night that comes on hot and humid and sticky, just like it is right now, then you can expect the monsoon to be right behind it, usually by the following morning." And when the monsoon starts, he said, the rain would come down heavy and relentlessly.

The following day as I was trudging up the hill with all the starch washed out of me, assigned as the Four Deuce FO to George Company, I felt the first huge drops of the monsoon rains pelt down. The heavy drops smashed down hard, cracking, drumming on my helmet, dripping off the front edge so that it seemed I was walking through a waterfall.

The punishing rain soaked me through and through in minutes. I was quite wet by the time I got into the trenches and headed to the bunker of the George Company skipper, a young captain. I got the standard welcoming speech. The words sounded like they were coming from far away, as though the captain was speaking into the wide end of a megaphone with the small opening pointed at my ears. "Sure happy to have you aboard, Sergeant Crawford. Your communicators are already on the hill. They're sacked out next to the FO bunker.

"We've got Chinese opposite us. They've been sneaking up on us at night. We call it their 'creeping war.' The chinks seem to want to occupy this hill.

"Find a bunker. Check in with the Top, here, if you need anything." I was dismissed with a quick handshake. The skipper was busy running his war.

My head was hot, feverish, and aching like there was no tomorrow, and pain spread down the leaders of my neck and into my shoulder joints. I was breathing hard. My chest physically ached with each lungful of indrawn air. My eyes were playing tricks, focusing and then not focusing, pulling my head—it seemed—forward and then back, forward and then back, and my eyelids were so very, very heavy. I was extremely tired. I was exhausted.

I found the company corpsman and scrounged some APCs and a collapsible stretcher from him. The Doc advised me to get off my feet for a while. I found an empty bunker. I dumped my Willie Peter bag, my weapon and map case, my pistol belt, my helmet, and my flak jacket inside the doorway. I felt so weak. I could barely manage the simple task of opening the stretcher. I pulled the coarse brown blanket I had carried to the hill over my body. I crashed out on the stretcher. My weight pressed the tough green nylon of the stretcher down to within four inches of the bunker deck. I closed my burning eyes. Relief avoided me. I was feverish, chilled, and shaking like a dog shitting peach pits.

My throat was dry and parched and swollen. Swallowing seemed too much of an effort, yet my tongue sought out the spit from around the front of my teeth, drawing the saliva to the middle of my tongue back around where my tonsils used to be, and I could feel my Adam's apple pushing, sort of catching everything, like a dusty grain elevator going up and down, but there was nothing to carry up or down, just me gagging and trying to puke and occasionally tasting bitter acid bile and then feeling all the sicker. I was so tired it seemed it took an effort just to feel sick. My actions were sluggish and apathetic. All I wanted to do was close my burning eyelids. I wanted to sleep, to sleep very deeply, but all I could manage to do was half close my eyes, manage to feel my eyelids burn on the inside, manage to feel the grit that had gathered on my eyelids and in the corners of my eyes. I just wanted to hold on tight to the edges of the stretcher to keep from being thrown off as it whirled and whirled.

And that was it for me. I do not remember another thing about being up on the hill with George Company. I do not remember the continuous, hard-driving, pelting rain that punished the trench line, collapsing many areas of it, washing out other locations. I do not remember the downpour that pelted the lines, coming down without letup. I do not remember the warnings passed by sentries that rainwater was filling the trenches, that sandbags needed to be placed in the entranceways of all bunkers, the better to keep out the rain and keep the bunker floors somewhat dry. I don't remember when it was that my bunker filled with rainwater or when that rainwater, by the process of osmosis, seeped and soaked the coarse brown blanket, then my clothing, and then water-puckered my skin. I don't remember my out-of-control temperature or my body-shaking, teeth-chattering chills.

Three days later the monsoon rains abated somewhat and my radioman found me in the bunker. He ran for the corpsman. The corpsman checked me out and ran for the company commander.

"We've got an emergency evacuation. He's gotta go right now. See if you can get a helicopter in. This guy needs to be sent to a MASH hospital where they have facilities to take care of him."

"Who is it, and what's he got, Doc?"

"He's the Four Deuce FO, Skipper. I don't know his name. I think he's got hemorrhagic fever, maybe malaria, too. He's definitely got pneumonia. His temperature is up outta sight. He's gonna die if we don't get him outta here most ricky-tick."

"Look up his name, First Sergeant, and contact the Four Deuces for another FO. We need one, with those chinks creeping in at night. I'll radio for a medevac by helicopter. Doc, get him down to the landing pad. Use whomever you need to help you."

I don't remember the quick trip by stretcher down the hill to the landing pad, a large flat, oval-shaped clearing halfway down the hill. Grunts sweated in the monsoon wetness as they carried me down the slight but extremely slippery incline of the hill. The grunts cursed the footing, cursed the awkwardness of the stretcher, and, I guess, cursed me. But I didn't hear their profanity. I don't remember the transfer from the doc's stretcher to the one strapped alongside the bubble-shaped helicopter.

I dimly heard the corpsman as he spoke to the grunts who had helped him, "Well, that's one of you fuckers getting away with a free ride. No fuckin' Purple Heart this trip. They don't give them away for what he's got. But at least the fucker's gettin' away free."

Vaguely, I seemed to have knowledge of a muted, heavy and insistent whop-whop-whop sound originating overhead and all around. It was the inelegant sound that rotor blades make as they whirl about and the sudden, awkward change of pitch when the blades bite deeply into surrounding air, causing the helicopter to lean forward and, with its nose down slightly, eggbeat its way down the valley, rippling the water in terraced rice paddies below. Flying just scant feet above the rice paddies, the medical helicopter hugged the ground, its camouflage exterior blending in naturally until the whirlybird seemed to be a moving part of nature, whump-whumping until it was well out of range of enemy view and bullets and shells.

When I tried to recall the events that followed, all I could bring to mind was the low, husky voice of an angel, a voice that insisted time and time again, "You cannot give up! If you want to go home again, then you must fight back! You cannot give up! You must fight back! You must help me! You must fight back! You must help me! You must fight back!"

I don't remember fighting back. I don't remember helping the angel. She was my lifeline and, like a fisher of men, she reeled me in all by herself.

When I opened my eyes and became aware of my circumstances, it was to see, overhead, the shit-brindle-brown coloring of the gently flapping, undulating, sloping canvas of the large medical tent. I could hear the comforting patter of rain, not smashing down now but gently striking in a soothing yet irregular and scratchy sort of way, forming from individual drops into a solid sheet of wet, sliding to the abrupt edge of the canvas and silently, gracefully dropping the final four-foot fall, ending in deep puddles below with a double-sounding Plop! Plop! The nearly two weeks of monsoon rains were ending.

"Well, thank Christ you're awake." I saw lips moving in a face topped with a nurse's hat. I looked up and saw a sort of round-faced, plump army nurse. She spoke in a full-toned, sonorous voice, a voice that had a rasp to it, a huskiness. "A couple times over the past ten days or so I thought I was gonna lose you! You've really been through the mill!"

She thumb-padded first my left and then my right eyelid, lifting up, looking in. Pleased with what she saw, she smiled the gentlest smile, one that covered her with beauty.

"In case you're wondering, you're at the Yong-Dong-Po MASH unit. That stands for Mobile Army Surgical Hospital, only we're not too mobile with all that mud out there.

"You're gonna be okay, now! There was some doubt about you there for a couple of days last week. But you're a fighter, by God! All you marine grunts are fighters when we get you in here!

"The doctor will be along in a minute or two. He's plannin' on transferrin' you out to the navy hospital ship for further treatment."

And then she was gone and I never saw her again.

CHAPTER
32

The following morning I was evacuated by helicopter to the USS *Repose,* a huge naval hospital ship painted stark white, with enormous red crosses on her port and starboard sides. The ship was at anchor in the mudflats off Inchon harbor. White-suited sailors helped me walk from the helicopter to an examining room, an area often used as a triage center, which was located inside the ship proper. I was examined quickly and competently by navy corpsmen. After a few questions and a couple of pokes and prods, the corpsmen seemed satisfied that, no, I did not have any gunshot or shrapnel wounds that needed either bandaging or rebandaging. Once that was determined, they seemed to lose interest in me; I was not a patient who needed their special skills.

My hospital chart was then picked up and read by a medical doctor. He asked questions concerning my present well-being, jotting down my answers. I watched him write August 12, 1952, as the date on my chart. That surprised me; I wondered what had happened to the last two weeks of my life.

"You don't have too much longer to go on your tour in Korea, Sergeant. Play your cards right and you can ride out the next couple of weeks here on board the hospital ship," the doctor said. "You could do with the rest. And I believe some of the doctors here would like to know more about the hemorrhagic fever you may have had."

The doctor assigned me to a hospital bed in a room that housed some other grunts. A corpsman helped me to the bed that had a thick mattress. The bottom white sheet was neat, with military corners. There was a huge pillow inside a white pillow case. The hospital bed was covered by a neatly turned-down heavy white wool blanket.

I made the move to the bed assigned to me with the help of a corpsman and so I did not see who else was in the room. I was, however, very much aware that I was the only one in the room not wearing bandages or plaster splints or a harness for broken bones.

I closed my eyes to the springs and mattress of the bunk above me. I didn't want to talk to anyone. I think I sort of felt ashamed that I didn't have any wounds or broken bones.

Suddenly a loud voice rasped out: "Okay, you people! Them that can use a broom I want them to use it on this deck. It's cruddy. Get it cleaned up!" It was a strident voice. I opened my eyes to see that it belonged to a navy nurse who wore the rank of commander. Although still weak, I raised up on an elbow and tried to swing my legs over the side rails of the hospital bunk bed.

"Not you, Sergeant Crawford," the navy nurse commander said in a more gentle voice, looking at me. "You lie back and let me get some vital signs. I'm talking to the rest of these goldbrickers in here!" She turned her head and looked at the other men in the room. They were giving her back as big a smile as she was giving them. The deck was spotlessly clean and tidy.

Conspiratorially winking at me, smiling broadly as if to cut me in on her private joke with the troops, she said, "I give them a little hell every so often. I don't want 'em to think they've got things easy just because they're aboard ship." All my vital signs tested okay.

"You'll want to know what happened, why you're here, why you spent about ten days at the MASH unit in Yong-Dong-Po," the nurse commander said.

She told me that I definitely had malaria: "You're gonna feel the shakes and sweats of that again. You need to keep on taking quinine tablets for it."

She told me I had had pneumonia: "That's part of why you're here. Your lungs are almost clean. You've been given penicillin for that. A day or two more will fix you up like new."

And she told me doctors thought I had had hemorrhagic fever: "That's the iffy part. You had something like it, at any rate. Most of you grunts who get it don't live too long with it."

I guess the nurse commander saw bewilderment on my face. She forestalled my question: "It's just another one of those rare Oriental diseases."

She guffawed and smiled, "Too bad it's not like that other rare Oriental disease 'lacka-nooky.' You marines seem to know how to get the right medicine for that, or so I've been told."

She smiled quite broadly at my embarrassment.

"There, now! See, you smiled! You're going to have to smile more often. That's part of the treatment you'll get here on this hospital ship. You marines heal better when you're smiling."

I stammered out my thanks to her. In minutes she had made me feel worthwhile about myself again. A grunt, I realized, could get hospitalized in a war even if he wasn't a candidate for a Purple Heart.

Most of the wounded grunts in the hospital room said they were from George Company.

"What the hell happened?" I asked. "I was up on the hill with you guys for just a couple of days at the end of July. There was no fighting going on then. Just the monsoon rain comin' down."

A corporal who had been a George Company squad leader said, "I thought I recognized you. Cautious? That's your name, ain't it? You're the Four Deuce FO who was evacuated off the hill with pneumonia or somethin' at the end of last month, right?" His left leg was heavily bandaged.

I nodded that he was right.

"I helped the Doc bring you down off the hill. He's dead now, did'ja know that? Naw, I guess you wouldn't. The fuckin' gooks shot him last week. He come out to Outpost Siberia when I got hit. The chinks got him before he got to me." The squad leader introduced me all around to the other wounded men. They told me what had happened up on the hill after I had been evacuated.

"When the monsoon rains stopped comin' down so hard, the chinks started probing an outpost we had out in front of our MLR. We started calling the outpost Siberia because nobody wanted to be there except the fuckin' chinks."

Other George Company grunts joined the conversation. Outpost Siberia, it was explained to me, was a small, insignificant hill, a spur, actually, out in front of the George Company position on the lines.

"We hadda man it, ya see. The hill blocked our MLR view of an approach to our lines. We stuck a reinforced squad out on Siberia, at first. The chinks just kept on creeping in, every damn night, hittin' us, throwin' a cuppla grenades at us, and then they were gone."

I quickly came to understand that while I was at the MASH hospital, George Company had been involved in a bloody battle for contested high-ground advantage. Within sight of the Panmunjon searchlights where truce talks were still at a standstill under canvas tentage, a steady stream of wounded and bloody grunts from George Company were brought to medical collection points for a quick patch-up and, when necessary, were helicoptered to the USS *Repose.*

Following up on their creeping war, a beefed-up Chinese platoon attacked Siberia during the first week of August. In a twenty-six-hour time period, Outpost Siberia—as the spur was being called—changed hands nine times.

Another Pfc said, "We'd of still been goin' back out, only we run out of grunts. All told, George Company had about seventy percent casualties. A lot of grunts got killed. I don't know how many. We'd still be gettin' the shit kicked outta us

323

if Baker Company hadn't 'a gone out and kicked the gooks off that Red Hill, Hill 110. They took the heat off us."

"Only they ain't callin' it the Red Hill anymore. They're callin' it Bunker Hill," the George Company squad leader said.

Baker Company marines, aided by hundreds of artillery and mortar rounds that suppressed the Chinese in their fighting holes, struggled up and then occupied Bunker Hill following a surprise jump-off and a brief, fierce fight during the hot afternoon hours of August 10. The marine grunts were now in fighting holes higher in elevation than those on Siberia. The grunts were in positions where riflemen and machine gunners looked right down the throats or at the back of the necks of Chinese troops on Outpost Siberia, some 250 yards away.

The Chinese commander was no fool; he counted his dead and knew that his position on Siberia was untenable. He pulled his troops back off the embattled slope. As quickly as the Chinese departed, so did George Company warily come out to retrieve their dead and wounded. For the present, fighting on Siberia was finished. Everyone knew the enemy had another bone to gnaw on.

Baker Company had taken a stick and stirred up a hornets' nest on Hill 110, the hill now called Bunker Hill. It wasn't the hill that was important anymore. It was simply that both the grunts and the Chinese wanted very badly to take a crack at each other, and Bunker Hill was the logical place for the fight to take place.

Sure, we got the word the Chinese had fresh troops facing us, soldiers who had been funneled in over the past several months. The word was the Chinese had doubled their strength in the trenches that faced positions held by the UN forces all up and down the line. The word also said that a helluva lot of heavy artillery, maybe twice as much as we had backing us up, had been spotted being moved into position near the front.

But, believing in our own invincibility when fighting an Asian soldier, we wanted to fight, perhaps as badly as the Chinese soldier wanted to fight.

324

That suited the top dogs on both sides, for they, too, for their own purposes wanted us to fight.

The high commands on both sides knew that the Panmunjon peace talks had come to a standstill. The Reds now were insisting the 38th Parallel be the line of demarcation and, in fact, demanded it be so. The Reds demanded this, knowing full well that United Nations forces held good and valuable territory and positions far to the north of the 38th Parallel. In Japan, General Ridgway and his UN negotiators wanted to force the issue, to stop the talks, to resume an active war; in Washington, D.C., President Truman and his advisers wanted to keep the talks going; the communist negotiator being manipulated by Moscow was very much aware of the difference in the view of the fighter and the politician and was attempting to capitalize on it.

On the battle lines, commanding officers could keep their men dormant in front-line positions just so long. The impasse at Panmunjon would soon open a Pandora's box and let loose platoons of fierce-fighting, howling, and shrieking Caucasian and Oriental soldiers.

Baker Company grunts knew it was a matter of time, a day or a couple of days, before the Chinese would come up from the still-muddy valleys around the base of Bunker Hill, come up again, perhaps, through the late-afternoon heat or in the cool dark of night, come up the sandy red scrub pine slopes behind a flurry of punishing artillery and, at the last moment, behind dozens of hastily thrown grenades come into our trench lines.

When I heard the helicopters buzzing businesslike, circling, hovering, waiting patiently like dragonflies over a creek bed, waiting to bump to a landing on the big red encircled X that marked their landing platform on the stern of the USS *Repose,* I had a hunch that my easy days of recuperation were soon going to come to a screeching halt.

The navy nurse commander came into the hospital room. She had taken a shine to me; there was no doubt I was one of her favorite patients. She said I reminded her of her younger brother, a marine buck sergeant killed on Okinawa.

"Come on, Sergeant Crawford. Let's take a look at what's going on." And then, out of character for her, for she was not usually crass, she said bitterly, "I think a bunch of marines just got their asses kicked."

We went out on the small patiolike structure and leaned against the waist-high piping, joining other men from the ward who were already there.

Five, six, seven, a dozen helicopters whirled overhead, with one whomping down, collapsing almost, to a landing in the center of the red circled X every sixty seconds or so. It seemed to me the rotor-whirling gooney birds had little grace and landed awkwardly.

The date was August 19, 1952, and the grunts of Baker Company had taken a beating. After five straight days of small-unit assaults on Hill 110, the Chinese had just one hour ago started an earnest attempt to knock Baker Company from the hill.

According to the scuttlebutt, Baker Company had, in the past hour, suffered more than 80 percent casualties fighting gooks who had finally gotten into Hill 110 trench lines. Chinese troops, taking cover advantage of an early morning low-lying ground fog, had carefully crawled up the forward slope of Hill 110. Unseen, unheard, the Chinese moved forward and stopped scant yards away from grunt gun emplacements. And then, to the fanatical sounds of bugles blowing off-key, to shrill whistle noises that worked them into a killing frenzy, to green flares bursting high overhead, the Chinese had in continuous human-wave assaults supported by thrown grenades and blazing burp guns attacked straight up the hill and could not, would not, be stopped, never mind how many were dropped by grunt small-arms fire.

During the past four days, the Chinese had tried time and again to push Baker Company off Hill 110. Now, in the trench line, the gooks fought Baker Company grunts in hand-to-hand combat. Both sides hacked away at each other with knives and bayonets and entrenching tools, shot at each other with pistols and revolvers and automatic weapons, stabbed and bit and locked each other in death grips.

An SCR-300 radio crackled: "We've been hit! We've been hit hard! Chinese have hit the hill in force! I don't know where the hell they came from." There was a long hissing pause broken only by the crackling sound of a transmitter key being held open. And then: "I can hold Hill 110 as long as I've got grunts that can shoot. I've already lost a lot of men! Be advised that I'm running low on grenades and small-arms ammunition." Again the sound of hissing air-waves as the transmitting microphone was keyed.

Suddenly, another voice cried out, a voice that bordered on hysteria: "They're in the trench line! Oh, shit! It's hand to hand!" And then the listening regimental communicators and staff officers heard the quick stutter of a burp gun followed quickly by the vacant hissing sound that signaled lost radio contact.

"Fuck!" spat out the regimental G-3, a colonel named Prescott of Boston, Massachusetts, a student of history who spoke through his nose with the broad, stilted accent of Massachusetts. Then, quickly gaining control of his emotions, he amended his order. "Who do we have in reserve? Item Company? Right! Send them right up! They'll relieve Baker Company in position! Damn! I must hold Hill 110! That hill's no higher than Bunker Hill back in the Charleston district of Boston!" Colonel Prescott was referring to the heights—connected by a ridge with another elevation just seventy-five feet high named Breed's Hill—heights that were made memorable as the scene of a mid-June 1775 battle commonly known now as the Battle of Bunker Hill. Great-great-great-grandfather Prescott, a Revolutionary War colonel, had successfully fought off two British assaults on Bunker Hill that long-past historic day, had used the massed rifle fire of his men to repulse in disorder a larger force of well-trained British troops. Present-day Colonel Prescott hoped to carry on a glorious family tradition. He had already renamed a Korean hill.

Item Company grunts commanded by Capt. Howard "Spike" Connolly were rushed quickly into position. Item Company grunts started bleeding and dying at the base of Bunker Hill as they shoved their way up and into the trench line, losing seven men KIA. None of their wounded accepted evacuation. "We'll stay on the hill with the Irishman," the patched-up grunts said.

They watched, quite pleased with themselves, as their skipper, Capt. "Spike" Connolly, ever the fighting Irishman, set the bright green flag of Saint Michael—made for his company by Korean orphans—in the sandbags that covered his command post bunker. During the next twelve hours, the flag would continue to fly under the most concentrated artillery and mortar barrage of the war. But that was still to come. I would help other FOs to fire thirty-two thousand artillery and mortar rounds forward of the eight-hundred-yard front held by Item Company. The Chinese would hit the Item Company position with fifteen thousand rounds.

Consolidating their gains, Item Company grunts—up on the hill now—saw Baker Company grunts and Chinese bodies in the trench line and in fighting holes, indiscriminately piled one on top of the other, intertwined in death postures. The brief, bitter struggle for Hill 110 ended with Item Company grunts taking potshots at gooks as they staggered falling down and drunkenly reeling off the hill, burdened gooks who presented fat targets as they dragged wounded comrades.

Three hours after their fight started, Item Company was firmly entrenched in Bunker Hill fighting holes.

Those few grunts remaining of Baker Company, gaunt-faced now and staring, dirt-encrusted lips dry and cracked, white-faced beneath gunpowder smears and with rips in their bodies, each one breathing shallowly, each one being very careful of every downward step they made as they came off the killing ground, were all grateful to be alive. They were survivors. They were temporarily out of action because of the exceedingly high casualty rates suffered by Baker Company, but they were survivors nonetheless.

CHAPTER
33

Earlier that morning, right after I saw the first of the wounded grunts from Baker Company off-loaded on the USS *Repose,* right after I heard the words "Bunker Hill" used synonymously with Hill 110 for the first time, I told the navy nurse commander I needed to get back to my outfit, the Four Deuces. Reluctantly she approved my request. "By rights you should stay a couple more days to completely regain your strength. But I know you marines. You remind me of my brother. He was a buck sergeant, too. A sniper killed him on Okinawa seven years ago." She put her hand on my arm: "I'll pray for you."

The only grunt clothing available on board ship was army utilities and army boots that had the lighter-colored leather straps and buckles at the top. That's what I was given; that's what I wore. The Four Deuces had been contacted by radio. Coordinating information had been passed. I would be helicoptered back to battalion headquarters within thirty minutes. I would fly back in one of the helicopters making a round-trip to pick up still more wounded.

The army utilities baffled the Four Deuce jeep driver, a

new man I did not recognize. He was reluctant to let me get aboard the jeep until I asserted my authority, turning the air blue with well-chosen profanities.

The Four Deuce first sergeant met me as we drove up to the command post bunker. He had a grim look on his face. His hands held familiar-looking 782 gear. He held my map case, binoculars, grease gun, pack board, and Willie Peter bag.

"You okay?"

"I'm okay, First Sergeant."

"Here's your gear. It's everything you left up on the hill. I had it sent down a couple weeks ago. I've been keeping it for you."

"Thanks, First Sergeant. That was decent of you. I'll come back up to the command bunker and get it after I've found a place to sleep."

"You're sleeping up on the hill, Sergeant Crawford. Up on Bunker Hill. I need you there."

"You gotta be shittin' me, First Sergeant. Goddamn! Less than an hour ago I got off the hospital ship."

"I need you up there, Sergeant Crawford."

"Well, goddamnit, First Sergeant, why can't you use Williams. He's available, ain't he?"

"Williams is dead. I guess you hadn't heard. Williams went up to George Company after you got medevaced out. He got killed on Siberia."

"Dead! Are you shittin' me, First Sergeant?"

"I wish I were, Sergeant Crawford. Think about it. That could have been you with a tag on your toe. I don't know why Williams went out to Siberia with his radioman. But he did, and now he's dead. So is his radioman. Grenades killed them."

"Goddamn, First Sergeant. That's a tough way to go."

"There are tougher ways, Sergeant Crawford. About two hours ago I sent Staff Sergeant Allbright up on Bunker Hill as the Four Deuce FO with Item Company. I sent him up on the hill after I had been informed that another one of my FOs had been killed. Sergeant Schmidt. Did you know him? I didn't think so. He just got in on the last draft. I sent

Allbright up with a team of men who were to bring the body of Schmidt back here.

"Less than five minutes ago I got the word that Allbright is dead. He's got about fifteen holes in him. Item Company didn't have but about seven KIAs going up Hill 110. That hill is being called Bunker Hill now.

"I told Allbright's radioman to take over as FO. But he didn't know what to do. You're my last FO, Sergeant Crawford. I need you up on Bunker Hill."

"Damn, Sergeant! I sure don't wanta go up. But I guess I better go relieve that radioman."

"You're not going to relieve him, Sergeant Crawford. You're going to replace him. Five minutes ago he tried calling in a fire mission. Only he read his map wrong. He was hit by his own short rounds. He's going to lose an arm, that's for sure. He's lucky. One Item Company grunt was killed."

I had no argument. I told the jeep driver to get me as close to Bunker Hill as he could without putting himself in any danger. I felt a dozen pairs of eyes on me. I knew that if I looked up I would see the business end of a lot of M1s. I hoped no one would get antsy and maybe ask me for the password or some dumb shit like that.

"I think he's a fuckin' grunt. But why the fuck's a grunt wearin' army clothes? I'll bet he's a fuckin' spy. Lemme get behind that machine gun. I know how to take care of spies!"

I couldn't see him but I would recognize the spy mentality of Castaglia anywhere.

"Castaglia, you dumb shit," I roared out, feeling better right away. "It's me, Cautious! You better get your goddamn finger off that machine gun trigger! Or else I'm gonna kick your ass so hard you'll have to take your shirt off to shit! You hear me!

"And how come you left me in that goddamn whorehouse with that goddamn nymphomaniac? I'm still hurtin'! I hope you caught the clap off that good-lookin' broad you had!" I felt better already.

It was like old home week in the trench line. Castaglia was a corporal again, the result of nonjudicial punishment through "office hours," punishment handed out at the discretion of Captain Connolly, punishment meted out because Castaglia had stayed three days longer in Japan than his R and R permitted.

"Easy come, easy go," he said, shrugging his shoulders. Castaglia explained to the grunts in the trench line that I was an old Item Company hand. "He'll back up muh story about how them east coast gooks use'ta send spies tuh check out our trench lines. A grunt's gotta be careful about things like that. Ya shoot 'em if they're spies, ain't that right, Cautious?

"And 'spose you tell me why'n the fuck yer wearin' that army getup. Are you tryin' tuh be a spy, or somethin'?"

I knew I was okay. Castaglia was smiling all around at everyone.

I checked in with Captain Connolly. Three hours earlier his men had taken control of Bunker Hill. I told him I would be on the hill calling Four Deuce shots. My wireman was already on the hill. He had kept the radio after the radioman had lost his arm to a called short round. I moved my gear into the bunker along with his. I planned our sleeping hours so that one of us would always be awake and have a weapon pointed toward the trench line outside.

I remembered Red and what happened when I shot at the rat and it seemed so long ago. Still, I would rather have one of our bullets on the way out bring down the roof than the concussion of a gook grenade. I sure didn't want to be wounded while I was in my sleeping bag. Sure, I wanted a Purple Heart, but I didn't want to get one like that. It seemed so undignified.

It was quiet on Bunker Hill all through the afternoon. I was a day late and a dollar short again. Except for a couple of sniping rounds peppering Bunker Hill and me and the gooks swapping a round or two every so often during the afternoon, life up on the hill was the same old grind.

Following the savage trench fighting that morning, everything went back to its status quo. We cleared the bodies of Baker Company grunts from the area, moving them downhill to be picked up by a graves registration team.

Marine losses on Bunker Hill during the early morning struggle amounted to 145 killed and 304 wounded. By an unofficial count, it was figured that 225 Chinese officers and men had been killed and that 825 had been wounded.

It figured that the Chinese would be back that night after licking their wounds during the afternoon. I had already placed my concentrations. I was in the FO bunker with the artillery officer, waiting.

Item Company had set out three long-range listening posts, one on each flank and another on a promontory straight down the center of our line. Each of the listening posts was to be manned from dusk to dawn by three grunts, an NCO, and two snuffies.

Because the middle outpost was the most hazardous position on line, Castaglia volunteered to man it. This position, unlike the two on either flank, had no cover whatever for Castaglia and his two men to use to get back into the main trench line if the shit should hit the fan again. If an action started, the three men would be stuck out about thirty-five yards in front, with not a thing in the world to protect them except the depth of their fighting hole and whatever luck they could draw upon. It wasn't the most enviable position on line, and yet Castaglia and his two Pfc's—one was his assistant machine gunner and the other was his ammo humper—seemed to thrive on the danger of it. They were a cocky bunch while it was still light during the early evening hours as they hunched over and made their way out to the outpost position, yelling and hollering lewd comments to the grunts behind them. That gay mood changed when they got into position and set up their light machine gun. I was pretty certain that Castaglia and his men would stay awake and alert throughout the long night. For communications, each outpost had a radio and a field telephone.

The grunts manning the listening post were in an excellent position to view our entire front. The listening posts were actually our first line of defense. Their main job was to protect the rest of the company from a surprise attack. The grunts who manned the listening posts were protected through their own vigilance and a deeply dug and sandbag-fortified foxhole.

In the FO bunker the artillery officer and I had an

overhead cover of wood and sandbags. We would be looking out of a thin aperture to call our shots. In comparison to the scant protection Castaglia and the other men had at the listening posts, FOs were very well protected.

The night sky was clear. A grunt could look up into an infinity of stars. There was no cloud cover at all. And that was bad news for Item Company. If there were no clouds, then the artifical moonlight from arc lamps could not be used, since cloud cover was needed to bounce or reflect the man-made moonlight downward. From about 2200 on, I threw up an occasional illumination flare that sizzled overhead, sending down an awkward light that cast running shadows. After about five such flares, the grunts said they would prefer to do without them, that they would rather trust their own night vision.

Item Company was on a 100 percent alert, with everyone in the trench-line fighting holes. Everyone was up. Everyone was anxious. Everyone was participating. Just knowing that gave me a spooky sort of feeling. A grunt who spends enough time in the trenches learns to trust those spooky feelings. I trusted mine. I sort of felt that something was going to happen, and that whatever would happen was going to happen soon. The feeling was nothing I could put my finger on.

I think Castaglia must have had the same kind of feeling. Just minutes before midnight Castaglia whispered into his sound-powered telephone: "They're out there. I can't see 'em and I can't hear 'em, but I know them fuckin' zipperhead spies are over tuh the left of me and some are right out in front of my position." He yelled loudly: "Okay, you fuckin' spies! Gimme the password." Moments later, even though he could not see the gooks, Castaglia instinctively felt their presence. Still later, and on throughout the night, those of us in the main trench line depended on the way Castaglia intuitively felt where the gooks were located even though we all knew for certain there was no way he could see them.

The first Chinese burp gun bullet that was fired barely touched the pupil of Castaglia's left eye as it zipped at great speed from left to right, taking away his eyelash and his ability to open and close his eyelid, taking away the cornea and the lens and fucking up something fierce his power and ability to look, or glance at, or gaze in wonder at all things, taking away his vision and leaving him with a permanent dull blue-gray-green line that constantly flashed as it stretched across an eternity, a bullet of almost insignificant size that significantly smashed the cartilage at the top of his nose and then turned inward and really fucked up his right eye. The rest of the bullets in the burp gun drum missed Castaglia completely. Some of the rounds hit his assistant gunner and some hit his ammunition humper.

Up in the FO bunker, at that same moment or two after midnight, the time of night when a grunt could expect gook visitors if his company on line was going to have any, all of us heard the sound of the burp gun and then the loud scream of Castaglia. I reacted by hollering into my EE-8 field telephone: "This is Cautious, FO Eight-Able! I want flares directly over Bunker Hill! I want lots of flares! I want you to keep them comin' until I stop them!

"And get some HE ready! I'm gonna want it right out in front of me. Prepare the HE to impact fifty yards directly out in front of my position. I want you to be ready to fire it on my command!

"And you tell the fuckin' first sergeant that the gooks are here, and I wanta be someplace else!"

Tracers flashed out in stuttering long red lines from Castaglia's listening post foxhole. He was still howling: "You fuckin' spies! You should'na climbed up out there!"

Under the merciless glare of smoking flares burning brightly overhead, we saw a half-dozen crumpled bodies in and around the listening post manned by Castaglia and his machine-gun crew.

"Castaglia! Listening post! Give me a report! What the fuck happened?" Captain Connolly barked it out over the sound-powered telephone in his command bunker. The Item Company commander's voice sounded tinny and small as it came through the telephone receiver in the FO bunker. The artillery FO lifted the sound-powered telephone and held it so all of us in the bunker could hear.

"Them fuckin' gook spies damn near come in and got a

hold of us, Skipper!" Castaglia said. "Nunna us heard 'em at all. Not 'til they started shootin'!"

"Are you hit? Are any of your men hurt?"

Castaglia was quiet for just a moment. "My assistant gunner's got four, mebbe five hits in his left arm. He's bleeding pretty bad, but I don't think he's got any broken bones or nuthin' like that. My ammo humper is all shot tuh shit in his legs. Them two fuckers is in a daisy chain, fixin' turnikets on each other. They'll be okay, Skipper, but the fuckin' gun pit here is all slippery with blood!"

"What about you, Corporal? Have you been hit?"

There was a long pause, and then, in a small voice: "I think I'm blind, Skipper. My eyes are all bleedin' or whatever the fuck eyes do when you get hit in 'em. I don't feel any pain, but my face is all sticky and I can't see for shit! But I can hear okay, Skipper. I can hear them fuckin' spies down at the bottom of the hill. It sounds like a whole shit pot full'a them, Skipper."

A flare popped overhead. I adjusted my binoculars and by the garish light looked to the bottom of Bunker Hill.

"Holy shit! Every fuckin' gook in the world is down there!" the artillery officer shouted.

I screamed into my EE-8 telephone to the Four Deuce FDC. I could hear both the 81mm mortar FO and the artillery officer loudly giving their firing instructions.

I gave my firing instructions. "I want you to open the sheaf using six guns. I want the rounds to land twenty-five yards apart. I want to cover one hundred and fifty yards of front. I want the rounds to impact one hundred yards directly in front of me. I want you to fire three rounds from all six guns at that target. Then I want you to bring the rounds in closer by twenty-five yards and shoot three more rounds from all six guns. Shoot the guns as soon as you can. I want some rounds landing in about one minute!

"There's a whole fuckin' bunch of gooks getting ready to come up on this fuckin' hill. I estimate at least three, maybe four hundred gooks are at the bottom of Bunker Hill in skirmish lines, like they're waiting to be inspected or something!"

Castaglia's shooting may have preempted the Chinese

336

attack on Bunker Hill by a minute or two. His keen hearing had picked up the sappers the Chinese always used prior to a concerted attack. The sappers, known for their skill and courage in cutting through dangerous mine fields, cleared lanes of approach to positions manned by marine grunts. Behind the sappers, on the ground and visible only to the Chinese attack troops, were yellow strips of tape marking a cleared path through our mine field. In the surprise shooting by a Chinese sapper caused by Castaglia's challenge, and with Castaglia's return fire that killed at least six gooks, Item Company was alerted of imminent danger by attack.

It was now just a minute or two after midnight. Through my binoculars I could see hundreds of Chinese in four rows, with about thirty feet between rows, move forward a hesitant step and then trot as they started a human-wave attack using businesslike skirmish lines. Side by side, elbow to elbow, the gooks started up the hill, spread across the company front, concentrated heavily at the center. Minutes later I would know these Chinese were just the first wave of a sustained, methodical assault in which an estimated thousand Chinese would take part. The G-2 would later inform Captain Connolly that the Chinese commander wanted to take Bunker Hill purely as a matter of prestige.

Just as the first wave of Chinese shuffled to the base of Bunker Hill, the first of my Four Deuce rounds landed among them, biting chunks out of their ranks. Still the enemy infantry charged up the open ground, ducking, falling down only to get up again, falling down to stay down. My second volley fell on the massed Chinese and was joined by artillery and 81mm mortar rounds. Marine grunts in the trenches held their fire; the Item Company gunnery sergeant walked courageously back and forth behind his troops, calming them with his rough tongue.

And then I lost track of what others were doing and concentrated only on my work, calling in accurate Four Deuce rounds. I saw a dozen gooks punish themselves by pushing constantly forward through shot and shell and run single file into a six-foot trench that exited out in front of a row of grunt foxholes. They ran through a screen of flying earth and metal. As a jack-in-the-box surprises, so too did a

337

handful of Chinese surprise as they popped out of the trench, hands and arms moving in a throwing gesture. Quick flashes lit the darkness as their grenades exploded, killing four young grunts. The gooks ran forward to Captain Connolly's command post, where his shrapnel-torn flag of Saint Michael was still flying. Grunts responded to Connolly's radio messages and moved in on each side, sealing the breach in Item Company lines. Quickly the Chinese fell to barking M1s and carbines.

Captain Connolly radioed back to battalion, continuing his running commentary of the battle: "My lines had been breached! They are now consolidated!"

I adjusted my fire again, extending it back into where the main mass of enemy might be located. Each time I changed target areas I would shoot a dozen rounds or more of high explosives.

"You got some, Cautious. But yer a little bit to the left of them," Castaglia would say, and I would adjust my fire. "Yer right on them fuckers. Give it to 'em!"

And that was the way it went throughout a long night. Castaglia would hear the gooks at what sometimes seemed impossibly long distances away. When it was possible for his assistant machine gunner to heave an incendiary grenade or a smoke grenade to the target area, I had, momentarily at least, something at which to aim. After his men had exhausted their supply of grenades, I depended entirely on Castaglia to tell me when and where he heard the gooks moving.

The hours to dawn passed slowly, one and then two hours, then a third hour and a fourth. And then, when there was the barest hint of a new day coming, Item Company got three grunts out as relief for Castaglia and his men. Castaglia would feel the outline of but would never see his Navy Cross and Purple Heart.

Before dawn, in a final attack, the gooks grenaded all three outpost positions, killing or wounding the grunts in them.

Suddenly, almost anticlimactically, the gooks were upon us. They were in the trench line before we knew what had happened. It had seemed impossible for them to have crossed that horrible, death-filled no-man's-land in front of

Bunker Hill, for them to have gotten that close to us without us knowing it.

I had my binoculars to my eyes, hoping the magnification would aid me in seeing through the lightening darkness of a coming dawn. I saw a bright yellow-orange flash almost directly in front of the FO bunker and superimposed on the flash, coming directly from the center of the flash or so it seemed to me, was a small projectile, a spinning projectile, a projectile that was on a contact course with my mind and I knew instantly it was my Purple Heart bullet.

EPILOGUE

A loud, rasping voice intruded: "Okay, you people! Them that can use a broom I want them to use it on this deck! It's cruddy! Get it cleaned up! I like a clean hospital!"

I struggled to open my eyes and managed to get the job about half done; in keeping with that effort, I knew I had a half smile on my face as well. It's good to be back, I thought to myself. I raised up on an elbow and made some very weak movement with my legs. There was nothing wrong with my right arm, but the left one was heavily bandaged and was bound across my body at just above waist level.

The strident voice softened. "Not you, Sergeant Crawford. You lay back for a minute or so and let me get some vital signs. I was barking at the rest of these goldbrickers in here."

I looked past the navy nurse commander, an old friend from just a day or two ago. She smiled conspiratorially. There were five other marines in the room. I knew they were marines. And I knew they were Item Company grunts because their eyes gave them away. I knew where they had been. The missing arm of one man, the missing leg of another, and the heavily wrapped bodies of the other three told me louder than words could say. One hospital bed was empty, but the rumpled sheets indicated that someone had recently been in it. The grunt with the missing arm waved casually with the other one: "Welcome aboard, Cautious. You saved my ass, just in case you didn't know it. I was on the outpost right in front of the FO bunker up on Bunker Hill with you. We'll talk about it later, okay?"

I nodded to him, and then the navy nurse commander stepped in the way, blocking him from my view. "I figured you'd be back," she said softly. She half smiled: "I think it's my figure that attracts you guys." She patted her ample hip with pudgy fingers. "Or maybe it's the way I do my hair," she said, her fingertips lightly cupping, touching, the tight salt-and-pepper ringlets showing below the starched white nursing cap with its black and gold bands of rank running from side to side.

The navy nurse commander smiled, and as I tried to smile back at her I winced with the sudden pain that shot down and over my face, a cold pain that hung on my forehead and melted, dripping down, seeping down, burning down to my cheeks. I had one helluva headache. I didn't need to see the bandages wrapped around my head. I could feel them. My head was swathed in bandage wrapping, turbanlike, heavily wrapped. My left arm was in a cast and lay, loosely bound, at right angles across my lower chest. My forearm felt uncomfortable, with an ache in it.

"You look great, ma'am. Better now than you did last week. I sure do like a full-figured woman, ma'am."

"Oh, I'm sure you do."

"Am I hurt bad? I sure don't feel like I'm hurt bad. It's just that I'm having trouble keeping my eyes open. They feel sort of tired-like."

"Nope. You've had a concussion, a bad concussion, I'd

341

say. From what we could figure out, you've been down that road before, though. That was the most serious problem. I recognized you down in the examining room. You know me; never forget a face, especially if it's worn by someone who reminds me of my brother. You do, you know. You remind me of my brother. He was a marine, too. In the Second World War. We talked about him, remember?"

"I remember when you told me about him. I'm sorry he got killed."

"Well, that was a long time ago. No need opening old wounds. And speaking of wounds, I'm going to need to take a look at that hard head of yours. Do you remember anything at all about what happened to you?"

"No, not really. The last thing I can really remember was being in the FO bunker up on Bunker Hill, and the fuckin' . . . , oops, I'm sorry, ma'am, I really am."

"That's okay, Sergeant Crawford. I've heard all those words before. They don't bother me if they slip out accidentally. It's just that I don't care for crassness, in speech or action. I'm a bit old-fashioned that way."

"Well, like I was saying—and as ridiculous as it sounds— the only distinct impression I have is that I thought I saw the round that hit me. I was hit, wasn't I?"

"Sort of. . . ."

"What does that mean . . . 'sort of'?"

"The other men in the FO bunker with you, well, they just knew you weren't going to believe it, so they made sure they sent it on with you when you were medically evacuated off Bunker Hill. Someone said you were shot at by a stray chink, almost the last round fired following a wild turkey shoot up there early yesterday when about a half dozen of them got into the trenches."

The navy nurse commander reached down at the bottom of my bunk. She brought up in her hands, of all the goddamned things, my helmet, the filthy camouflage cover brown side out. She pointed to the very slightly downward-curved and forward-jutting edge at the front of the helmet.

"You can see where the bullet went in, right here, right between the helmet liner and the steel helmet. It's still in there. You can feel the lump of it. No wonder it knocked you out and gave you a concussion, the way it smacked your helmet. You ended up with an awful welt on your head, I'll say that. We put that thick bandage on so you wouldn't jar your head as we moved you around in sick bay down below to take care of your arm."

"What's wrong with my arm?"

"Your arm is broken. You had a compound fracture. And the navy is really sorry about that. I personally made certain the navy made it up to you, though."

"That bullet that hit my helmet . . . it didn't break the skin of my head, is that what you're telling me?"

"That's right."

"No Purple Heart is what you're telling me. Is that what you're saying to me?"

"Well, Sergeant, it was wet weather when you were helicoptered in and those steel decks are slippery enough under the best of conditions."

"So?"

"When the corpsmen—and they are very, very good corpsmen—they're not careless or anything like that. . . ."

"You don't have to sell me on corpsmen. I think those guys are the greatest."

"Well, the corpsman carrying the front end of your stretcher slipped on the wet deck and you went ka-blooey all over the place. You fell on your left side, against a metal bulkhead. Your arm was broken, a compound fracture. You know what a compound fracture is, don't you?"

"I'm not sure. Tell me."

"A compound fracture is a bone fracture in which broken ends of the bone have pierced the skin."

The navy nurse commander gave me her wonderful, warm smile: "I just added it to your casualty tag. You'll get a Purple Heart for it."

All I could think of was Lob Stratton. Singular meritorious action, my ass.

343

And all I could hear was the loud voice of the grunt who belonged in the other bed in the ward and who, with bandages covering his eyes, was being brought back to that bed in a wheelchair: "I'm gonna tell you straight, that fuckin' gook should'na never have tried tuh have been a fuckin' spy!"